THE LAST GREAT FIGHT

The Extraordinary Tale of Two Men and
How One Fight Changed Their Lives Forever

JOE LAYDEN

ST. MARTIN'S PRESS ⚞ NEW YORK

www.stmartins.com

Design by Phil Mazzone

Library of Congress Cataloging-in-Publication Data

Layden, Joseph, 1959–
    The last great fight : the extraordinary tale of two men and how one fight changed their lives forever / Joe Layden.—1st ed.
        p.   cm.
    ISBN-13: 978-0-312-35330-8
    ISBN-10: 0-312-35330-8
    1. Tyson, Mike, 1966–   2. Douglas, Buster, 1960–   3. Boxing.   4. Boxing matches.
I. Title.
    GV1133.L39   2007
    796.83—dc22

                                                                                        2007022461

First Edition: October 2007

10   9   8   7   6   5   4   3   2   1

For Sue . . . who made this possible

Understand me on this, kid. Everything in boxing is backwards to life.

—F. X. TOOLE

Freedom's just another word for nothing left to lose . . .

—KRIS KRISTOFFERSON

PROLOGUE

July 4, 1994

So exhausted that he lacks even the strength to drive, the big man surrenders the keys to his wife, a woman who has always tried to keep him in line and care for him, who saw potential and goodness where some saw laziness and complacency. Bathed in sweat, he lets out a little groan and slides awkwardly into the passenger seat. This simple act takes all his energy and leaves him gasping for breath. Finally he settles, slumped against the door, a short tangle of dreadlocks spilling over his forehead, his thick legs curled beneath the dashboard.

"Hang in there, baby," she says. "We'll be there soon."

He moans, mumbles something beneath his breath.

"What's that, honey?"

"I'll be all right."

As the flatland of central Ohio whizzes past in a blur, the big man drifts away. His wife talks to him, tries to keep him awake and alert, but the struggle is lost. Funny, isn't it, that a man who made his living as a fighter—who once, precisely once, battled like no one before— hasn't an ounce of fight left in him? It's been that way for months now, maybe years. James "Buster" Douglas was, for a very brief time, the heavyweight champion of the world. He was the conquering hero, the man who beat the unbeatable. But that was more than four years ago. The man in the front seat of the car bears almost no resemblance to the Buster of 1990, the Buster who stepped into a ring in Tokyo, Japan, and provided boxing with the greatest upset it has ever known.

Then he was a sweet-tempered journeyman who preferred basketball to boxing . . . a 42 to 1 long shot (if you could actually find a gaming establishment, legal or otherwise, willing to take your bet) . . . who somehow dismantled and humbled a brutal young fighter almost preternaturally suited to the role of champion.

But now?

James Douglas tips the scales at a Sumo-esque four hundred pounds, his belly so swollen that it would snap the championship belts he once owned. His eyes are slits barely visible through veils of flesh, and there is an odor hanging in the air, the sweet, sickly smell of fruit gone bad. It is the smell of diabetes, of a quiet killer shaken from its slumber. By the time they reach the hospital in Columbus, Douglas is unconscious, having lapsed into a diabetic coma.

He dreams . . . and in the dream, he will later explain, his wife, Bertha Douglas, is gone. So is everyone else he knows and loves. He imagines that he is alone in the back bay of an ambulance, strapped to a gurney. In the front, a nurse sits in the passenger seat; an orderly in a crisp white uniform is behind the wheel. They are silent, stoic. It's dark outside. Rain is falling. Buster struggles to lift his head from the gurney; he peers out the window and sees a light at the end of a long mountain road. They are climbing now. Slowly . . . steadily. He hears the groan of the engine as it strains against the incline, and the rhythmic clicking of the wipers against the window. His head falls back and the dream dissolves away.

Meanwhile, two hundred miles down the road, in Plainfield, Indiana, the most famous resident of the quaintly named Indiana Youth Center—inmate No. 922335—passes another day in captivity. Now more than two years into his sentence for a rape conviction, he has become, by most accounts, a reasonably docile and cooperative prisoner. No more disputes with the guards, no more confrontations with other inmates. For the time being anyway, the bad has been removed from the self-proclaimed baddest man on the planet. Word is that he's found religion, that he spends peaceful, solitary time with the Koran, and that fighting no longer captivates him the way it once did.

Maybe.

Despite its cheery moniker, which evokes images of robust, energetic kids playing ball under the tutelage of thoughtful, well-meaning mentors, the Indiana Youth Center offers few outlets for the fighter. There are no boxing rings, no gloves, no speed bags or heavy bags. Nothing to promote testosterone and aggressive behavior. So inmate No. 922335 eats, sleeps, and prays. He takes classes in the hope of earning a high school equivalency degree. He tries to stay fit through calisthenics and jogging. Mainly, he says, he reads, grazing endlessly and somewhat aimlessly from a literary buffet table that includes Ernest Hemingway and F. Scott Fitzgerald, Arthur Ashe and Mao Tse-tung (the latter two will be paid tribute through tattoos on the fighter's biceps), among countless others. Like his counterpart in Columbus, he's bigger now than on the day they met in the ring. Not really overweight, as he was when he entered prison (at 250 pounds), but thicker. The teenage fighter who used to stand nearly naked in front of a mirror at a dusty, spartan gym in a small town in upstate New York and marvel at his own lines, at his youthful, clean-cut musculature, is long gone, replaced by a grown man hardened by time and circumstance and his own penchant for self-destructive behavior.

Things will get worse, too, before they get better for inmate No. 922335, also known as Michael Gerard Tyson. There will be another "bid," the counterintuitive term that convicts sometimes use to describe their time behind bars. There will be comic and tragic incidents of rage, snapshots of a life and career gone horribly wrong: a bloody chunk of a human ear, ripped from an opponent in midfight and spat with disdain upon the canvas; a seemingly insane and full-throated promise to eat the children of another fighter; bankruptcy, assault charges, multiple lawsuits, and, ultimately, a series of pathetic encounters with boxers so lacking in skill that they once wouldn't have dared even step in the ring with him.

In August 1986, at barely twenty years of age, he had become the youngest heavyweight champion in history. By the time he met James Douglas, on February 11, 1990, the erosion had begun, although few people recognized it at the time. He was still undefeated then, a vicious puncher with stunning speed and technical acumen and an almost primeval taste for blood . . . a terrifying fighter who *threw every punch with bad intentions,* and who seemed worthy of comparisons to the great ones: Muhammad Ali, Rocky Marciano, and Sonny Liston— especially Liston, as it turned out, since his, too, was a life and career punctuated by violence, sadness, and chaos.

And then came Buster, and a single night (afternoon, actually, since the fight, broadcast late in the evening to an American television audience, was fought at lunchtime in Tokyo) that altered the lives and careers of the combatants. In many ways, the most memorable night that boxing has ever known.

They are linked in the public consciousness, Tyson and Douglas, as surely as Louis was linked to Schmeling, Dempsey to Tunney, Frazier to Ali. It is Independence Day, a time to celebrate hard-earned freedoms, and the sad, unmistakable irony is that each man is at this moment a captive, confined to a prison of his own making.

But there was a time . . .

1

In the fall of 1967 Bruce Trampler was a freshman at Ohio University. An energetic Easterner with vague designs on a career in sports journalism, Trampler, like a lot of kids from New Jersey, was a self-proclaimed boxing nut who loved nothing so much as spending a few hours in the sweat-soaked atmosphere of a smoky club or gymnasium.

For him the love affair had begun only recently, just a few months earlier, in fact, when he'd been treated to the grotesque but undeniably enthralling spectacle of Joe Frazier—then at his brawling best—disfiguring and defeating a courageous but overmatched Canadian fighter named George Chuvalo in a heavyweight championship fight at Madison Square Garden. How could one not admire Chuvalo, a tenacious pug seemingly impervious to pain and unfazed by the sight of blood—particularly his own? Chuvalo grew up in a working-class neighborhood in Toronto, not far from the city's meatpacking district; his father, in fact, worked on the slaughterhouse floor, and Chuvalo seemed to have inherited from him an innate toughness. He dropped out of school at the age of fifteen, supporting himself by working alongside his father and training on the side for a career in boxing. By seventeen he was the Canadian amateur heavyweight champion, and the following year he turned professional.

Chuvalo fought all of the best heavyweights of the 1960s and 1970s, which by definition meant he faced some of the greatest fighters in history: Joe Frazier, Muhammad Ali, George Foreman, Floyd Patterson. And he backed down from none of them; not once was he even knocked off his feet. He didn't always win, but he never quit. That decision was best left in the hands of the referee, for if it were up to Chuvalo, every match would have been fought to the death. Foreman swatted him around the ring, beat him to a pulp, and still, when the fight was stopped in the third round, there was Chuvalo, staring ahead blankly, holding his gloves up to referee Arthur Mercante (whose blood-spattered shirt spoke volumes), as if to say, *What's the big deal?* He was Monty Python's Black Knight incarnate, forever proclaiming, in the face of graphic, irrefutable evidence to the contrary, "It's just a flesh wound!"

Against Frazier the end came in the fourth round, with Chuvalo, his face a knot of purple welts and open wounds, taking a stinging hook to the head and then turning away briefly. For anyone who had followed Chuvalo's career, it was a startling sight, indicative that something unusually bad had happened. And, indeed, shortly thereafter the fight was stopped and Frazier declared a winner by technical knockout. As it turned out, Chuvalo had suffered a fractured right orbital bone, an injury so severe and potentially dangerous that it precluded a return to the ring for nearly a year. (To this day, Chuvalo carries a reminder of that fight: a tiny piece of plastic, surgically implanted, that helps keep his eyeball from straying where it shouldn't.)

This was Trampler's not-so-sweet introduction to the sweet science, and it made an immediate and lasting impact on him. It mattered not in the least that Trampler had never stepped into a ring himself, had never laced up a pair of gloves. He understood the sport on an elemental level, and was attracted to it in a way that went beyond the merely visceral. And so it was one afternoon that Trampler and a friend found themselves on the side of a highway, thumbs extended, hitching a ride to Columbus. There they would catch a local boxing show, have a couple beers, and later Trampler would report on the night's activities for the school newspaper, thus justifying the time and expense of the trip.

That was the plan, anyway.

Strange, though, how life can take an unexpected turn. For Trampler, a career in journalism gave way serendipitously to a life in the fights, and it happened with the shake of a hand in a musty, postfight dressing room. There Trampler was introduced to one of the main-event fighters, a lean and muscular middleweight named William Douglas. No one called him that, of course. William Douglas was a name reserved for his father, who had been an amateur boxer. This guy, with the long arms and close-cropped hair, and an uncanny ability to stare right into your soul, had a fighter's name: Billy "Dynamite" Douglas.

"He was very friendly and accommodating, for a hard guy," Trampler recalled. "He was the kind of guy you met and immediately sensed: This is a tough man, not some goofball athlete. This is a serious, mature family man."

Indeed, Douglas was already twenty-seven years old at the time, with a long and unusual résumé. A Golden Gloves champion in 1963 (in an era when that title really carried some heft), now a factory worker by day and a musician in a rock-'n'-roll band by night, Bill Douglas earned his nickname with a brawler's approach to boxing that seemed to border on the masochistic, if not the insane. As the years would go by, the legend of Dynamite would grow. He was a fighter to the core, a man who would travel anywhere, anytime . . . to fight anybody. Didn't matter how big the opponent was, didn't matter how small the purse was (okay, maybe that mattered a little bit). If there was an opportunity to fight, Bill Douglas was first in line to accept the offer. It wasn't merely that he had a family to support (although that was clearly paramount in his mind) or that he was prone to self-destructive behavior. He just liked to fight. And anyone who stepped into a ring with him knew that in fact they had been in a fight.

Trampler talked with Douglas for a while that evening. They chatted amiably about boxing and life. Douglas introduced the young writer to his family: his wife, Lula Pearl, and his children (there would be four of them, all boys), the oldest of whom was named James (and quickly dubbed "Buster" by his grandfather, because it seemed to be

the kind of nickname befitting such a big and playful kid). Trampler
was impressed by Dynamite's skill and ferocity in the ring, as well as
his presence outside the ring. Here was a man who commanded respect simply by walking into a room, and yet, beneath the surface,
Trampler sensed, there was a thoughtfulness that warranted investiga-
tion. He would prove to be right. There was a complexity to Bill
Douglas that he would take to his grave. He was as intense as he was
indecipherable, a man who "wore his emotions, good and bad, on his
sleeve," as James would later say. But praise did not always spill easily
from his lips, especially when it came to his children. More than anything else, Dynamite Douglas was a man who followed his own
compass, and woe to anyone who dared suggest he was traveling in
the wrong direction.

Trampler was taken by the fighter, and the fighter, in turn, was
impressed by the young man's interest in and knowledge of boxing.
Thus was born a surprising alliance. Douglas did not have a manager
at the time, so Trampler, despite having no formal training for the
job, gradually stepped into that role. In the beginning he toiled as a
publicist for a variety of promoters and matchmakers. He wrote press
releases on Douglas's behalf, in his naïveté hammering out breathless
prose trumpeting the *awesome punching power of Billy "Dynamite"
Douglas.*

Trampler took to the role of publicist with gusto; unfortunately, it
never occurred to him that by touting Bill Douglas as the hardest-
hitting middleweight in the game, he might not be meeting his client's
needs, since such proclamations typically served only to frighten away
potential opponents. What Trampler had not yet learned was the fine
art of sandbagging, of whispering rather than shouting from the
rooftops. Boxing was a tricky game in those days, in many ways
more credible than it is today, but in other ways shadier, more subject
to backroom deals and careful matchmaking. Imagine trying to promote a sport without the benefit of twenty-four-hour cable television
and eight-figure pay-per-view bouts . . . without the Internet or cell
phones or even fax machines.

Professional boxing was a more popular and legitimate mainstream sport in the 1960s and 1970s than it is today, especially in the
middleweight and light heavyweight divisions, where Bill Douglas

tried to make his name in a crowded field that included the likes of Carlos Monzon and Matthew Saad Muhammad, formidable men who were at once technically proficient and blessed with a fighter's spirit. They were artful boxers, but more than willing to stand toe to toe if necessary. And behind them, waiting in line, were a hundred other hungry fighters eager for a shot at a title.

Getting that opportunity was often the biggest hurdle, and it was cleared only through a combination of guile and guts. A smart manager carefully protected his fighter, nurturing and propelling his career forward through a series of increasingly difficult encounters, culminating with a championship bout. Once at the top of the heap, the goal was to stay there as long as possible, and that was accomplished by not taking risks against unknown commodities or challengers who seemed just a bit too capable. In a modern market, the exploits of Bill Douglas would have been apparent to all who followed boxing; his prowess would have been reported, his victories and his heart applauded. But this was a shadowy time, and so while insiders knew of Bill Douglas and respected his talents, there was no outrage over his relegation to the game's periphery. There were unspoken, even counterintuitive, rules in the fight game, and one of them was this: If you want to be a champion, try not to fight like a champion. At least, not every night.

Douglas ignored this rule. He fought fifty-six professional fights in a career that spanned thirteen and a half years, compiling a record of 41-14-1 (thirty-one of the victories came by knockout). Boxing aficionados will tell you he never put on a bad show, that he always came prepared to fight. As his reputation blossomed, though, the list of people willing to face Dynamite grew shorter. As J. Russell Peltz, a prominent Philadelphia promoter who worked closely with Douglas, said, "At a time when the middleweight division, and later the light heavyweight division, was filled with talent, he held his own and was feared by all. No one stood in line to fight him."

Trampler traveled the second-tier boxing circuit with Douglas, publicizing fights in Ohio, West Virginia, and Indiana—wherever the paycheck took them. Over a period of time Dynamite got to know the young publicist, appreciated his effort and enthusiasm, and when Trampler reached the age of twenty-one, Douglas offered him a job as manager. Trampler accepted, and for the next half-dozen years or so they traveled the world together, facing any and all comers. This in an era when a manager's role was less restricted than it is today, when he not only handled the paperwork and negotiations, but sometimes, in the boxing backwaters where a purse of a few thousand dollars represented a princely sum, doubled as a trainer and cut man. Trampler did all of this and more in a career that spanned the better part of four decades (most recently, and notably, as a matchmaker for the promotional giant Top Rank), handling an array of duties with such aplomb that in 1999 he was inducted into the Boxing Hall of Fame.

Bill Douglas never made it to the Hall, never wore the crown of a world champion. But no one in the fight game made a greater impact on Trampler. And this is a man whose coworkers included heavyweight champion George Foreman, the great trainer Angelo Dundee, and the brilliant, charismatic Oscar De La Hoya—just to name a few. In the winter of 2005 Trampler got to thinking of Douglas one night while watching forty-year-old Bernard Hopkins, a revered and seemingly ageless middleweight, lose for the second time to a lightning-quick youngster named Jermain Taylor. A few days later Trampler dashed off an e-mail to Peltz, his friend and business associate, wondering whether he, too, felt that Hopkins, far from being a future Hall of Famer, was one of the sport's most overrated practitioners. How many of the beastly middleweights who called Peltz's stable home in the 1970s would have dismantled Hopkins with little trouble?

Peltz responded quickly with a list of ten names. A short time later another e-mail message landed in Trampler's in-box, an addendum to Peltz's earlier missive. Seems he'd forgotten about Bill Douglas, who was not technically one of Peltz's fighters, but often worked in the Philadelphia area. Dynamite, Peltz explained, was an "honorary" Philly middleweight who belonged on the list. Oh, and by the way—"he would have bounced right hands off Bernard Hopkins all night long."

In his youth Trampler was impressed by Douglas in ways large and small. Something of a smart-ass himself, Trampler found it fascinating that Dynamite's children were so well-spoken and courteous. They didn't seem to fear their father, but clearly there was a respect that went beyond the norm. Bill was a man who spoke in clipped sentences, rarely wasting a word. He said what he believed, and felt no reason to explain the rationale behind those beliefs; his brevity conveyed a sense of seriousness that was not easily mistaken.

Dynamite's toughness ran deep, too. He was not a caricature or a bully, the kind of person who would drop his shoulder to make contact with someone on the street, just to let everyone know who was boss. There was no need to mark his territory, for it was clearly defined. And yet, what a contradiction. Douglas was a professional fighter whose second love was music. Although he kept his own hours and "did what he wanted to do," as James Douglas noted, Bill was not exactly a raconteur. In all their years together on the road, Trampler never saw Dynamite avail himself of the women who were fond of fighters. Douglas wasn't a drinker, either. Didn't smoke, didn't curse; when he found something—or someone—particularly unpleasant, he would respond with an odd expression of disgust that became familiar to all who knew him, but that seemed inexplicable to those who didn't: "Kiss me!" Dynamite would snarl. And then, for good measure, "Kiss me again!"

In 1972 Bill Douglas traveled to Cape Town, South Africa, to face light heavyweight Sydney Hoho. Although the card was among the first in South Africa to be granted approval for an interracial audience, the country remained deeply segregated, as Trampler and Douglas, an African American, discovered when their flight landed in Johannesburg. They were greeted at the gate by the fight's promoter, who extended his hand to Dynamite and assured him that he was a welcome guest. In fact, the promoter gushed, as an international athlete, Douglas would be granted, for the duration of his stay, status as . . . an *honorary white man!*

A few minutes later, as they strolled through the terminal, Dynamite took his new designation to heart, marching right past the bathroom marked "blacks" and into the one reserved for "whites." As hundreds of horrified passengers of all races and nationalities looked on, Douglas disappeared from view to take care of business. Trampler insists to this day that he's pretty sure he heard the words "Kiss me!" as Dynamite walked away.

Anyone who knew Bill Douglas has a favorite story to tell. There was the time, for instance, that he flattened Billy Lloyd in the first minute of a fight at the old Philadelphia Arena, followed by an exuberant and thoroughly unexpected victory dance that lasted longer than the bout itself; or the night he hit Tom "the Bomb" Bethea so hard that Bethea's mouthpiece landed in the third row; and there were the fights late in his career, the decision he lost to World Boxing Association (WBA) light heavyweight champion Victor Galindez, and a brutally memorable 1977 fight at the 18,000-seat Philadelphia Spectrum against Saad Muhammad (then known as Matthew Franklin), a future World Boxing Council (WBC) champion. Dynamite was thirty-seven years old at the time, and yet he put the younger Franklin on the canvas and nearly knocked him out before losing on a controversial and unpopular stoppage. It was a prototypically feral Bill Douglas performance, one that left longtime fight fans shaking their heads in awe. There was no quit in the man, no backing down.

Without question, though, the story that best illustrates the character of Bill Douglas is the one involving his February 6, 1976, fight against Pedro Soto, a twenty-two-year-old rising star in the light heavyweight ranks. Trampler had parted amicably with Douglas by this time, citing his concern for Douglas's health, particularly in light of the way in which Douglas fought—his willingness to absorb punishment in pursuit of victory. When Trampler, then based in Florida, received a call from Teddy Brenner, the matchmaker for Madison Square Garden, one morning in early February, asking for Douglas's phone number, Trampler was at first reluctant to part with it. Soto, a Garden house fighter, had been scheduled to meet Tom Bethea, and when Bethea backed out with an illness on the morning of the fight, Brenner found himself in need of an opponent. And not just any opponent—it had to be someone willing to take a fight on virtually no notice. Who better than Bill Douglas?

Trampler believed that Soto, with his size and youth, was a bad and potentially dangerous match for the thirty-five-year-old Douglas. He also knew that it was no longer his place to determine which fights were or were not appropriate for Dynamite. So he shared the phone number with Brenner (although not before asking Brenner to call someone else), and of course Brenner did his job: He reached Douglas at home, and within a few hours Douglas was on a plane bound for New York City. For anyone else it might have been an act of lunacy, but it was entirely in keeping with Dynamite's code of conduct. Besides, it had always been his dream to fight at the Garden, and this was his chance. How could he turn it down? The purse, a measly two grand, was almost beside the point.

The fight itself has become the stuff of legend, unfolding in a blur of combat that thrilled the Garden crowd and surely stunned Soto. Twice Douglas put Soto on the canvas—in the fifth and tenth rounds—and in the end he walked away with a ten-round decision. He made it back to Columbus in time to work the next morning.

You couldn't spend much time with Dynamite and not have some of that toughness rub off on you, as Trampler discovered early in his tenure as Douglas's manager. Trampler loved the fight game, but he was not a fighter, a fact that gnawed at Dynamite. If you love the sport that much, Douglas reasoned, you owe it to yourself to give it a try. Not just a few rounds on the heavy bag or speed bag, either—real fighting, against real opponents. Eventually Trampler relented. He sparred a few times, even fought seven amateur bouts (and won five of them), which was enough to determine that he really preferred being on the outside of the ring. It was also enough to satisfy Bill Douglas, to assure him that Trampler was suited to the task of managing his career.

"Bill was the kind of guy who would go to the wall for you," Trampler remembered. Then he paused and laughed. "He was also the kind of guy who liked to be around people who had some balls."

Mention the name of James "Buster" Douglas and you'll find no shortage of people in the boxing world who will shake their heads and say, with a dismissive laugh, *If only he had the old man's balls.* Trampler knew them both, father and son, and as much as he liked both men, he states rather matter-of-factly that Bill Douglas spent a good portion of his life unsuccessfully trying to instill in his eldest son the same traits that had made Dynamite such a compelling boxer. Theirs was a complex and sometimes fiery relationship. That is a truth that even James is willing to acknowledge. If there was sometimes disappointment on the part of the father and frustration on the part of the son (and when isn't it so?), there was also no shortage of mutual affection. But it wasn't easy being the firstborn child of Dynamite Douglas, especially for someone who carried such an ambivalent outlook toward the sport his father loved, and the attitude that shaped his life.

All of Bill Douglas's sons found their way to the gym while they were toddlers, but it would be unfair to say that he dragged them there. They liked watching their father work out, thrilled at the sight of him sparring and sweating and snorting. James was no different in this regard, but in most ways it was obvious from an early age that father and son were cast from different molds. Buster was a big kid, soft around the edges, with an easy smile and a gentle demeanor. Born while Lula Pearl was still in high school, James spent most of the first six years of his life in the care of his grandmother, Sarah. She doted on the boy, treating him precisely the way one might expect the family's first grandchild to be treated. They were best friends, James and Sarah. He slept in her bed at night, took naps curled into a tight ball against the warm belly of her dog. Like a prince, he was protected and cared for.

And then Bill and Lula Pearl made their union official, presented a marriage license to Sarah, and off went James to live with mom and dad. There would be three more children, and they were reared in an atmosphere of love and tension. Lula Pearl offset the sometimes volcanic presence of Bill, stood her ground when he lost his temper and stormed out of the house. Or when he butted heads with one of his boys.

"My mom was the mediator between me and my dad," James said. "She was strong. In a lot of ways, she was tougher than my dad. She was no joke. I don't think they fought more than any other couple, but my dad was my dad, you know? He loved my mother and she loved him, but Bill Douglas did what he wanted to do. My mom ran the house. She ran everything. And she kept him in line—as much as anybody could."

To the extent that he became a heavyweight champion, James was a fighter made, not born. Whether watching his father beat the dust out of a homemade heavy bag hanging from the rafters in the basement of their home or sitting in the stands and hearing the bloodthirsty cries of the drunken crowds at one of Dynamite's professional brawls, Buster felt nothing so much as awe. He couldn't deny the urge to follow in Bill Douglas's substantial footsteps, to make his father proud, but neither could he squelch the voice in his head, the one that told him he was different.

Boxing was in many ways the Douglas family business. In addition to William Senior and Bill, the clan included pugilists on the distaff side, most notably in the person of Lula Pearl's brother, J. D. McCauley, who would later become one of Buster's trainers. McCauley was introduced to the sport by Bill Douglas and fought for the better part of a decade before settling into the role of trainer and teacher. McCauley and Bill Douglas were the closest of friends back then, before Buster's evolving career and disputes over the manner in which it should be handled drove a wedge through the family. McCauley felt for the young James Douglas, a thoughtful, introspective boy who had no taste for conflict, and who really didn't like the sport of boxing all that much.

James has sometimes disputed this take on his early life, claiming that his relationship with the sport was more tempestuous. As a dreamy ten-year-old he would stand in front of a mirror and throw jabs at invisible opponents, sweating until his arms ached. You couldn't keep Buster out of the gym in those days; you couldn't keep him away from his father. He loved boxing, which is not to say that he enjoyed fighting. The truth is, even the young James preferred the path of least resistance. And, oddly enough, it was Lula Pearl who pushed him into boxing, not because she longed for a champion in the family, or because she wanted him to emulate her husband, but simply because she feared for his safety.

There was the time in fifth grade when James, one of the biggest and most athletic kids in his elementary school, spiked the ball into the face of another boy during a volleyball game in gym class. James knew he'd made a mistake right away, for the boy was tough in a way that James was not, tough in a way that Bill Douglas might have admired. He rose from the ground, pointed a finger at the bigger boy, and said, "I'm gonna get you for that!" James stood frozen with fear, so anxious was he that the boy might make good on his threat. They met outside later, in the grand schoolyard tradition, but James escaped injury, and even battle, by simply refusing to take part. *Keep moving,* he told himself. *Just keep walking.* When he got home, he ran straight to Lula Pearl. Short of breath, his voice catching as he explained what had transpired, James leaned into his mother and waited for her to comfort him. Instead, Lula Pearl grabbed him by the collar and pushed him to the floor, planting a knee in his chest for good measure.

"What's wrong with you?" she yelled in disgust. "He ain't nothing but a sissy! Next time this happens, you fight that boy, or you're going to have to fight me!"

A few years later, when James's younger brother, Robert, was badly beaten in a street fight, Bill Douglas was appalled to learn that James had been in the vicinity but had done nothing to prevent the attack. James explained to his father that the assailant had been armed with a baseball bat. Bill scoffed: "That ain't no excuse. If he got a bat, you get a brick."

And so it went in the Douglas household.

In early adolescence, from roughly the ages of ten to fifteen, James threw himself into boxing with a zeal that surprised even his parents. Motivated at least in part by admiration for his father, he did roadwork without complaint and shadowboxed for hours, often biting his lower lip and feinting as he watched himself in the mirror, wondering whether he looked as much like Ali as he hoped. And he began fighting—real bouts, at county fairs and on local amateur cards. Eventually James became a Golden Gloves champ, and it seemed for a while that he might surpass his father's exploits in the ring. Then came the night he traveled with his father to New York to watch Dynamite trade blows with Tom Bethea. The brutality of that confrontation was startling to the fifteen-year-old James. He was struck by the intensity of the violence, and the way the men might as well have been smacking each other with their bare knuckles, so light and flimsy were the ten-ounce gloves they wore. Hell, it hurt enough to get hit in the face with the pillows Buster wore while sparring with other boys in the amateur ranks. He couldn't imagine what his father must have endured. And, frankly, he didn't care to find out, especially when he watched Dynamite nursing his battered body in the days that followed. Boxing held some appeal to James as a competitive endeavor . . . as a *sport.* But whatever it was that drove men like

Tom Bethea and Bill Douglas, whatever anger or animalistic instinct that carried them through the battle . . . well, that was lacking in James. And he knew it.

Before long, boxing was competing with other sports, most notably basketball, for a place in his heart. James was a terrific athlete, graceful and gifted and strong. Basketball, which rewarded those qualities and had the added benefit of being *fun,* soon eclipsed boxing as his game of choice. Given half a chance, James would skip a session at the Blackburn Recreation Center on the east side of Columbus, where his father worked, to play pickup hoops with other kids from the neighborhood. By the time he was a sophomore in high school James had quit boxing completely and turned his full attention to basketball. If it was a decision that disappointed his father, it did not seem at the time to be an entirely foolish or self-indulgent act. A six-foot-four frontcourt player with a lively body and soft touch around the basket, James was a legitimate Division I college prospect. What he lacked was an academic profile to match his athletic résumé, and so, even after leading Linden-McKinley High School to an undefeated season and a large-school state championship in 1977, Douglas went unrecruited by the nation's basketball powerhouses. He enrolled at Coffeyville (Kansas) Junior College, hoping to earn a scholarship via the community college route, but homesickness brought him back to Columbus within a year. James fared better at nearby Sinclair Community College in Dayton, and even earned a scholarship to Division II Mercyhurst College in Erie, Pennsylvania. Again, however, he felt the tug of home and dropped out of school.

Faced with the realization that his dream of becoming a professional basketball player was vanishing into the ether, James began toying with the idea of a return to the boxing ring. He was an athlete, after all, still in his early twenties. More to the point, he was the son of Dynamite Douglas! Somewhere inside beat the heart of a champion. It was simply a matter of finding it. And who better to assist in the quest than Bill Douglas?

"I was going to be a basketball player," James said. "That was my thing. It only went so far, and after that I started thinking about boxing again. You know why? It was the team concept that I loved about basketball. When you've got a team, and everything's working right, it's a special thing. The friendships and bonds you make are so important. I never really had that again after high school. We won a state title, and that was great, but the college teams I was involved with weren't a unit. It was a bunch of individuals. Boxing is different. It's only you. You mess up, guess what? It's on you, man. All of a sudden that started to appeal to me again. I wanted to compete, and I knew I could depend on myself."

James wasn't sure how Bill would respond to his dropping out of college, but he had a feeling the old man wouldn't lose much sleep over it. And he was right. Bill had continued to train fighters even after James went away to school, and as often as not he'd come back to the house shaking his head in disgust at what he'd seen: fat, lazy heavyweights who had neither the talent nor the guts to fight. "Jesus!" he'd rail at Lula Pearl. "Buster could knock out any one of these guys. I got the damn heavyweight champion of the world right here at home, and he doesn't have any interest in the game!"

But all of that was about to change.

Buster called his father from Mercyhurst, told him he'd had enough of college, enough of basketball. He was returning to Columbus, and he wanted to get back in the gym.

There was silence on the other end of the line. And then came the kicker.

"Will you train me, Dad?"

More silence . . . and then a single word from the father, and the sound of ice melting at the edges.

"Beautiful."

2

June 27, 1988

Butch Lewis apparently *never got the memo. Still, there are certain things a prudent man knows better than to do: tug on Superman's cape, spit into the wind, pull the mask off the ol' Lone Ranger . . . agitate Mike Tyson moments before he's scheduled to meet your fighter in the ring.*

Then again, it's unlikely that any man whose idea of formal attire is a tuxedo without a shirt (Lewis's outfit on this night, and most fight nights, for that matter) has anything more than a passing acquaintance with the concept of prudence. So here is Lewis, the promoter and manager of a beefed-up light heavyweight named Michael Spinks, in all his smiling, blustery glory, swatting recklessly at a hornet's nest in the bowels of the Atlantic City Convention Center.

It is customary in boxing for representatives of one camp to visit the opponent's dressing room before a fight. They are permitted, encouraged, even, to witness the ritual of "gloving up," and to inspect each other's equipment, a practice that harkens back to the sport's darker and dirtier days, when it wasn't unheard of for a fighter to tamper with his gloves, the better to inflict serious damage on an opponent. Over the years these transgressions have become somewhat apocryphal—Jack Dempsey's handlers allegedly soaking his bandaged hands in plaster of paris before the fighter's 1919 pummeling of Jess Willard; Walk Miller, the manager of future world middleweight champion Tiger Flowers, accusing Jack Delaney of using a "gimmick" (specifically, a three-inch iron rivet hidden within his glove) following Delaney's knockout of Flowers at Madison Square Garden in the winter of 1925—the stuff of pulp fiction and movies, but there was a time when they presented a legitimate concern. (In fact, just two years earlier, junior middleweight Luis Resto and his trainer-manager, Carlos "Panama" Lewis, had been sentenced to prison for removing half the padding from Resto's gloves prior to a 1983 fight against Billy Ray Collins Jr.; Collins absorbed such a beating that he never fought again.) And so the practice continues today, albeit with an emphasis on more mundane matters, such as ensuring that gloves are properly tied and taped.

Lewis is a feisty showman who has skillfully guided Spinks to an unlikely position as a legitimate threat to Tyson's heavyweight crown and helped secure for the challenger the biggest payday of his career. Now, whether fueled by hubris or arrogance or a healthy sense of competition (or whether he is simply "pulling his usual bullshit," as Tyson's trainer, Kevin Rooney, will later claim), Lewis is standing in the champion's dressing room, questioning what appears to be a small bulge protruding from the athletic tape that binds Tyson's left glove to his wrist. (The abnormality was first detected by another member of the Spinks camp, who, after failing to convince Tyson's handlers that the gloves should be retied, summoned the manager.)

"Get rid of that," Lewis demands, "or we don't fight."

Given what is about to transpire, one might wonder if this is a threat or a last-ditch effort to opt out. But here, in the gambling capital of the East, Lewis plays the bluff for all it's worth. Rooney, at once amused and irritated, argues that the bulge is nothing more than the knotted laces of his fighter's glove, and surely poses no threat to Spinks. Reluctant to accept that explanation, Lewis demands that the glove be examined by Larry Hazzard, chairman of the New Jersey State Athletic Commission, which oversees the event. Hazzard finds the bulge to be harmless and the glove perfectly legal; nevertheless, Lewis continues to protest. Meanwhile, Tyson, surly and lathered, grows more agitated with each passing second, as his skin cools and the sweat from his prefight ritual evaporates into the musty air.

For a few tense moments, as Lewis digs in deeper, it almost seems as though the fight might not happen. Tyson is so angry that he punches the wall *of his dressing room. Finally, a cooler head prevails, that belonging to Eddie Futch, the esteemed seventy-seven-year-old trainer of Spinks. Futch calmly inspects Tyson's wrist, runs his hand over the glove and the laces, and casually declares all to be fair and right. This assuages Lewis, who leaves the champion's dressing room and walks down the hall to check on his fighter.*

The manager is barely out the door when Tyson leans into Rooney. In a voice barely above a whisper, a voice thick with confidence and menace, he says, "You know, I'm gonna hurt this guy."

While the passing of years is never kind to athletes, perhaps none feel its sting quite so acutely as boxers. The fighter first seems not to age at all, and then so quickly that we can scarcely recall the day when he was young and vital. The story of the athlete who overstays his welcome is not a new one, of course, and it rarely turns out well. For every Roger Clemens, throwing heaters like a kid even as he crosses the threshold of middle age, there are ten (or a hundred) men who stagger on well past their prime, leaving only when injuries or the vagaries of the business (i.e., no one is willing to pay their salary) force them to the sideline. It's a hard thing, knowing when to quit. Harder still to admit the game is over.

Boxers, historically, have demonstrated a particular stubbornness in this regard. Why? The cliché is that "fighting is in their blood," and maybe that's true; some of them really don't know anything else, any other way of life. Maybe it's a matter of simple economics—God knows there is a sad tradition of fighters making countless millions and somehow flushing it all away. Whatever the reason, this much is undeniable: Rare indeed is the boxer who walks away on top, championship belt in hand, faculties intact. The vast majority, even the greatest (Ali comes to mind), continue to fight, some well, some not so well, until eventually the losses come with greater frequency than the victories, and the purses shrink dramatically, and the opponents show neither fear nor even respect. When the gloves are finally unlaced for the last time, if the fighter is lucky, he leaves with enough money to carry him comfortably into old age, and nothing worse than a badly splayed nose and arthritic hands. All too often, though, the fallout is significantly worse: from postconcussive syndrome to the uncontrollable tremors of Parkinson's that afflict Ali, rendering virtually mute and docile one of the most eloquent and entertaining athletes of the past fifty years.

No one knows how the story of Mike Tyson will end, but by 2005 it seemed to be on the downslope of a rather tragic arc. The twenty-first-century model was the monster in the closet, released once every few months to issue an invective-filled tirade against an undistinguished opponent, or the media, or society in general, all in advance of an utterly forgettable fight. Would he win? Would he lose? It almost didn't matter. On the cusp of middle age, his skills having eroded and his personal life having become calamitous, Tyson's career had devolved into little more than a circus sideshow. He was hopelessly and almost incomprehensibly broke, and utterly lacking in options. So he fought on, whether anyone cared or not.

If you knew Tyson at all, there was poignancy and even perverse beauty to this stage of his life, for it was, in many ways, exactly as he had predicted it would be. Twenty years earlier, as a teenager about to burst on the international scene, he was just a juvenile delinquent looking for direction. He sometimes foreshadowed a life of sadness and self-destruction, even as he recognized the likelihood that he was destined for some sort of greatness. The demons were always there, scratching at the surface, trying to claw their way out.

Even by boxing's sordid standards, Tyson's fall was precipitous and ugly. But it needs context. His place in athletic history, while not what it might have been, remains secure. The fact is, from 1986, when he first became heavyweight champion, through 1990, when he lost the title to Buster Douglas, Mike Tyson was arguably the greatest heavyweight champion boxing has ever known. Hyperbolic? Not really, although the term "greatest" is open to interpretation, and boxing fans and historians, like baseball fans and historians, are a particularly knowledgeable and feisty lot. Theirs is an arcane world, and they know it well and protect it with great vigor.

Here are the facts: For more than five years, from his very first professional fight until the loss to Douglas, Tyson cut an unparalleled swath through the heavyweight division. His record going into the Douglas fight was 37-0, including nine successful title defenses (trailing only Louis, Ali, and Larry Holmes); thirty-three of those victories came by knockout, many within the first few rounds, or even the first few minutes. On occasion, a bout would end mere seconds after the opening bell. By that point Tyson had established himself as perhaps the best puncher in boxing history. But he wasn't a brawler. The casual observer was often fooled into thinking that Tyson was nothing more than a one-punch fighter, a knockout artist with bulging biceps and a penchant for throwing wild, lethal uppercuts. In reality, for a time, anyway, he was much more than that.

Look at the young Tyson. Look at the hand speed, the punches coming with such alarming frequency that it almost seems as though the tape is on fast-forward. Often regarded (again, by the casual observer) as a bull in the ring, Tyson was actually a marvelous defensive fighter. How could he have been anything else? This was the style taught by the great trainer, Cus D'Amato, who took Tyson in when the kid was fourteen years old, who either forgave or overlooked his troubled past and violent, sometimes sociopathic tendencies, and concentrated instead on molding him into the greatest fighter the game had ever seen. Watch Tyson bobbing and weaving, slipping three, four, five consecutive punches, the upper half of his body shifting wildly and unpredictably, like a human bobble-head doll. And then, finally, there is an opening, and Tyson pounces on it. We remember the knockout, the awful sight of a body spilling to the canvas. We forget the speed and athleticism . . . the *schooling* . . . that set it up. Tyson was a boxer, a deeply devoted student of the sport who spent endless hours reviewing films of the great ones, of Louis and Dempsey and Marciano.

That said, there is no denying the sheer visceral impact of a Tyson fight. He resurrected boxing, brought it to a place in the public consciousness that it hadn't held for two decades, and he accomplished this not through style but swagger. Truth be told, it was menace and bloodlust that brought people to the arena, that compelled otherwise frugal and sensible consumers to spring for a Home Box Office subscription (long before *The Sopranos* had made the premium cable network must-see TV, HBO featured Tyson as a cornerstone of its basic programming) or to shell out somewhere between thirty and forty bucks for a pay-per-view event unlikely to last more than a few minutes. Indeed, they felt cheated if Tyson did *not* vanquish his opponent swiftly and heartlessly; the 1980s-era Tyson fight that stretched on for four or five rounds was viewed as an anomaly by boxing analysts and a disappointment by fans. At no other time in modern history has the boxing ring so closely resembled the arena of the Roman gladiators. Tyson's fights were not unlike public executions: violent, primal, cathartic.

"There were all kinds of questions about Tyson, but none of them could ever be answered because he was knocking people out so quickly," observed boxing historian and author Bert Sugar. "And, of course, that was part of his appeal. After an entire decade of champions who were, at best, drab, going to fifteen-round decisions in every fight, here we had a guy—finally!—who did what heavyweights should have done, which was lay people endwise. So there was an interest and investment in him that led to people giving him all kinds of wonderful nicknames, and using words like 'invincible.' Now, anytime I see the word invincible in front of someone's name, I'm running to the goddamn window to bet on the opponent. But Tyson was given the mantle of invincibility."

The nicknames progressed ominously as Tyson matured: Kid Dynamite became Iron Mike, which gave way to the Baddest Man on the Planet. If these represented little more than marketing strategy, they were nonetheless effective and, for the most part, accurate. The young Mike Tyson was indeed an explosive fighter, so mesmerizing in his power that one dared not look away for an instant, for fear of missing the climactic moment. And, of course, as he outgrew youthful innocence (if ever that phrase applied to Tyson), he became darkly fascinating as a public figure, prone to indiscretions that ranged from small lapses in judgment to the outright criminal. All of these things—the good, the bad, and the ugly—combined to make Tyson perhaps the most fascinating athlete of his generation.

Timing is everything, and there is no question that Tyson came along at precisely the right moment, rescuing the sport of boxing from a malaise that had lingered for years. With the decline of Ali and Frazier in the middle to late 1970s came an attendant decline in professional boxing. Admittedly, these were big shoes to fill. Ali remains the most charismatic figure in the history of boxing, a multidimensional fighter who could jab and dance or deliver a knockout punch. Handsome and well-spoken, with a gift for sparring in press conferences as well as in the ring, and a heart so big that it carried him through countless battles—personal, political, and athletic—Ali stands as a figure of almost incomparable prowess.

How could anyone replace him?

Charged primarily with that task was Larry Holmes, a tall (six-foot-three) but doughy heavyweight from Easton, Pennsylvania (by way of Cuthbert, Georgia), who ruled the division for the better part of a decade. Nicknamed "the Easton Assassin," Holmes was the owner of a quick and stinging jab (courtesy of an eighty-one-inch reach) that belied his soft appearance and gentle manner. For a big man he moved exceedingly well, methodically but effectively cutting down the ring and wearing down his opponents with repeated jabs and counterpunches. Despite his size and obvious strength, he was no knockout artist. In fact, only forty-four of his sixty-nine career victories (he lost just six times) were by knockout. But give this much to Holmes: He knew how to fight, and he knew how to win.

In fact, from March of 1973, when he made his professional debut with a four-round decision over Rodell Dupree in Scranton, Pennsylvania, until September 21, 1985, when he lost the International Boxing Federation (IBF) title to Michael Spinks, Holmes did not suffer a single defeat. He won his first forty-eight professional fights, falling just one short of Rocky Marciano's record for consecutive victories at the start of a career. Holmes gained possession of his first heavyweight title in 1978, when he upset Ken Norton for the World Boxing Council crown. Two years later, in October of 1980, Ali came out of retirement to challenge Holmes for the title. If it was a fight that signified a passing of the torch, it was nevertheless a sad day for boxing, and even a bittersweet one for the champion, who seemed reluctant to hurt the slow and aged icon that Ali had become. Holmes, who had once worked as a sparring partner for Ali, danced and jabbed, but never tried to put his opponent away. The end came after the tenth round, when Ali's trainer, Angelo Dundee, stopped the fight.

Holmes defended the WBC title seventeen times before relinquishing the belt (in part due to an ongoing feud with promoter Don

King, who ruled the WBC) in late 1983 and assuming the championship of the newly formed IBF. He defended that title three times, until being upset by Spinks, a former light heavyweight champion who had embarked on a rigorous (and, at the time, revolutionary) training regimen to gain entry into the more glamorous and lucrative heavyweight division. The smaller but fitter Spinks wore down the champion over the course of fifteen rounds and walked away with a unanimous decision. It turned out to be a bad night all the way around for Holmes. As naturally reticent as Ali was loquacious, he had, in the weeks leading up to the fight, strained under the weight of repeated questioning about his pursuit of Marciano's record. When pressed, Holmes would point out, rather ungraciously, "I'm thirty-five fighting young men and he was twenty-five fighting old-men-to-be." Afterward, visibly shaken by the decision, Holmes bristled noticeably as the reporters' questions turned again to the subject of Marciano and the record that now was out of Holmes's reach.

"If you want to get technical about it, Rocky Marciano couldn't have carried my jockstrap," Holmes said, and with that he was instantly transformed from a marble-mouthed fighter who was respected, if not beloved, into a bitter, self-absorbed ex-champion. Forget for a moment that the comment had little basis in fact—by any reasonable standard, Marciano was one of the sport's all-time greats. Instead, view it through the prism of common sense. With that single, ridiculous proclamation, Holmes sealed his fate as a champion who would never get his due—not from boxing fans, anyway. It didn't help that seven months later, after again losing to Spinks (this time on a split decision), Holmes, before embarking on a temporary retirement, offered this parting shot: "I can say to the judges, the referees, the promoters, to kiss [me] where the sun don't shine. And since we're on HBO, that's my big black behind."

Neither Holmes nor Gerry Cooney (the Great White Hope of his generation), nor any of the other heavyweight champions and would-be champions of the late 1970s and early 1980s was able to capture the imagination of the sporting public. But even as Cooney and Holmes were staging a not-so-epic 1982 confrontation with the epic moniker "War by the Shore" (the fight was held in Atlantic City), Mike Tyson was in the process of being "discovered."

Much of what passes for the Tyson mythology had transpired by this point: Born on June 30, 1966; raised by his mother, Lorna Smith Tyson, in the Brownsville section of Brooklyn, after his father, Jimmy Kirkpatrick, leaves home when Tyson is two; falls into a thuggish life on the streets while still in grade school; arrested numerous times as a preteen; eventually sent upstate to the Tryon School for Boys in Johnstown, where he catches the eye of a counselor and boxer named Bobby Stewart; introduced by Stewart to the iconoclastic trainer Cus D'Amato, a tough old bastard who had earned the respect of just about anyone associated with the sport, not only because he had guided Floyd Patterson to a heavyweight title, but also, and perhaps more important, because he famously had stood up to the mob that controlled boxing in the 1950s.

The conduit between Stewart and D'Amato was Matt Baranski, who ran a gym in nearby Albany. Baranski had once trained and managed Stewart, and would later become the cut man for Team Tyson. It didn't take long for Baranski to recognize that Tyson had the potential to be something special. Stewart, after all, was a highly skilled and experienced fighter (in 1974 he'd won the U.S. National Golden Gloves Light Heavyweight title), and here he was, in a sparring match, getting all he could handle from a thirteen-year-old boy.

"Yeah, Mike was thirteen," Baranski recalled with a laugh, "but he weighed 186 pounds. And it was a solid 186 pounds."

Two decades earlier Baranski had experienced something similar. He'd been introduced to a young fighter who had been released from a reform school in Albany. The kid had no family, just a keen interest in boxing and a desire to straighten out his life, so Baranski took him in, acting as surrogate father, as well as trainer, for more than two years. Perhaps, Stewart suggested, Baranski might be interested in rescuing Tyson, as well. The kid was due to be discharged soon and had no desire to return to Brooklyn, where he'd certainly find trouble all over again. But too much time had passed for Baranski. He'd recently retired from a career with the U.S. Postal Service. He liked working with kids, hanging out at the gym, spending time at home with his wife. The energy and commitment required of this assignment was beyond him now, and he was smart enough to realize it.

Rather than drop the kid, however, Baranski referred Tyson to D'Amato, who lived a tranquil life in Catskill, some forty miles south of Albany. D'Amato and Baranski were longtime friends, and though D'Amato still worked with fighters, even opened to some of them the rambling old farmhouse he shared with Camille Ewald, the widow of his brother, he never expected a return to the game's biggest stage. Quietly, though, he longed for it. Sometimes he would tell Baranski and others that if only he could find a young heavyweight with potential, someone like Patterson, it would reinvigorate him. A kid like that, D'Amato would say, wistfully, "he'd put ten years on my life."

And then came Tyson, and with him, the roller-coaster ride of D'Amato's life.

"It's funny," Baranski said. "After Mike had five or six professional fights, Cus said to me, 'This son of a bitch is going to take ten years *off* my life!'"

But that was later, after Tyson had been expelled from Catskill High School and D'Amato had assumed the role of legal guardian . . . after Bill Cayton and his business partner Jimmy Jacobs had developed a management strategy that, if successful, would take Tyson to the top of the heavyweight division and make him wealthy beyond his wildest dreams. At thirteen, though demonstrably capable of violent outbursts, Tyson was an insecure and sometimes stunningly affectionate boy, "an angel," as Baranski said. "He'd throw his arm around me, put his head on my shoulder and say, 'You're my man, Matt. You're my man.' He was such a sweet kid."

Many of those closest to Tyson would argue (and have argued) that he was always a magnet for trouble, that the world into which he was born imprinted on him a prodigious capacity for antisocial behavior, and that to this day he struggles to reconcile the trauma of his youth with the man he has become. Tom Patti has known Tyson since their days together in Catskill, when both trained under D'Amato and lived in his home. While Tyson has shucked off virtually all connections to the Catskill era of his life, Patti (now a businessman in California) remains a friend and advisor.

"Mike, I think, is still battling his past, and when I say that, I mean his history from his childhood," Patti said. "That's probably the biggest cross that he bears."

Less forgiving and diplomatic is Steve Lott, a New Yorker who worked in the offices of Big Fights, Inc., the boxing video company owned by Cayton and Jacobs. Lott was also a proficient handball player, and it was through his accomplishments in the sport that he came to know and work with Jacobs. Lott wore several hats as part of Team Tyson. Officially, his title was assistant manager, but Lott also worked Tyson's corner for early fights and even shared an apartment with Tyson for a few years in the mid-1980s. As Lott saw it, sure, Tyson had a brutal and unfair start in life, but he had opportunities to transcend that life, and eventually those opportunities were squandered.

"Mike lived in my apartment in 1985, '86, '87," Lott recalled. "We were a block from the *Daily News* [offices], so why weren't they over there once a month for some incident involving Mike Tyson? Not once. Because Mike was happy then. He was getting as many women as he wanted, making millions of dollars a fight. Guys would kill for that. He was happy. You could see it in his eyes."

And now?

According to Lott, "I think it's easier for Mike to say, 'I've always been a bad kid,' than to say, 'I've been a chump and I've been conned out of the most wonderful life I could have had. I'm sure that Mike in Brooklyn, in 1977 or 1978, was horrible, worse than anything I saw with Cus in the early days. But that was the beauty of Cus: He knew that Mike would evolve."

In the ring, at least, Tyson did evolve, as quickly and effectively as any fighter in history. The ascent was punctuated by moments of tenderness and compassion. Just as Tyson had once been a violent juvenile delinquent with the improbable hobby of raising pigeons, so, too, did he become a young fighter whose brutishness was balanced by open displays of gentleness and vulnerability. How much of this was innate, and how much was the work of D'Amato, playing a sort of Henry Higgins to Tyson's Liza Doolittle, is impossible to say. Surely D'Amato made an indelible mark on Tyson the boxer, and it seems fair to suggest that he at least tried to school Tyson in the art of manners, to create a fully realized human being, as well as the perfect fighting machine.

At the 1984 Olympic Trials, for example, after dispatching a fighter whose pedigree could not have been more dissimilar from his own (he was a student at Princeton), Tyson offered this courtly assessment: "My opponent was game and gutsy. What round did I stop the gentleman in, anyway?"

Such delicate phrasing was a far cry from the venom that Tyson would later spew on a regular basis. By the latter part of the decade boxing fans (and readers of the New York tabloids) were accustomed to hearing of Tyson's graphic expectations and desires—how he wanted to literally rip out an opponent's heart, or, failing that, "drive his nose bone into his brain." If he harbored such grisly sentiments, the barely adolescent Tyson kept them mostly to himself. When he showed any emotion at all, it was likely to be of a more sensitive nature, as, for example, when he lost to Henry Tillman—twice—at the Olympic Trials. Tyson wept openly after that defeat, so loudly that his sobbing could be heard outside the dressing room. It would be quite some time before he would shed tears in public again; it would also be quite some time before he would taste defeat.

There was nothing accidental or serendipitous about Tyson's rise to prominence in the heavyweight division, no detail left to chance or fate. Cayton and Jacobs (himself a former athlete who once was a nationally ranked handball player) were smart and polished businessmen who did not permit their love for the sport or their desire to make money to cloud their judgment. They had a holistic plan for Tyson, one that would, hopefully, sharpen his social and interpersonal skills as well as his boxing ability. Within a few years, if all went according to plan, Tyson would be the undisputed heavyweight champion of boxing and the king of Madison Avenue. Seven-figure endorsement deals would be his for the asking. To that end, Tyson trained furiously in the gym and studied films of the game's greatest fighters. He could converse freely and adeptly on the subject of boxing history, knew exactly what weapons the champions had in their arsenals. Over time he would take on some of the characteristics of these men: the whitewall haircut and minimalist presentation (no socks, no robe) of Dempsey; the menacing habit, borrowed from welterweight and middleweight champion (and brazen challenger of heavyweights) Mickey "the Toy Bulldog" Walker, of hovering over a fallen opponent, if only briefly, as if to signal complete and utter dominance. (Walker, a wildly popular and self-indulgent Prohibition-era brawler, was a particular favorite of Tyson's; not coincidentally, Walker drank excessively, chummed around with the likes of Charlie Chaplin and Al Capone, married seven times, burned through most of the money he earned in the ring, and later in life indulged a passion for art by becoming a painter.) Tyson learned from the best, and for a while his ascent to their ranks seemed an absolute certainty.

A foundation of the master plan included a frenetic training and fighting schedule that would keep the young boxer in the gym as much as possible. The rationale was simple: If Tyson was training, he'd stay out of trouble; and if he had a fight coming up, he would have to train. And so he became a throwback to an earlier era, a fighter who entered the ring with alarming regularity: fifteen times in 1985, his first year as a professional, a statistic that becomes even more impressive when one considers that he didn't make his debut until March. Fifteen fights in less than ten months. For the most part they were close encounters of the briefest kind. Each fight ended with Tyson knocking out his opponent, and eleven of those opponents were vanquished in the first round. The challengers hardly represented the best that boxing had to offer; nevertheless, there was something about those early performances, most staged either in Tyson's backyard (in Albany or Latham, or an hour and a half downstate, in Poughkeepsie) or in Atlantic City, that provoked an almost unparalleled sense of anticipation.

From opening night, on March 6, 1985, when he flew out of his corner at the Empire State Plaza Convention Center in Albany, rushed across the ring like a young man who couldn't wait to throw his first punch, and leveled a chunky fighter named Hector Mercedes (in exactly 107 seconds), Tyson announced his intentions with clarity. He was just eighteen years old at the time, still a raw and unrefined talent, but there was so much power and athleticism and determination. Even in those early fights, some against men so hopelessly overmatched and frightened that they couldn't wait to hit the canvas, it was apparent that Tyson was unique.

Kevin Rooney, who had spent the better part of a decade training under and assisting D'Amato, had the distinction of headlining the card on which Tyson made his debut. Rooney's career as a boxer had peaked in 1982, with a knockout at the hands of welterweight champion Alexis Arguello; ostensibly retired and working as a trainer, Rooney put on the gloves twice more in 1985 to help promote local cards on which Tyson appeared. He won both fights, but quickly turned his full attention to training Tyson.

"I knew he had potential," Rooney said. "I just didn't know how good he'd be."

Rooney had witnessed Tyson's rise firsthand, having assumed the role of chief assistant from Teddy Atlas, who departed in the wake of an infamous confrontation with the then-fourteen-year-old Tyson. According to Atlas, who still trains fighters and works as a boxing analyst for ESPN, the dispute stemmed from an incident involving Tyson and the eleven-year-old sister of Atlas's wife. Atlas, who had grown increasingly disturbed by Tyson's propensity for violent and sociopathic behavior (as well as D'Amato's inclination to overlook or forgive such behavior), tracked Tyson down and threatened the young fighter at gunpoint. Shortly thereafter, Atlas was dismissed from the Tyson camp; in his 2006 autobiography, *Atlas: From the Streets to the Ring,* Atlas asserted that as part of the separation agreement he was offered by D'Amato (through an intermediary) 5 percent of Tyson's earnings, for life. Atlas's response to the offer, which he considered to be the equivalent of hush money: "Go fuck yourself." Rooney has long disputed some of the details of Atlas's account, and the two have been adversaries ever since. Perhaps a more objective opinion might be offered by Steve Lott.

"Let's say it was true, what Teddy said. Well, Mike was not exactly a college graduate; he was an asshole at times, first class. I'm sure of that. So I'm going to agree with Teddy. Whatever Mike did at that time, it was wrong. Now, Teddy's opinion was this: You cut Mike loose and let him go. Cus said, That's one possibility; the other possibility is to hope and pray he learns from his mistakes. And succeeds. If I do it your way, Teddy, he'll go back to the streets and no one will ever hear from him again. We do it my way, I think he'll learn and he'll be better. Teddy said, No, he won't. Cus said, Yes, he will."

D'Amato, naturally, prevailed in this discussion. Atlas left Team Tyson, replaced, for the most part, by Rooney. It was D'Amato who taught Tyson the fundamentals of boxing, who worked with him daily in the ring, at the musty old gym above the Catskill Police Station. But the mildly reclusive D'Amato, who by this time was not in the best of health, had no desire to travel or to work Tyson's corner when he fought. That job was left to others: first Atlas, then Rooney, along with Baranski and Lott. Whether D'Amato was Tyson's guardian angel, looking out for his welfare and hoping to shape him into a complete and mature person (that, too, is part of the Tyson mythology), or merely an old trainer so desperate for one last championship that he was willing to turn a blind eye to the young fighter's misdeeds . . . well, that is a point of contention that has been argued effectively on both sides. Rooney and Lott believe D'Amato, aided by Cayton and Jacobs, did everything in his power to help Tyson evolve as a human being, as well as a boxer. Rooney, in particular, has been a staunch D'Amato supporter, often using the word "love" to describe the old man's feelings toward Tyson.

Among those less certain of D'Amato's motives is Bert Sugar.

"Cus D'Amato, who was held out as the Second Coming, was no great help," Sugar said. "He took Tyson out of Tryon and promised to give him a high school education. Then why [ten years later] was he taking his GED in prison in Indianapolis? I can't buy that D'Amato was the sainted man he was made out to be. He wanted a heavyweight champion, so he took Tyson in. And he favored him. Jimmy Jacobs once told me when Tyson was fighting every month that the reason they did that was to keep him out of trouble."

The truth about D'Amato and Tyson probably lies somewhere in the middle, though just about anyone who saw them together in the early days acknowledges a genuine affection that ran in both directions. Regardless, D'Amato never got the chance to realize his dream of training another heavyweight champion. He died of complications from pneumonia on November 4, 1985, three days after Tyson ran his record to 11-0 with a first-round knockout of Sterling Benjamin. Nine days after D'Amato's death, a grieving Tyson flew to

Houston and knocked out Eddie Richardson—again, in the first round.

The pace continued unabated for the next twelve months. Tyson continued to live in Catskill, in the same house D'Amato had shared with Ewald. He trained every day with Rooney, fought, on average, once a month, in bouts whose scheduled duration increased as time went on; not that it mattered, since Tyson's practice of knocking his opponents into oblivion was becoming something of a habit. There were lapses—for example, consecutive ten-round decisions over James "Quick" Tillis and Mitch "Blood" Green in May of 1986— that gave at least a glimpse into the Tyson who would emerge later, a fighter who could be frustrated and slowed by a taller opponent who did not cower in his presence. But these were generally dismissed as growing pains. He was, after all, still a teenager, a professional neophyte, unblemished record notwithstanding. And anyway, far more common, and compelling, were the explosive first-round knockouts that became part of the Tyson iconography and were, let's face it, chiefly responsible for the resurrection of the heavyweight division.

Whatever limited popularity boxing had sustained in the late 1970s and early 1980s was attributed primarily, and rightly, to the efforts of a handful of brilliant middleweights and welterweights, most notably Thomas Hearns, Ray Leonard, Roberto Duran, and Marvin Hagler. To galvanize the sport, though, a heavyweight is needed. The emergence of Tyson, with his seemingly Dickensian story and propensity for displays of power and violence, was a tonic for the heavyweight division, and as such a tonic for the sport. On November 22, 1986, in Las Vegas, he became the youngest champion in history by knocking out Trevor Berbick to win the WBC title. Of Tyson's early victories, that was among the most memorable, and not merely because it made him a champion. The image of Berbick, reeling and stumbling around the ring after absorbing one of Tyson's lethal uppercuts, his body fighting furiously and vainly against the darkness falling over his mind, remains one of the indelible images of the Tyson era. As Berbick twitched and fell, stood, wobbled into the ropes, and fell again, Tyson merely watched, bemused, as if almost unable to comprehend his own handiwork.

Within seven months Tyson had completed his dominance of a

unification series sponsored by Home Box Office and become the undisputed heavyweight champion (the first person to hold that title since Ali). Along the way he survived a twelve-round waltz with WBA champ James "Bonecrusher" Smith (who earned the nickname "Boneclutcher" for his reluctance to engage Tyson), a twelve-round decision over IBF champ Tony Tucker, and a sad but necessary fourth-round knockout of Larry Holmes, who probably should have known better.

As spring gave way to summer, Tyson found himself not only at the center of the sporting universe, but in the glare of an increasingly bright pop culture spotlight; whether by design or happenstance he had accomplished the unlikely feat of transcending his sport. A Tyson fight became the hottest ticket in sports. Casinos bid vigorously for the right to host his events; celebrities flocked to ringside, figuring there was no small amount of PR cachet in being spotted at a Tyson fight. No longer did a subscription to HBO necessarily entitle one to view Tyson's latest performance. For that privilege, boxing fans (rapidly becoming an eclectic lot) would have to hand over an additional $34.95 (the cost of the Tyson-Spinks fight, Tyson's first as a pay-per-view headliner). But no one seemed to mind. A Tyson pay-per-view event, in those days, was considered a worthwhile investment, providing a quick fix for anyone in need of a vicarious thrill, a safe and sanitized twentieth-century version of the public execution, as well as ammunition for the inevitable water-cooler conversation at the office on Monday morning.

It's difficult to pinpoint the precise zenith of Tyson's . . . well, "popularity" might be the wrong word; even at his peak, Tyson was held in awe more than he was admired. But, then, that's often the case with boxers, whose chosen profession evinces all manner of contradictory emotions. In some circles it is socially unacceptable to proclaim one's fondness for a sport in which the objective is to render another man unconscious. Rare is the boxer who overcomes this stigma and finds himself embraced at all levels of the socioeconomic strata. Ali came close. It might be a stretch to suggest that affection for Tyson ever rivaled that of Ali; unquestionably, though, he occupied a unique position in the pantheon of world-class athletes. If one were to insist on circling a particular date on the calendar and to declare that to be the apex of Tyson's brilliance, the instant before he stepped off the top rung and began the inevitable fall, then this one is as good as any: June 27, 1988.

On that date (actually the magazine hit newsstands a week earlier, although June 27 was the official publication date), a tight shot of Tyson's glistening face, scowling and sweat soaked, adorned the cover of *Time* magazine, accompanied by this headline: "Why the Fascination with Boxing?" Inside, over the course of a few thousand words, writer Tom Callahan wrestled admirably and artfully with precisely that question, offering the usual suspects—a fascination with violence, cathartic release, admiration for those who are willing to risk their health in pursuit of a better life (since boxing, after all, has always been the province of the downtrodden)—and ultimately admitting that no single explanation suffices. But, Callahan wrote, "If the allure of boxing is hazy, the awe of the champion is clear. Regional vainglories like the World Cup or the World Series only aspire to the global importance of the heavyweight champion. [John L.] Sullivan, Jack Dempsey, Joe Louis, and Ali truly possessed the world."

True enough, and Tyson, at this moment, stood poised to join their ranks as a champion whose following knew no boundaries, geographic or otherwise. Twenty years down the road, at a time when most sports fans would be hard-pressed to name any titleholder in the heavyweight division, it seems almost absurd to imagine professional boxing eliciting such a passionate response or enjoying such a massive and diverse audience. If a national magazine were to devote a cover story to the sport today, it would more likely be accompanied by a much different type of headline, something along the lines of "Whatever Happened to Boxing?"

But on June 27, 1988, the night Mike Tyson defended his title against Spinks, the public's appetite for professional boxing—or at least professional boxing that involved the heavyweight champion—seemed insatiable. It was the richest fight boxing had known, with Spinks guaranteed $13 million and Tyson at least $20 million (depending on pay-per-view revenue), and the attendant publicity was predictably breathless. "Tyson vs. Spinks: Once and for All" screamed (or at least promised) promotional materials for the bout. The consensus among boxing analysts was that the unbeaten twenty-two-year-old

Tyson, weighing 216 pounds, was simply too quick and strong for the thirty-one-year-old Spinks (who weighed 212¼ pounds). But there existed as well a faction that supported Spinks, that gave the challenger a reasonable chance of an upset, thanks to his experience, ring savvy, height advantage (Spinks was six two and a half; Tyson was usually listed, generously, as five eleven) and, not least of all, heart.

Like Tyson, Spinks had never tasted defeat (his record was 31-0); like Tyson, he'd grown up surrounded by urban squalor, in the projects of St. Louis; unlike Tyson, Spinks was a mature adult, a single father apparently content with who he was and what he had done with his life and career. So far as anyone could tell, there was little or no inner turmoil. Spinks's older brother, Leon, who briefly held the heavyweight title in the late 1970s, thanks to a victory over an aging Muhammad Ali, was the clown of the family, a fighter whose misdeeds outside the ring overshadowed his accomplishments in the ring. Michael was a calmer sort, well-spoken and polite, and genuinely liked by most who came to know him.

Sensitive demeanor notwithstanding, Spinks was a true fighter. His résumé included a gold medal in the light heavyweight division at the 1976 Olympics; a courageous fifteen-round decision over Dwight Qawi (just two months after Spinks's girlfriend, and the mother of his young daughter, had been killed in an automobile accident) to win the undisputed light heavyweight championship; and, of course, the two victories over Holmes that established Spinks as a legitimate heavyweight champion. (Although unbeaten at the time of the Tyson fight, Spinks held no titles; the IBF had stripped him of the heavyweight crown in 1987 when he ignored a mandate to defend his title against Tony Tucker, the IBF's top-ranked contender, and instead opted for a more lucrative bout with Gerry Cooney.) In Tyson he would be facing a fighter unlike any on his résumé, but Spinks had banked enough goodwill and respect to be considered at least a threat to Tyson's crown. By fight night he was a 3½-to-1 underdog—significant odds, to be sure, but hardly reflective of the long-shot status accorded most Tyson challengers. If anyone could slow the Tyson onslaught, if anyone could withstand the withering barrage of the first round, and then slowly, methodically wear down the champion, it was Spinks. That, at least, was the conventional wisdom.

As it happened, Spinks was beaten before he set foot in the ring.

"I was with Gil Clancy two days before the fight," said Matt Baranski, recalling an encounter with the Hall of Fame trainer and respected television boxing analyst. "He said, 'Matt, your honest opinion'—there had been a lot of stuff written about Spinks being able to outbox Mike—'what do you think Mike is going to be able to do?' I said, 'Mike is going to wipe him out completely, blow him right out of there. It won't surprise me if it happens in the first round.'"

Any lingering concerns Baranski might have had were alleviated when he visited Spinks's dressing room shortly before the fight.

"When I worked with Mike, I was the guy who went into the other locker room to see the other fighter get wrapped and put the gloves on," Baranski explained. "And I could see it in Spinks. He was so scared."

Entering first, as is customary for the challenger, Spinks appeared lean and fit; unmistakable, though, were the signs of a fighter unprepared for the battle of his life. Whether Spinks was frightened to the point that he was reluctant to leave his dressing room (a rumor that has been widely circulated over the years, although never substantiated) is beside the point. All fighters, Tyson included, know what it's like to be scared. Fear comes with the territory. The trick, as D'Amato was fond of saying, is knowing how to channel the anxiety. "Fear is like fire," the old trainer philosophized. "You can make it work for you: It can warm you in the winter, cook your food when you're hungry, give you light when you are in the dark. Let it get out of control and it can hurt you, even kill you . . . Fear is a friend of exceptional people." Tyson learned early on how to use fear—his own and that of his opponents—to his advantage. And as Tyson walked to the ring, one could see in the flitting eyes of Michael Spinks something less than enthusiasm about the evening's activities. Even more telling: when Spinks removed his robe, it became apparent that he was completely dry. Not a drop of sweat was visible on his skin, clear evidence that he hadn't warmed up sufficiently. Conversely, Tyson entered the ring looking like a man who had just stepped out of a shower; rivulets of sweat poured from his body as he climbed through the ropes and sauntered menacingly around the ring. As was his custom, Tyson ignored all introductions and pleasantries, preferring instead to focus entirely on the task at hand; in this phase of his career Tyson often seemed genuinely annoyed by prefight pageantry—the introduction of celebrities and other dignitaries, even the singing of the national anthem. There was work to be done; everything else was merely a distraction.

"Most fighters, all fighters, really, at some point in time, they lose their desire to just fight the fight," Rooney said. "It becomes a question of money. You see guys come back because they're broke and they need a payday. But the true fighters love to fight. And that's what Mike was—for a while, anyway. We used to say, 'We just want to fight. Who cares about the money? Fuck the money! Let's get in the ring and knock the guy out. Knock him out and go home and have a little party.' That was the glory of it."

Tyson, to the surprise of absolutely no one, pounced at the sound of opening bell; the surprise was that Spinks met him in the center of the ring, apparently prepared to match might with might. Interestingly enough, this was not a unique approach when facing Tyson, for, if nothing else, it provided an opponent with a reliable exit strategy: Absorb the first blow, hope it doesn't hurt too much, hit the canvas . . . and stay there. Then cash the check. Spinks likely had something more ambitious in mind; nevertheless, the strategy backfired spectacularly. Tyson immediately landed a left hook to Spinks's head, and the challenger, obviously stung by the blow, tried to wrap Tyson in a clinch. Referee Frank Capuccino separated the two men, and as Spinks attempted to create some space, Tyson caught him with a left uppercut to the head, followed by a right hook to the ribs. The combination dropped Spinks to one knee. It was the first time in his career that he had ever been knocked down, although he seemed to be more stunned than incapacitated.

"I hurt him with the first punch I threw," Tyson said after the fight. "He wobbled a little, but I knew he would try to fight back. There were only two things he could do: Try to get lucky or try to run around all night."

As Capuccino's count reached four, Spinks struggled to his feet and pronounced himself fit to continue. Tyson, sensing the kill, charged in again. Rather than retreat, Spinks gamely but ineffectively tried to ward off the attack with a weak and slow right hand.

Tyson countered with a left hook and, finally, a perfectly timed right hook to Spinks's jaw. It was a devastating punch, the kind that turns out the lights so quickly and efficiently that the body continues to struggle even after the brain has ceased to work. Spinks's knees buckled and he toppled backward. As Capuccino stood over him, counting, Spinks tried to stand, only to crumple to the canvas once again, this time with his head flopping almost through the ropes.

The fight lasted precisely ninety-one seconds, or, as many reporters noted in their coverage of the event, four seconds less than singer Jeffrey Osborne's prefight rendition of the national anthem. It was over almost before it began; and yet, few observers, if any at all, seemed to feel as though they had been cheated. This was the Tyson they had come to see: a flawless fighter. A work of art.

In reality, Tyson was already inching toward a precipice. The system put in place by D'Amato and tuned perfectly by Cayton and Jacobs was straining under the weight of Tyson's increasingly complicated personal life, which would unravel in spectacular fashion in the coming months (and years). For now, though, he remained a singularly compelling force in the sport of boxing. The Spinks fight is generally regarded as Tyson's greatest achievement, and yet Rooney believes to this day that even then, on that night in Atlantic City, Tyson had barely scratched the surface of his potential.

"In my opinion, Mike was maybe fifty percent of what he should have been, fifty percent of what he was capable of being," Rooney said. That's how good he could have become. But he got caught up in all that bullshit."

As for the challenger . . . Well, there would be no bullshit for him. Michael Spinks took his $13 million and quietly walked away; he never fought again.

3

On his twenty-fourth birthday, April 7, 1984, James Douglas decided it was time for a change.

Again.

The professional boxing career he had embraced, albeit loosely, had been turbulent and inconsistent. Despite what he had promised his father upon returning home to Columbus, James's attitude toward boxing had been, at best, ambivalent, and his performances reflected nothing so much as talent unfulfilled. In the beginning, with Bill Douglas in his corner, serving as trainer, manager, and all-around taskmaster, James expressed shock at the level of devotion required to compete in the professional ranks. As an amateur he had relied primarily on natural athleticism—size, speed, strength—to overpower his opponents. Now, though, the protective headgear was gone and the atmosphere was markedly more intense. The men across the ring were adults, some just as big as he was, some even bigger. Most, regardless of their physical attributes, had a more refined taste for the nastier elements of the sport: the sweat and blood of training, the pain of competition. Buster had left home for a few years, tasted success and defeat, and had come to the conclusion that boxing was his ticket to a better life. It sounded good, and not entirely implausible, that he might even become a heavyweight contender. In reality, the affirmation was half-hearted. At times James trained with intensity and purpose; at other times he had to be dragged out of bed in the morning.

Not coincidentally, James's performances in the ring reflected this inconsistency. After beginning his professional career with five consecutive victories over a five-month period in 1981, he turned in a disturbingly lackluster effort at the Civic Arena in Pittsburgh against six-foot-three, 271-pound David Bey, a mountainous, though not exactly muscular, carpenter and army veteran. Whether intimidated by the prospect of getting hurt, or simply overwhelmed by Bey's size advantage, Douglas, for the first time in his short tenure as a professional, appeared to lack both the conviction and the arsenal to compete. Midway through the second round Bey began landing a series of heavy punches to the head and midsection of an apparently defenseless (or uninterested) Douglas. Between rounds, with Douglas sitting on his stool, the fight was stopped.

The official record of the Bey-Douglas fight shows only that Douglas lost by technical knockout in the second round. It does not reveal the sad postfight exchange between father and son, fighter and trainer, as related by boxing writer Wallace Matthews, who some years later would record this moment in Douglas's career as follows: "The first major blowup between father and son came in 1981, when Buster, in his sixth pro fight, inexplicably quit after two rounds against David Bey. Billy slapped his son around the ring in disgust."

Disappointing though it was, the loss to Bey did not sidetrack Douglas for long. By late 1983 he had compiled a record of 18-1-1 and seemed to the casual observer to be poised for a run at the upper ranks of the heavyweight division. Then, on December 17, in Atlantic City, came a ninth-round technical knockout at the hands of a lowly regarded journeyman named Mike "the Giant" White, a lumbering six-foot-ten former basketball player. It was the first time in Douglas's career that he'd been in a fight that lasted more than eight rounds, and clearly conditioning was a factor. As was the case against Bey, Douglas appeared, at the time the fight was stopped, to have lost interest in the proceedings. Not long after that defeat, exasperated boxing observers, who had trouble reconciling James's periodic ring reticence with the combustible presence of Bill Douglas in his corner, began whispering the word "quitter" in the same breath as the name "James Douglas."

"I don't think any significant punches hit him," observed J. Russell Peltz, the Philadelphia promoter who had helped sell the fight against Bey. "After that one I said, 'I'm bailing out.' I released him."

Douglas, however, did not think of himself as a quitter, and could not, in fact, stomach the idea that others might think of him that way. He wanted to realize his potential as a fighter, but wasn't quite sure how to make that happen. In his heart he knew he lacked the fire that fuels so many boxers—the hunger born of abject poverty or an abusive home life, or even just some innate hardness that draws a man to violence. Even as he refined his skills and studied at the knee of his father, Buster found it difficult to focus on becoming a heavyweight champion. A champion's money would be nice, he sometimes thought, but it didn't drive him the way it drove others. The fame? He could do without that, too. But there were other considerations: a son from a previous relationship named Lamar Jefferson Douglas (James and Lamar's mother never married), who by this time was five years old; and the ghost of James's little brother, Arthur, a talented kid who might have grown up to be the best boxer in the Douglas family, had he not bled to death after suffering an accidental gunshot wound while cleaning a pistol in '83, just as James was beginning to show promise in the ring.

"Artie was tough," James recalled. "He inspired me. When Artie died, it was then I found out . . . shit . . . I'm not afraid of anything."

If not fear, then what was it that provoked fits of inconsistency from Douglas? To this day he remains amused (rather than offended) by the notion that others have ever questioned his courage or character, preferring instead to toss off the losses and pedestrian performances that pock his résumé with a smile or a shrug. There was clutter back then, he will say, when pressed, as if that explains anything. And maybe it does. Although eventually there would be a night of astonishing achievement, rendered all the more remarkable for the hardship endured en route, Douglas generally abhorred all manner of clutter in his life. Arguments with his trainer and father, the pressure of being a young father himself, the tragic death of his brother—none of this was likely to bring out the best in Douglas. Indeed, when things got hard he was more likely to fantasize about returning to his old job driving a truck for the Rite Rug Company in Columbus. That was simple enough. No demands, no pressure.

But what would Artie think? What would their father think?

No, the answer was to diminish the clutter, to create a world in which James would be able to focus on boxing; the way James saw it, that meant a world without Bill Douglas. Or, at least, a boxing ring without Bill Douglas.

"Number one, it's very hard for your father to train you if you're a professional fighter," observed John Russell, James's former trainer and still one of his closest friends. "Bill Douglas was a nice guy, but very tough, and I think it was difficult for a nice, bighearted guy like Buster to follow that. Bill Douglas was the kind of man who, if you ever went into battle, you wanted him beside you. He was old school, didn't put up with any nonsense."

Buster turned first to his uncle, J. D. McCauley, and asked him to assume the role of trainer. McCauley agreed; he also said that if James was serious about changing the arc of his career, he needed new management. (It is worth noting that Douglas's early career was not free of questionable managerial decisions, including one that, memorably, placed him in the ring twice in a period of forty-eight hours in February 1982.) McCauley suggested John Johnson, a former football coach who had taken a long and circuitous path to becoming a capable, if not wildly successful boxing man. Johnson had grown up the son of a coal miner in West Virginia. Perhaps not surprisingly, for someone whose mother's name was Maria Angelina Millimigi, Johnson developed a fondness for the great Italian-American fighters of the mid–twentieth century. He and his brothers (and their buddies) would assemble a makeshift ring in the backyard and pretend they were Rocky Marciano or Jake LaMotta and knock each other senseless— sometimes just for fun, other times to settle disputes.

"I grew up with boxing being a part of the love of my life," Johnson said. Another love was football. As a young man Johnson settled in

Columbus and began building a career in business. Although he achieved a degree of success, emotional fulfillment remained out of reach. What Johnson really wanted was a life in sports. So, in 1972, he sought the help of Woody Hayes, the revered Ohio State University football coach, with whom Johnson had developed a friendship (and for whom he had even provided unofficial recruiting assistance). Johnson told Hayes he was willing to trade in his suit for a whistle, even if it meant longer hours and shorter pay. The coach assessed Johnson's seriousness and commitment, and offered him a position as a graduate assistant. Johnson was twenty-eight years old at the time, a bit on the mature side for a graduate assistant, but he was undeterred. For the next five years he took classes (Johnson eventually earned undergraduate and master's degrees from Ohio State, as well as a good chunk of his doctorate) and studied from a man widely acknowledged, especially at that time, to be one of the greatest (and most demanding) coaches in all of sports.

"It was the best thing that ever happened to me," Johnson said. "Everything I know, everything I accomplished, I give credit to Coach Hayes. He was not only a great coach, he was the most compassionate, caring man I ever knew."

Hayes was also volatile, profane, and outspoken, traits that would come to describe Johnson as well. The connection to Hayes helped Johnson land a pair of high school coaching positions, neither of which lasted more than a year. Johnson said that his fondness for colorful language had contributed to his dismissals. He boasted, jokingly, "The last job, I left with a police escort. Supposedly I had said I was going to kill the principal, which was a damned lie. I said I would *like* to kill the principal."

Like his mentor, Johnson lacked neither confidence nor ambition, characteristics that helped him carve out a niche in boxing, a sport (and business) notorious for eating the weak. A small but not insignificant break came in the mid-1970s, when he began guiding the career of a Columbus middleweight named Steve Gregory. A former Ohio State and Golden Gloves champion, Gregory enlisted the services of Johnson, who was then employed by the Ohio Department of Youth Services, in making the transition from amateur to professional. Johnson, in turn, wisely sought the assistance of Angelo

Dundee in shaping Gregory's career. With Dundee as his trainer and Johnson as his manager, Gregory built a solid professional résumé, winning twenty-eight of thirty-three fights and challenging for the world middleweight title in 1979.

That success notwithstanding, Johnson was hardly a towering figure in boxing when he was approached by Buster Douglas in the spring of 1984. In reality, neither fighter nor manager had much to show for his efforts. When they gathered around the dining-room table at Johnson's home (shortly after the birthday call from James), the manager told Douglas and McCauley matter-of-factly that they would all be starting from scratch. There was no money, no prestige, no power. To illustrate his point, Johnson walked into the kitchen and returned with a paper plate, which he placed, empty and white, on the dining room table.

"This is all we got," Johnson said.

Years later he would add, "That paper plate shouldn't even have been on the top of the table. It should have been under the table, because we didn't even have that much."

Like so many intense working (and personal) relationships, the one forged by Douglas, Johnson, and McCauley would evolve over time, passing through stages of courtship, trust, success, happiness, betrayal, anger, sadness . . . and eventually a parting of the ways. But even at this early phase there were ramifications for all parties, most notably Douglas. The split, to Bill Douglas, represented an affront on a personal and professional level. That his son would turn to another man for guidance in the ring was unimaginable to Bill. How could anyone know Buster better than his own father? It didn't help matters any that the person who would assume the mantle of trainer was Bill's brother-in-law, J.D. Wasn't that, too, a betrayal of sorts, a breaching of unwritten family law?

Worse, in Bill's estimation, was the introduction of Johnson to Team Douglas. Bill had known Johnson from the Columbus boxing scene and had no real quarrel with the man. But this was different. Now Johnson was largely responsible for Buster's livelihood, and Bill questioned his suitability for the role, in part, he would later admit, for reasons that had nothing to do with Johnson's business or boxing acumen.

"I didn't trust white people very much," Bill acknowledged. "Maybe I was wrong, but that was just me."

Odd that he would feel that way, considering the friendships he had fostered with white men in and out of boxing over the years, men like Bruce Trampler, who in all their years on the road together never saw a hint of bigotry from Bill Douglas—only toughness that was dispensed unflinchingly, without regard to race or ethnicity. And yet, there it was, unavoidable, smack at the front of Bill's mind: the white manager stealing away his baby boy. With the help of his brother-in-law, no less!

And so the rift was born between father and son, eventually to be repaired, cracked again, repaired again . . . and so on. For J.D. and Bill, though, the split would be harder and more permanent, complicated by the fact that they were bound by proximity and marriage, if not blood, and thus compelled to spend time with each other once in a while. Business would bring Bill, J.D., and Johnson together for short periods of time over the years, but never were they more than cordial with each other, and often their relationship was acrimonious, if not downright hostile.

"Bill and I were real close, the best of friends," McCauley said. "Then Buster came to my house and asked me to take him over and help train him. That was Buster's idea. So I brought him to John Johnson, and that was the breaking point in our relationship. Bill was mad because he thought he could do a better job of it, and he wanted to be a part of it. But Johnny and Buster's dad—they couldn't get along. And I was in the middle of it."

Neither Douglas nor Johnson disputes McCauley's assessment.

"We were friends way back when, in the younger days," Johnson recalled, somewhat wistfully. "And then Bill, I think, you know . . . some fathers can be . . ." Johnson paused for a moment. "Bill was his trainer and his everything for his first twenty-something fights. Then James called me, and we ended up signing a contract, and Bill resented that. That's all. Bill just had tremendous resentment toward me and J.D. But it was the best thing that ever happened to [James]."

Fifteen years down the road, viewing matters through the prism of hindsight and experience, James Douglas is less appreciative of his time with Johnson.

"When we first got together it was cool," Douglas said. "John would do shit from time to time, but I would just ignore him, try to keep my eye on the prize. But once we got the prize, it all came apart."

For a time, though, they chased the prize together, lunging after it in fits and starts. Johnson worked the promotional and managerial end of the business, while McCauley assumed the challenging task of motivating and training Douglas. It was, by most accounts, a ceaseless struggle. Though physically gifted and charming enough to talk a good game, Douglas remained ambivalent about boxing. There were days when he attacked his training and looked like the champion he would eventually become; there were other days when he offered a litany of excuses for failing to complete roadwork or bailing out of sparring sessions. McCauley often accompanied Douglas on training runs that became walks, and when he'd grow tired of his nephew's complaining, he'd give Buster a shove in the back and exhort him to be stronger. Sometimes Buster would resume jogging; sometimes he wouldn't.

"James, at heart, is a laid-back, supernice guy," Johnson said. "But there were times he didn't train hard. There's no question about that."

In the summer of 1984, a few months after meeting with Johnson and establishing a new management team, Douglas faced Dave Starkey in a fight that didn't exactly portend greatness. It was, in fact, the strangest encounter of Douglas's career, ending as it did with Douglas knocking Starkey down, and the enraged Starkey responding by trying to throw Douglas out of the ring. The fight was stopped when the two men began wrestling each other to the canvas and both corners spilled into the ring; it went into the books as "no contest," meaning it might as well not have happened, which was fine with the Douglas camp. Better things were to come, at least in the short term.

On November 7, 1984, Johnson received a last-second offer for Douglas to fight Randall "Tex" Cobb in Las Vegas. Cobb was one of the more interesting fighters in the annals of boxing. Hirsute and heavy-browed, with a flattened nose and nodules of scar tissue accenting his face, he looked every inch the battle-hardened fighter. That appearance, coupled with a surprisingly sharp intellect and wit, and a background in martial arts, eventually helped Cobb ease into an acting career, where, typically, he played the part of a bad guy or a biker or a fighter. Sometimes all three at once.

In his prime, Cobb was no slouch in the ring. A promoter's dream, he would invariably endure an enormous amount of punishment, donate some blood, and fight to the final bell. He was never knocked out, although his fights sometimes were so gruesome that referees were compelled to call a halt to the proceedings. (Indeed, after watching Larry Holmes's grisly dismantling of a bloody Cobb in 1982, the famed broadcaster and fight commentator Howard Cosell was so repulsed that he vowed never to work another professional fight; it was a promise he kept.) Although he lacked the tools of a champion, Cobb boasted an impressive 25-3 record and was widely considered to be a dangerous opponent; anyone who stepped into the ring with him understood that there was risk involved. Johnson knew it, Douglas knew it. Complicating matters further was the realization that Douglas would have only two days to prepare for the fight. That was the deal. Take it or leave it.

Douglas accepted the offer on a Wednesday, flew to Vegas on Thursday, and on Friday night proceeded to win the fight by a majority decision. Next came a first-round knockout of Dion Simpson in Atlantic City, in March of 1985. Then, just as he seemed to be getting on a bit of a roll, Douglas lost a ten-round decision to Jesse Ferguson, a setback so jarring to his confidence that Douglas reached out, once again, to his father. Bill Douglas accepted the olive branch and returned to his son's side. The plan was for Bill and J. D. Mc-Cauley to work as cotrainers, with John Johnson continuing to serve as manager. In reality, the arrangement was far more complicated, tarnished as it was by the residue of Bill's prior estrangement from James, James's ongoing attempts to both please his father and escape his shadow, and Bill's contempt for McCauley and Johnson.

It was the last of these things that made the Douglas camp such a tumultuous, often dysfunctional place in the late 1980s. Although Bill Douglas and McCauley were listed as cotrainers, it was Bill who ran the show in the gym, who directed training sessions and tolerated no interference from McCauley or Johnson. McCauley was not easily intimidated, however. He'd been a fighter, too, after all, and wasn't about to cede complete authority to Bill without an argument. And there were plenty over the years. Sometimes these were merely turf wars, each man marking his territory with spit and sweat, cursing the other out for being too hard on James . . . or not hard enough, depending on the day. Typically, in the end, Bill would emerge with his alpha status intact, perhaps because he had more at stake. James was his flesh and blood, after all, and how could J.D. or anyone else for that matter, possibly understand what made the boy tick?

Regardless, the constant fighting was exhausting for all involved, especially Buster.

"My dad was bickering with John and J.D. all the time," Douglas remembered. "There was so much turmoil. They would come to work, man, and be scared to death to say anything. John and J.D.— my dad would look at them like, *You open your mouth and I'm gonna smack your teeth out!* And they knew he would, too. So they were scared, and it was really intense. They'd wait until my dad left the gym to talk to me. J.D would say something once in a while to me, but if he said a little bit too much, my dad would tell him to shut up, and then J.D. would say, 'Hey, you can't tell me to shut up!' Then they'd get to arguing. But Johnny wouldn't say anything. J.D. would, because, you know, they were like that ever since he started dating my mother. My mother was J.D.'s sister, of course, and J.D. and my dad at first started out pretty good friends. He admired my dad, really liked my dad, but somewhere along the line it went bad."

If the volatility of his boxing family affected Douglas, the impact, for a time, was largely unnoticeable to outsiders. The first time Douglas stepped between the ropes following the return of Bill Douglas to his corner, James posted the biggest victory of his career, an improbable ten-round unanimous decision over former champion Greg Page on January 17, 1986, in Atlanta. Given his spotty record to that point, and the loss to Ferguson in his previous fight, Douglas's performance against Page, a former WBA heavyweight champion who was still one of the top fighters in the game, seemed nothing short of stunning. Those accustomed to witnessing a soft and fatigued James

Douglas had to wonder what was behind this transformation, for here was a fit and fearless fighter, flicking off jabs with precision, countering with devastating hooks, and generally acting like a man on a quest.

On the heels of that victory, which once again catapulted Douglas into the ranks of serious contenders, came consecutive victories over Dave Jaco and Dee Collier. By this time it was September of 1986, and Mike Tyson's reign was nearly under way. (Tyson would knock out Trevor Berbick in November to capture the WBC title and become the youngest heavyweight champion in history.) For Douglas, though, a title shot was not far off. It came in the form of an offer to meet Tony Tucker for the vacant International Boxing Federation crown on May 30, 1987, in Las Vegas; coincidentally, that fight would be the highlight of an undercard of Tyson's defense of the WBC and WBA crowns against Pinklon Thomas. So, for Douglas, the Tucker fight represented not only a championship opportunity, but a chance to prove himself on a grand stage. A win, in all likelihood, would make him more than just a heavyweight champion, but a probable challenger to Tyson in a fight that would surely result in the biggest payday of Douglas's career; a loss, especially one that offered little entertainment value, could relegate him to the slag heap of heavyweight boxing.

What Douglas needed in the months leading up to the Tucker fight was a clean and orderly training camp; what he got was a family feud. Tension between the warring factions—Bill Douglas on one side, Johnson and McCauley on the other—escalated nearly to the point of parody. There had been fights before. After the fiasco of the Starkey fight, for example, Bill had gone ballistic and blamed the chaos, at least indirectly, on what he perceived to be incompetence on the part of James's handlers. With Buster looking on, Bill and J.D. exchanged words in the dressing room afterward; then they exchanged punches.

"Nothing too serious," McCauley said. "Nobody went to jail or anything, but it was kind of crazy for a hot minute or two."

There was another time J.D. responded to Bill's bullying not with a fist, but with a golf club. Once, during a fracas at a family picnic, J.D. waved a gun at Bill. Was it any surprise that in this atmosphere James found it difficult to focus on Tony Tucker?

And Tucker was not a man to be taken lightly. At six feet five, with good hand speed and an athlete's gift for moving swiftly and effortlessly around the ring—characteristics that helped him compile a 34-0 record prior to the Douglas fight—Tucker was considered one of the top fighters in the heavyweight division. Stylistically and aesthetically, he bore at least a passing resemblance to Muhammad Ali, although Tucker's list of opponents was largely unimpressive, and already he, like every other heavyweight, had been relegated to undercard status beneath Tyson. Still, no one could deny that Tucker had earned his distinction as the top contender for the IBF title (Douglas was ranked No. 2), and oddsmakers appropriately made him a 4-to-1 favorite going into the Douglas fight. Tucker was approaching a peak in the spring of '87, and indeed would stagger Tyson in the first round of a subsequent meeting before losing a twelve-round decision.

While his career would eventually unravel in the wake of a series of injuries and a debilitating cocaine addiction, there is no denying that for a time Tucker was a formidable fighter. Clearly, Douglas would have to be in top form to beat him. As it turned out, he was not.

"Going into that [training] camp, there was just so much going on," Douglas recalled. "It was the worst camp possible."

On that much, all parties seem to agree. As for who was responsible for the ensuing debacle . . . well, that is a point of contention. Douglas, to his credit, takes much of the blame—he was in the ring, after all. Johnson claims that he and McCauley were basically shoved aside as the camp progressed, to the point that Bill Douglas was in charge of virtually everything. If Bill was committed to his son's cause, he also seemed oddly drawn to the spotlight. A week before the fight, for example, as James skipped rope in a public training session for the media, Bill picked up a rope himself and began working out right next to James. An armchair psychologist might have had a field day with that one—the father flexing his muscle in front of the son, nudging the son out of the way.

Then there was the statement, subliminal or otherwise, that Bill made on the night of the Tucker fight. It is traditional in boxing for cornermen, in a show of unity, to be attired in garb bearing the name of their fighter. And, indeed, Bill entered the ring wearing a T-shirt adorned with the Douglas name: *BILL Douglas!*

Regardless, by fight night, Johnson said, he and McCauley were little more than spectators.

"J.D. and I sat in the audience," Johnson said. "We didn't even work the corner."

In James's version of the story, all three men were in the corner (with Bill clearly in charge, to the extent that eventually Johnson and McCauley abandoned the scene in favor of a safer vantage point), tensely coexisting as their fighter danced and jabbed his way through the early rounds, apparently on his way to a convincing victory—and a heavyweight championship. Then something happened. Suddenly it was the tenth round, and there was James, on the ropes after taking a shot from Tucker, not hurt, really, but tired, or uninterested (if that was possible), covering up, trying to withstand a barrage of punches from Tucker, who must have been amazed at this sudden reversal of fortune. Referee Mills Lane gave Douglas every opportunity to assert and protect himself, but Douglas declined the offer. Finally, at the 1:36 mark, with Tucker flailing away mightily and Douglas refusing to fight back, Lane stepped in.

And just like that, the fight was over. Tony Tucker was the IBF champion by technical knockout, and James Douglas . . . well . . .

"He had shown that he had no heart," said Bert Sugar. "He had quit in a fight. Just stopped. And everybody said, 'What the hell is this?'"

What it was, according to Douglas, was the public unraveling of a man who didn't care whether he won or lost. There were too many distractions, too much clutter. He wanted out, and so he took the nearest exit.

"I was just going through the motions," Douglas said. "Watch the tape. You can still see it if you look in the corner. J.D. would go to give me water, and my dad would snap the water bottle out of his hand. And Johnny would just be standing there, saying nothing.

"It was all mental. There wasn't any problem with me, physically. They always say that bullshit about me running out of gas. I was in great shape. I was 227 pounds. Physically, I was ready for that fight.

Mentally? Man, that's something else. I'm telling you, I was on cruise control. I'm lucky I didn't get hurt, because I was just going through the motions. Shadowboxing—that's what I was doing. I guess I just got tired of everything."

Mention the name James Douglas to almost anyone who closely follows the sport of professional boxing and they will invariably invoke two events: the upset of Tyson and the loss to Tucker that preceded it. The former was startling not only because of Tyson's seeming invincibility, but because it was unfathomable that he could lose to the man who had collapsed and surrendered to Tucker. How could one athlete be capable of two such dissimilar performances? Hard-core (and hard-boiled) boxing fans are prone to slapping Douglas with the label of "quitter" and rationalizing the upset of Tyson as the reasonable outcome of a confluence of events: Tyson had already begun to slip and did not take his opponent seriously; Douglas trained seriously and fought bravely for the first (and only?) time in his life; Tyson's support team was incompetent.

Some of these things are true, and yet they tell only a portion of the story. Moreover, it seems harsh and simplistic to suggest that Douglas was an inveterate slacker who merely got lucky on one night in Tokyo. A more measured and thoughtful assessment was offered by Larry Merchant, the color commentator and boxing analyst who covered the Tyson fight for HBO, and who had followed Douglas's career for several years prior to their meeting.

"Tony Tucker was a very good fighter," Merchant said. "One of the best amateurs, I'm told, that we ever had. He was a big, strong guy, well schooled, but didn't have the athletic talent that Buster had. Buster was beating him and then just didn't have the energy to keep going. Whether it was a lack of conditioning or the other guy was better, I can't say, but Tucker was more persistent and beat him."

Unlike Bert Sugar, and many others, Merchant is reluctant to paint Douglas with too broad a brush. A quitter?

"I don't really remember that," Merchant said. "I think his reputation was more of being a guy who just didn't have the desire to go as far as his talent could take him. I never thought he was a quitter; I just thought he, for whatever reason, maybe how big he was . . . Sometimes it's body language—he had a kind of indolent way of movement—and even the way he talked . . . There was no visible fire there. But you knew he had some competitive juices, otherwise he never would have gotten even that far."

As the story goes, Bill Douglas was so disgusted by his son's lack of resolve in the Tucker fight that he walked away from Buster and vowed never to work his corner again. But that, too, is more fiction than fact. Bill later said on several occasions that he and James agreed to a parting of the ways; more likely, it seems, is that James realized, once again, that he needed distance from the man. Dynamite was a great fighter, maybe even a great teacher. But some things just don't work, despite the best of intentions, and the pairing of Bill Douglas and James Douglas was one of those things.

The morning after the Tucker fight, uncertain of his status as manager or even whether his fighter would continue in the sport, John Johnson visited James Douglas's hotel suite. To his surprise, Johnson listened as James told him it was time to make a change. Bill Douglas would have to go.

Not long after that, James sat down at a table at his father's house, with Lula Pearl present for moral support (and, realistically, to act as a referee in the event things turned ugly), and broke the news to Dynamite.

"Dad, this isn't going to work anymore," James said. "I have to work with these guys, and they're scared to death with you around. I have to do this, and I have to do it my way."

Bill understood, accepted what amounted to a dismissal with nothing more than a nod and a simple pronouncement.

"You're going to be on your own, you know, because those guys don't know anything about boxing."

"Yeah, Dad, I know," James said. "But I've learned so much from you already. It'll be okay."

And it was okay. For a while, in fact, it was much more than that. With Bill out of the picture, supporting his son quietly, from a safe distance, James returned to the gym. Together with Johnson and McCauley, he went about the business of picking up the pieces of his career. Whether his reputation could withstand the fallout of the Tucker loss remained to be seen. Buster would have to prove himself all over again. He would have to prove that he wasn't a quitter.

4

It's very simple: For a while [Mike] was with people who were very positive, and then he met people who were exactly the opposite. And it changed him. Mike was smart. When he traveled, he knew that if he did anything wrong, he'd have to face Jimmy Jacobs and Bill Cayton. You know how some kids hate doing anything wrong because they don't want to go home and face their parents? Well, Mike said to himself, "Screw it! I'd rather get shot in the streets of Brooklyn than face Jim and Bill."

    I've been in a room when Jim scolded both of us. This was 1987. Mike did an interview from Las Vegas—he was the heavyweight champion, and he did an interview with [New York Times reporter] Phil Berger, on the phone; usually I listened to these things just to try to monitor them. Well, the interview comes out the next day and Jim says, "Steve, how come you let him say that? What happened?" Phil had asked Mike, "How are you doing?" And Mike had said, "I'm bored." Jimmy didn't like that. He said, "Steve, how could he be bored? He's the heavyweight champion of the world, making millions! People think he's stupid when he talks that way. And by the way, Steve, why did you say that stuff about Leonard and Ali?"

    A week before this I was interviewed, too, and I had said, stupidly, that Mike was so good he was going to make people forget about Muhammad Ali and Sugar Ray Leonard. Jim said, "Steve, I'm coming out in three days; I want to see both of you." So Jim comes out to Vegas, where we were living at the time, and says, "Mike, Steve, come with me." He closes the door, sits us down, like he's Mike's father, and Mike is hanging his head like a baby. Jim says, "Mike, how can you say that stuff to Phil Berger? It makes you look stupid." Mike says, "I'm sorry." Jim looks at me, says, "Steve, you told that writer Mike is going to be so good . . ." And as Jim is railing at me, Mike's foot is right next to my foot, under the table, and Jim didn't see this, but as Jim is digging into me, Mike is taking my foot and gently popping it with his foot, saying, "Now you're getting yours, huh?" We were like two kids in school.

Mike didn't make that mistake again, and I didn't make that mistake again. But that's the kind of critical insight Mike got from Jim. Mike wasn't perfect, but for a kid from Brooklyn, he was pretty good. So when people say he was never good . . . well, I beg to differ. You can't hide that stuff.

—Steve Lott

If Bill Cayton and Jim Jacobs were ostensibly equal partners in the business of managing and guiding Mike Tyson's career, it is fair to say that their roles were not identical. Owing in large part to his enduring relationship with D'Amato, Jacobs enjoyed a more personal connection with the fighter, one built on a foundation of friendship and love, as well as mutual economic interests.

Jacobs's history with D'Amato could be traced back to the early 1960s, when Jacobs was a sales manager for a company that distributed business equipment and supplies. That was his vocation. By avocation, Jacobs was a handball player and avid boxing fan who had already spent many years (he started at the age of twelve) amassing a substantial collection of fight films (these would later become part of the inventory for Big Fights, Inc.,). Jacobs would sometimes screen the films for boxing writers in New York, and it was at one of these screenings that he was introduced to D'Amato.

Bound by their passion for the sport, D'Amato and Jacobs developed a lasting friendship. Jacobs lived for several years in D'Amato's Manhattan apartment, and when the trainer moved upstate to Catskill, to a life of semiretirement, Jacobs and Cayton provided financial assistance to D'Amato's fledgling Catskill Boxing Club. Never one to be preoccupied with money, D'Amato in those days, and for the last fifteen years of his life, willfully became a man with no traceable source of income, in part because he felt the most sensible way to settle (or, rather, win) a long-standing dispute with the Internal Revenue Service (the agency claimed he owed somewhere in the neighborhood of $250,000) was to not have any money at all. And so he took none or gave it away, living a quiet, modest life with Camille Ewald and a small, ever-changing stable of fighters.

As the late Phil Berger wrote in *Blood Season: Tyson and the World of Boxing,* "In Catskill D'Amato became a kind of boxing Father Flanagan, welcoming the outcasts from the neighborhood, and sometimes from beyond. At any one time there were usually a select few who were invited to stay in the Ewald house. Most of the lodgers were amateurs, and before Tyson, only Kevin Rooney would go on to fight professionally for D'Amato, while being managed by Cayton and Jacobs."

Not surprisingly, Rooney, himself a wayward kid from New York (Staten Island), became a devout disciple of D'Amato, reinforcing to Tyson not only the trainer's philosophy and techniques, but also his faith in the management team of Cayton and Jacobs.

"Mike moved into Cus's house in 1980, and it took Cus a good two years to get Tyson's trust," Rooney recalled. "I was still living in the house then. What you had was a black kid surrounded by all these white people. And the kid was only twelve, thirteen years old, whatever. But Cus loved Mike, supported him, tried to give him confidence. He was very smart about Mike. Cus showed him films, really taught him, in and out of the gym. And Bill and Jimmy were the brains behind the operation. I just inherited Mike. That's all."

Like D'Amato, Jacobs would sit for hours with Tyson, watching old fight films, dissecting the strengths and weaknesses of fighters from a bygone era. By most accounts Tyson considered Jacobs to be much more than a manager: He was a friend and mentor, the adult male (and father figure) to whom he was closest following the death of D'Amato. By the time Tyson so impressively dismantled Michael Spinks on June 27, 1988, however, Jacobs, too, had passed away, and much of the discipline and order that had been integral to Tyson's success both in and out of the ring had substantially eroded.

Whether this was a byproduct of Tyson's naturally growing up and taking control (or losing control) of his own life, as adults are wont to do, or whether it was attributable largely to interference (fueled by greed and malevolence) on the part of others has long been a point of dispute when those concerned with such matters begin debating the rise and fall of Mike Tyson. Interestingly, Tyson, occasional fits of madness notwithstanding, has rarely strayed from a stance of self-flagellation, typically preferring to hold himself accountable for all transgressions and mistakes, and imploring anyone who might be inclined to think otherwise that sympathy would best be directed elsewhere.

If 1988 will be remembered by boxing historians as the apex of Tyson's career—the year he knocked out Larry Holmes, Tony Tubbs, and, most notably, Spinks, bringing a clarity and fervor to the heavyweight division that it had not known since the glory days of Ali and Frazier—then it will also be remembered as the year in which Tyson became a fixture on the front page of the tabloids as well as the back page. There had been prior incidents of an inflammatory nature—the propositioning of a sales clerk at an Albany, shopping mall (and subsequent ejection from a movie theater in that mall) in 1986; an incident in 1987 at a Los Angeles parking lot, in which Tyson allegedly tried to kiss a female employee and struck a male attendant (the case was settled out of court)—but 1988 brought a seemingly endless string of unfortunate events, and an inexhaustible supply of fodder for gossip columnists and sports reporters.

To the extent that any single event could be considered the catalyst (or at least the defining moment) for the train wreck that Tyson's life became, then his marriage, on February 8, 1988, to the actress Robin Givens is as suitable as any other. Tyson had become infatuated with Givens nearly two years earlier, after seeing her on television (Givens, then in her early twenties, had appeared in several movies and been a star of the ABC series *Head of the Class*). Tyson reached out to Givens through intermediaries. The young actress was smart, attractive, fashionable (traits that inevitably led to a spate of "Beauty and the Beast" headlines in newspapers around the globe) and the product of a background that was decidedly different from Tyson's. Givens had grown up comfortably middle-class, been educated in private secondary schools, and attended Sarah Lawrence College. (According to her résumé, she had also attended Harvard Medical School, although that claim, along with the accuracy of others, was called into question as the Tyson-Givens affair descended into the uniquely depraved soap opera hell that is reserved for doomed celebrity marriages.)

There were two distinct but overlapping layers to the Tyson-Givens story: the first involved their personal travails; the second focused on control of Tyson's burgeoning financial empire. When Jacobs, who had been waging a battle with leukemia, died on March 25, 1988, Tyson became vulnerable to entreaties from any number of persons who stood to gain by currying favor with him. A story often has been told of a framed photograph of Tyson delivering a blow to Marvis Frazier (Tyson knocked out the son of former champion Joe Frazier in the first round of a fight in Glens Falls, New York, in 1986) that Cayton proudly displayed on his office wall. Tyson autographed the photo with the following inscription:

To Bill
From your boy Mike
8-22-86.
To my dear friend and the man I love greatly

In reality, though, it was Jacobs to whom Tyson felt a particularly strong bond; by comparison, the fighter's relationship with Cayton was more professional and businesslike. It is fair to say that while Tyson certainly respected and liked Cayton (at least in the beginning), the two did not enjoy the same level of intimacy experienced by Jacobs and Tyson. So it wasn't surprising that Jacobs's passing left an immense void in Tyson's life and set in motion a chain of events that would ultimately result in a complete and irrevocable disruption of the athletic, personal, and financial structure that had so successfully been implemented by the original Team Tyson.

With Jacobs out of the picture, Tyson's new wife, along with her mother, Ruth Roper, found it much easier to convince Tyson that Cayton did not have the fighter's best interests at heart, and that there might be a better way to manage Tyson's career and finances—matters that, to be perfectly blunt, had never been of much concern to Tyson in the past. He had been content to fight and party and enjoy the fruits of his labor, without expending too much thought or energy on the minutiae of investments, endorsements, and deferred income. Almost from the outset, however, the new women in Tyson's life expressed mistrust toward Cayton and, to a lesser extent, Jacobs.

Roper was painted in the press as either a shrewd businesswoman or a conniving and manipulative gold digger who instilled within her daughter at an early age the value of networking and, even more important, *marrying right*. A single mother, she had once retained the services of the renowned palimony attorney Marvin Michelson in a lawsuit against baseball player Dave Winfield, whom she had dated, and from whom, Roper claimed, she had received a sexually transmitted disease. Roper had worked an assortment of jobs while raising her two daughters (mostly on her own, although she had twice been married), and eventually built a successful New York–based business known as R. L. Roper Consultants. By the summer of 1988, she was also handling the day-to-day administration of a new business entity, Mike Tyson Enterprises, and in that capacity she, along with Givens, stood at, or at least near, the helm of one of the most powerful sports franchises in the world.

Roper and Givens were not the only ones trying to gain control of Tyson's fortune. So, too, was Don King, a onetime numbers runner from Cleveland who had served nearly four years in prison before transforming himself into the most powerful figure in professional boxing. With his electrified hair, transparently jolly countenance, and penchant for creative language (this is the man who coined the term "trickeration"), King played the role of the buffoon with an almost perverse glee. In reality, though, King was far from the cartoon character he pretended to be when surrounded by a sea of microphones and television cameras. In his youth he had been a ruthless, physically imposing (he stood six feet, four inches tall and weighed 240 pounds), at times charming street hustler who had survived at least two attempts on his life by rival gang members.

Initially convicted of second-degree murder for the April 1966 beating death of a man named Sam Garrett, a sickly, 134-pound "customer" who had been slow to pay his debts, King avoided a life term when a judge reduced the conviction to manslaughter. In his aggressively reported biography of King, *Only in America: The Life and Crimes of Don King,* the late Jack Newfield presents a compelling argument that the judge presiding over King's trial, Hugh Corrigan, had been corrupted by the Cleveland mob and had in all probability received some type of compensation in exchange for treating King delicately. A decade later, for example, King secured a public endorsement from Muhammad Ali on behalf of Judge Corrigan, who was then campaigning for a position on the Ohio Court of Appeals. As Newfield wrote, "Ali recorded a commercial . . . that said he was endorsing Corrigan because of what he did to help 'my good friend Don King.' "

King was released from Ohio's Marion Correctional Facility on September 30, 1971, and soon began the process of making over his life and reputation. With the help of a handful of high-profile benefactors (including Lloyd Price, the 1950s-era singer-songwriter best known for the hits "Stagger Lee" and "Personality"), King acquired wealth and fame in equal measure, first through sometimes shady real estate investments and later through his role as boxing's P. T. Barnum. He rose to international prominence by promoting the 1974 heavyweight championship fight between Ali and George Foreman, an event staged in Zaire, Africa, and thus famously remembered as the "Rumble in the Jungle," and over the years worked with most of the sport's biggest names, many of whom eventually parted ways with the promoter acrimoniously, or litigiously, claiming they had unwittingly signed onerous promotional contracts with Don King Productions. (Tyson would later fall into this category as well.)

King invariably emerged from these disagreements with his smile and stock portfolio intact. Like a carnival barker, he had a gift for making the tawdry seem sublime, but in order to maintain control over the sport of boxing, he had to find a way into Tyson's heart and mind, as well as his pocket. Getting past Cayton and Jacobs proved an almost insurmountable hurdle for King, but as the balance of power shifted toward Givens and Roper, he sensed an opening.

"Don King is the most notorious con man that boxing has ever had," said Kevin Rooney. "You can go all the way back to the '20s, the 1900s, when Dempsey and Jack Johnson and those guys were fighting. Boxing has always been a con game, but King is the best. He's the king. In the 1980s he corralled the whole market. Whenever anyone was fighting, he had nothing to lose, because he always had contracts with both fighters."

It was King's predictable and not unwise desire to arrange with Tyson a long-term deal that would give King the exclusive right to promote Tyson's fights and thus ensure a steady and enormous stream of revenue well into the future. If worded carefully, the contract would effectively usurp the power of Cayton, Tyson's manager, and even that of Mike Tyson Enterprises.

Throughout 1988, King doggedly went about the business of courting Tyson, using every tool at his disposal to gain the fighter's trust and friendship, including, most obviously, one that would cleave a racial divide between the black fighter and his white manager. Following the death of Jim Jacobs (Tyson, it should be noted, was unaware of the severity of Jacobs's illness, since the manager had kept it hidden from Tyson until the final days), a distraught and vulnerable Tyson began spending time with King at the promoter's estate in Ohio. While it seems unlikely in retrospect that Tyson considered King a friend, or even a trustworthy ally, he was willing to listen to King's sales pitch, which included a theme of racial solidarity and criticism of Cayton and Jacobs, two men who reflected, in King's estimation, the disturbing trend of boxing being controlled by Jews. Whether King believed any of this or not is irrelevant; it was merely a wedge to be driven between Tyson and Cayton, who was now the fighter's sole manager. And, perhaps, there was a loophole in the Cayton-Tyson agreement, since it had been signed without Tyson having knowledge of Jacobs's illness.

In a thoughtful and thought-provoking article that first appeared in the Fall 1996 issue of *Transition,* author Gerald Early tells the story of an encounter between Tyson and King that ended with the promoter handing Tyson a copy of Jawanza Kunjufu's *Countering the Conspiracy to Destroy Black Boys,* "a very short and easy-to-read piece of racial paranoia—a poorly reasoned, wretchedly researched, badly written book that is enormously popular in Afrocentric circles and among the black reading public generally. It argues in almost laughably reductive Freudian terms that whites fear people of color because they [whites] lack color, and so want to rule and destroy them: women have penis envy, whites have melanin envy. Racism is thus a form of hysteria which is perfectly immune to remedy, a kind of genetic disorder."

According to the author, King kept at least a dozen copies of the book in his home, so that he would always have one handy in the event that a young, impressionable black fighter came to visit. He recommended the book "not to calm or cure their insecurities, but to worsen them."

Whether this cynical strategy worked on Tyson—indeed, he may not have even bothered to read the book—is difficult to say. This much is certain: By the end of 1988, Don King would be the most influential man in the life and career of Mike Tyson. Aiding him in this transition were Rory Holloway and John Horne, a pair of men who had grown up in Albany and who were first acquaintances of Tyson's, then friends and running mates, and eventually, some years down the road, his comanagers.

Holloway, a youth counselor whose family owned a grocery store in Albany, had known Tyson for some time, dating back to the fighter's rambunctious teenage years. (Tyson was introduced to Holloway through Holloway's younger brother, Todd, a standout basketball player at Christian Brothers Academy in Albany.) Even now, when Tyson the millionaire wanted to get away from the pressure of boxing (and from his fraying marriage) and just hang out and party, he often turned to Holloway for support and companionship. In return for his serving as the champion's wingman, Tyson assisted Holloway financially. (While the two men likely enjoyed a legitimate friendship at one time, their relationship seems to have been corrupted by fame and wealth, and exploited by King.)

Horne had left New York several years earlier and relocated to Los Angeles, where he had attempted to fashion a career as an actor and stand-up comedian (he would later try his hand at producing movies). It was through Holloway that Tyson became friends with Horne, and by the summer of 1988 the three of them were nearly inseparable.

The majority of what has been written about this period of Tyson's life depicts Horne and Holloway as little more than pawns in King's grand scheme to secure control of Tyson's life and career. If this is so (and it is a claim both have rejected over the years), they did their jobs well. In *The Inner Ring,* Tyson's former limousine driver, Rudy Gonzalez, describes a series of meetings between King and Horne and Holloway supporting the notion that Tyson's buddies were already on the King payroll in 1988 and that their job description included assisting the promoter in his attempts to steal Tyson from Cayton. To that end, according to Gonzalez, Holloway and Horne "began continuously pounding Mike Tyson with a 'black rap.' The white man, Bill Cayton, was using him and stealing his money. And his white trainers didn't give the champion the same respect they would give to a white fighter."

To a man, Tyson's original team members echo this unflattering view of King and his subordinates and embrace the idea that they conspired to break Tyson's allegiance to Cayton. A slightly more generous perspective (of Horne, anyway) was offered by Donald McRae in *Dark Trade: Lost in Boxing:* "Horne exuded an instinctive sharpness at odds with media sketches of him as just another fool in the expanded Tyson asylum of gangbangers, homies and assorted crazies. There was an aloof arrogance about him, a cutting vitriol in most of his dealings with the white media. And yet he had a certain sophistication, élan even, which suggested that there was something beyond the coarse caricatures of him as a snake-like hustler."

Like King, both Holloway and Horne would one day be targeted in a multimillion-dollar lawsuit filed by Tyson. For now, though, they were his closest allies, standing by to pick up the pieces—and hand them over to King—as Tyson's marriage to Robin Givens, along with the rest of his personal life, disintegrated in public.

First, in May, came a fender-bender in New York, after which

Tyson tried to give away his $183,000 Bentley convertible to the two patrolmen investigating the accident. On Friday, June 17, just ten days before Tyson was scheduled to defend his title against Michael Spinks, Givens appeared on a New York newscast to defend herself and her mother against accusations that they were interfering with Tyson's career. Two days later a story in *Newsday* depicted Tyson, with supporting quotes from Givens, as a man prone to violent physical outbursts. His wife, allegedly, had been a recent victim.

Meanwhile, the struggle for control of Tyson's financial empire continued unabated. Remarkably, none of these things seemed to have any noticeable impact on Tyson the fighter. In fact, on June 27, 1988, the very day he knocked out Spinks, Tyson sued Cayton in an attempt to break their contract. One month later, on July 27, Tyson and Cayton settled their dispute out of court, with Cayton agreeing to accept a significant reduction in his managerial fee.

"At the time of the Spinks fight, Don King, Robin Givens, and Bill Cayton are three entities looking over Mike," explained Steve Lott. "Robin has control because she's married to him. Don is behind Robin's back, giving Mike a promotional contract to sign that would lock Mike up to Don. Mike, being the dutiful husband, gives the contract to Robin to look over. Mike says, 'Don gave me this. I'll do whatever you want.' Her lawyer reports that even though they're about to sue Bill to break the [managerial] contract, this contract with Don King . . . if Don was Mike's promoter, he'd be able to steal every buck from Mike—before she could [get at] it! . . . So what she did, after a month of a lawsuit with Bill, going through all the books, and realizing that Bill actually overpaid Mike, she rehired Bill, bringing the contract down from thirty-three and a third to twenty percent. While Bill didn't like that idea, he said, 'Let's be done with it, let's get Mike fighting, let's get him back in the ring.'"

Easier said than done, for while Tyson might have been capable of casting aside distractions while preparing for the Spinks fight, he now seemed to be collapsing beneath the weight of his own negative publicity. Among the more infamous events in the bad behavior canon of Mike Tyson was an off-duty encounter with heavyweight contender Mitch "Blood" Green shortly before dawn on the morning of August 23 at an all-night boutique in Harlem. Tyson later said he was visiting the store to pick up a custom-made white leather jacket bearing the inscription "Don't Believe the Hype." While exiting the store he ran into Green, whom Tyson had beaten by unanimous decision in a 1986 fight. Words were exchanged. As to the precise nature of those words, well, choose your version. Tyson painted Green as the instigator; Green claimed he merely wanted to talk with Tyson about perceived injustices directed at him by Don King. Regardless, the two wound up scuffling in the street, with Green initially appearing to have gotten the worst of the brawl. Published photos showed Green with a badly swollen left eye and a gash on the bridge of his nose that required four stitches to close.

The more lasting damage was done to Tyson, who not only suffered another blow to his crumbling reputation, but also sustained a hairline fracture in his right hand, an injury that would force the postponement of a scheduled October title defense against Britain's Frank Bruno. Misdemeanor assault charges were also filed against Tyson, although Green somewhat miraculously had a change of heart the next day, when he walked into the Twenty-fifth Precinct headquarters and withdrew his complaint . . . without explanation.

As it happened, there was a perfectly good reason for Green's sudden generosity, and it had nothing to do with a forgiving spirit.

"Robin's lawyers called Bill and said, 'There's a warrant out for Mike. You have to bring him down to the station house just to get the paperwork done, and then he'll be released,'" said Steve Lott. "Bill said, 'There's no way Mike is going to be arraigned. Let me handle this.' This was the type of thinking that Don King could never do in a million years. Bill gets on the phone with Mitch Green's mother, says, 'Hello, Mrs. Green, I understand that Mitch is very unhappy about what happened, but let's do this. Would you consider asking your son to please drop the lawsuit, and we'll put Mitch Green on the undercards of Mike's next two fights, and by the third fight we'll have him ranked number ten, and he'll get a shot to fight for the championship?' Boom! Done! History! Mike never had to go anywhere. Donald Trump's lawyers wanted to get their pictures in the paper with Trump next to Mike in the station house! Bill's only thinking—and this is the tough part—is what's best for the fighter. I learned that early on: It's not what's best for me; it's what's best for the fighter. That's what made Mike so good: the thinking processes of the people around him. For Don, it's not like that. It's what's best for Don. I find it interesting that every single decision made for Mike by Bill, Jim, Cus . . . almost without exception . . . resulted in something positive for Mike. On the other side, almost every single decision made by Don King resulted in something negative. It's shocking . . . almost unbelievable! Every fight, every payday, every press conference."

Bad as it was, the incident with Mitch Green, and the schadenfreude that seemed to fuel the gleefully reported mayhem that was now Tyson's daily life, paled in comparison to what happened on September 4.

It was on that morning that Tyson, a notoriously bad driver (penchant for expensive automobiles notwithstanding), drove his BMW into a chestnut tree outside Camille Ewald's Catskill home. Tyson, who was unconscious when Ewald reached the vehicle (she had witnessed the crash from her front porch), was taken by ambulance to Catskill Hospital, then transferred to the larger Columbia-Greene Medical Center, located in nearby Hudson, so that he could receive a more complete evaluation, including a CAT scan. In *Bad Intentions: The Mike Tyson Story*, author Peter Heller describes in vivid detail both the accident and Tyson's time in the hospital, portraying the fighter as lucid, comfortable, and, above all else, hungry (shortly after regaining consciousness, Tyson began asking for food, which was delivered by his friend Jay Bright). Although Cayton had been told by doctors at Columbia-Greene that tests indicated Tyson appeared to have sustained no serious injuries, he was transferred that evening to Columbia-Presbyterian Medical Center in New York, at the insistence of his wife and mother-in-law. Over the course of the next three days, as Tyson underwent further evaluation, Roper and Givens attempted to exert control over the natural ebb and flow of visitors. Security guards blocked the entrance to Tyson's room, and only those on a preapproved guest list were permitted access. Among those on the list was Donald Trump, a friend of Givens and Roper who had recently taken on a formal role as a Tyson "advisor" (Tyson would eventually receive a bill from Trump for services rendered, in the amount of $2 million); among those not on the list were Bill Cayton and Kevin Rooney.

Media outlets predictably had a ball with the Tyson accident and subsequent hospitalization, the coverage of which reached a pinnacle on the morning of Wednesday, September 7, with a story by New York *Daily News* columnist Mike McAlary, who reported in the purplest of prose, beneath a headline that screamed "Exclusive: Tyson Tried to Kill Self," the "real" story behind the accident in Catskill. According to McAlary's sources, Tyson had deliberately driven his BMW into the tree following a distressing phone conversation with his wife. The columnist also reported that Tyson had threatened to kill Givens, and that Givens and Roper had been trying for some time to convince the fighter that he needed psychiatric help in dealing with his violent mood swings. Numerous sensational accusations were made in the story, including that as an adolescent Tyson had taken medication to quell his violent urges (but had since been weaned from the drugs), and that he had repeatedly abused his wife. In general, it was a story that cast the champion in a brutal and unflattering light, while depicting Givens as a mostly sympathetic victim.

In the aftermath of the *Daily News* story, two distinct and opposing camps were formed: those who believed Tyson was a deeply disturbed man in need of serious help, if not incarceration; and those who believed he was being used and manipulated by his wife and others (including Don King). Most of the original members of Team Tyson, including Cayton, Rooney, and Lott, publicly derided the story and its author. Tyson, too, denied the most serious allegations in the story, saying he had never hit his wife, and that the accident was merely that, an accident. Not a suicide attempt.

"Mike wrecked a lot of cars in his life," remembered Paul Antonelli, a former reporter for the Catskill *Daily Mail* who covered Tyson in great detail during the mid-to-late 1980s. "I remember him smashing a car into a convenience store in Catskill. Mike would just laugh and say, 'I'm the worst driver in the world.' Usually, no one found out, because Cayton would keep it out of the press."

Not this time, though, and Team Tyson's attempts to downplay the significance of the accident fell mostly on deaf ears. The damage had been done, and certainly events that followed not only served to heighten interest in the Tyson-Givens affair, but simultaneously had the unfortunate effect of diminishing Tyson as a purely athletic figure. So relentless was the media barrage, so twisted and depraved was the reported version of the Tyson-Givens marriage, that it became difficult to view the champion as anything other than a freak show.

When the end came, it came quickly and dramatically—and, of course, publicly. On September 30, 1988, Tyson inexplicably agreed to appear with Givens on a segment of the ABC News program *20/20*. The couple was interviewed by Barbara Walters in their Bernardsville, New Jersey, mansion, and together they offered up to the viewing public one of the most riveting and shamelessly surreal confessionals in the annals of television. As Tyson sat quietly, betraying virtually no emotion, Givens described their marriage to Walters: "It's been torture. It's been pure hell. It's been worse than anything I could possibly imagine . . . Michael is intimidating, to say the least . . . He gets out of control, throwing, screaming. He shakes, he pushes, he swings."

As Givens catalogued her husband's bad behavior, expressing at once her fear of him and her love for him, Tyson sat emotionless and unresponsive. Givens asserted her belief that Tyson suffered from manic depression; in a soft voice, Tyson eventually said he realized he had a problem, but that he was capable of handling it without chemical intervention. Later, though, as friends expressed to him their dismay at the interview, and his apparent unwillingness to challenge Givens's accusations, Tyson said his nearly somnambulant appearance could be attributed to the fact that he had taken a prescribed dose of lithium and Thorazine shortly before the ABC crew had arrived at his house. The drugs, he claimed, had rendered him docile and compliant.

These, to be sure, were adjectives no one would have used to describe the man encountered by police summoned to the Tyson-Givens mansion on October 2. According to Givens, this Mike Tyson had threatened her in a violent rage, and then, as an exclamation point, tossed a few chairs through a window. When police began searching the house to assess the damage Tyson had done, he reportedly erupted at them, too, shouting, "Fuck you all. Fuck you, cops, you scum. Get the fuck off the property, and fuck off."

Amazingly, Tyson emerged from the incident without being

arrested, primarily because Givens opted not to file a formal complaint. Five days later, however, on October 7, Givens filed something more serious and permanent: a petition for divorce and annulment.

"Robin and me," Tyson would say years later, in a moment of clarity, "we were two young kids who never should have been married in the first place."

More lawsuits followed. Tyson countersued for divorce on October 14. On November 16 Givens sued Tyson for $125 million, accusing him of making libelous statements to the media. One week later Tyson sued Cayton—again—in an attempt to sever their managerial contract (which would not expire until 1992). Along the way Tyson formally and legally became partners with Don King, signing a long-term, exclusive contract with the promoter; reinjured his hand while training; allowed his weight to balloon to nearly 260 pounds; and jettisoned much of what was left of his original network of support.

When Tyson finally returned to the ring, on February 25, 1989, in Las Vegas, to defend his title against Frank Bruno, an entirely different cast of characters was assembled in his corner. Gone were Kevin Rooney, Steve Lott, and Matt Baranski. In their place was a pair of relatively unknown cotrainers, thirty-year-old Jay Bright and twenty-nine-year-old Aaron Snowell. Bright, a friend of Tyson's dating back to their time together at Ewald's house in Catskill, earned the job through a personal invitation from Tyson; Snowell, who had been around boxing since his teenage years, came to the team through a friendship with Carl King, Don's son.

While some boxing analysts openly questioned the expertise of the two men, their roles turned out to be rather insignificant in the short term. Though Tyson clearly lacked the precision that had defined much of his professional career, there seemed to be no shortage of ferocity and fitness. He knocked Bruno to the canvas in the first minute of the fight, and though Bruno subsequently landed a punch that seemed to straighten and perhaps even momentarily stagger Tyson, the champion quickly regained his composure. Over the course of the next four rounds Tyson shook off the rust that had accumulated over nine months of inactivity. Bruno, a strong and muscular fighter, survived numerous onslaughts, mainly by using his size to clutch Tyson, and by pawing at the back of Tyson's neck, a practice that resulted in several warnings and eventually a formal deduction of points from referee Richard Steele. Not that it mattered. Late in the fifth round, with Tyson unleashing a series of brutal uppercuts and hooks to Bruno's head, and the challenger bleeding profusely from the nose, Steele stopped the fight.

For Tyson, this was not the first step in a return to the type of busy schedule that had defined his ascent to the top of the heavyweight division; rather, it was an interlude to the gossip and legal wrangling that had come to define his existence. In the next six months he would be charged with striking a parking lot attendant outside a Los Angeles nightclub (the charges were later dropped) and twice receive tickets for speeding. Meanwhile, the battle between Cayton and King for control of Tyson's career continued in the courtroom, with Cayton suing the promoter for "tortious interference" with his managerial contract.

As a reminder, both to himself and to others, of what the relationship with King had cost Tyson, Cayton kept on his office desk a single piece of yellow paper, torn from a legal pad. On that sheet of paper were the names of five heavyweight boxers, and next to each name was a dollar figure, representing the amount of money Tyson was likely to earn against each opponent. At the bottom of the pad, in blue ink, was a sum, conservative in Cayton's estimation, that Tyson would have taken home: $56 million. By July 1989, on the eve of a title defense against Carl "the Truth" Williams, Cayton figured that Tyson's alignment with King, noteworthy for its extraordinary periods of inactivity, as well as a greater percentage of his earnings being siphoned off by the promoter, had cost Tyson at least $25 million. For that reason, Cayton insisted, he would not acquiesce in his fight with King.

"I have integrity as a manger," Cayton said. "I'm happy to see Mike fighting. The best life for Mike is the discipline of training and fighting regularly. It would have been so easy to say, 'Okay, just go away.' The only reason I didn't was that I couldn't live with myself if I let Mike Tyson commit economic suicide. I felt I owed it to Jimmy and Cus. It sounds so sickly sentimental, but it's true. We all wanted this kid to retire as the richest and most successful fighter in history."

If Cayton was not quite the saintly benefactor he was sometimes portrayed to be, there is little question that he was an attentive and scrupulous manager (in a business with no shortage of managers who are neither) who established a brilliant framework for Tyson's career, one that promised to provide a lifetime of security. For example, it was Cayton who decided that the first $2 million earned by Tyson should be applied to a pair of single-payment life insurance policies. Together, the policies would provide Tyson with $250,000 of tax-free annual income—for life—beginning at the age of twenty-six. The policies, however, never matured: Tyson cashed them in to help pay enormous legal fees stemming from his conviction on rape charges in 1992.

"Mike could have been a billionaire if he had stayed with Bill Cayton," said Kevin Rooney, who was officially dismissed as Tyson's trainer in December 1988, shortly after commenting publicly on the Tyson-Givens marriage. "Bill was a smart businessman. And he was honest, contrary to what Robin Givens was saying on television. All that was bullshit."

By the summer of 1989, bullshit had, in effect, become the operative word in Tyson's life. And yet, somehow, he remained apparently unbeatable. Certainly Carl Williams proved to be an insignificant opponent, bowing to Tyson in exactly ninety-three seconds. By this time interest in Tyson the fighter was far exceeded by interest in Tyson the celebrity. And just when it seemed that Tyson's personal life might have reached a state of quietude, there would be another "incident." Tyson's reputation received no boost from Jose Torres, the former champion (trained by D'Amato) whose biography of Tyson, *Fire and Fear,* released in 1989 (the same year Heller's *Bad Intentions* was first published), painted a particularly disturbing portrait of the fighter, in no small part because the author had once been a close friend of Tyson's, and indeed the fighter had at first enthusiastically cooperated with the author, only to withdraw his support shortly before publication. That Torres knew his subject intimately gave the book a certain gravitas it might otherwise have lacked, and somehow made the lurid stories of Tyson's sexual conquests and his attitude toward women not merely creepy, but truly disturbing.

When Torres quoted Tyson thusly—"I like to hurt women when I make love to them. I like to hear them scream with pain, to see them bleed"—one tended to believe the statements were truthfully and accurately recorded, if not necessarily issued with conviction. (Tyson was known for speaking hyperbolically, sometimes merely to elicit a strong reaction.)

What Tyson needed, more than anything else, was a fight that mattered, one that would galvanize boxing fans and compel the media to focus on events within the ring, rather than outside it. Evander Holyfield, an undefeated former cruiserweight champion who had added sufficient muscle and bulk to be considered the top contender in the heavyweight division, was an obvious candidate for the role of "worthy opponent." So obvious, in fact, that almost no one in boxing could come up with a suitable explanation for the fight not having already taken place. Even greed, always a powerful motivator in boxing circles, seemed an unlikely excuse. After all, Tyson stood to make at least $20 million by agreeing to face Holyfield. King, however, seemed more interested in avoiding the No.1-ranked challenger in favor of less lucrative fights against weaker opponents in far-flung locales. Why? Well, here's a possibility. Perhaps the promoter was waiting for the expiration of Tyson's exclusive contract with Home Box Office (an eight-fight, $27 million deal signed in 1987). Three fights remained on that contract, after which King would be free to negotiate with the highest bidder for the right to broadcast future Tyson fights. And King's promotional deal with the champion, it is worth noting, naturally included a cut of pay-per-view revenue.

Regardless of the motivation, it seems reasonable to suggest that King saw no harm in making Holyfield wait a bit longer. Anticipation would only serve to drive up the price of the fight. In the meantime, Tyson needed an opponent. Unfortunately, with the champion's overwhelming and yet somehow perfunctory throttling of Carl Williams, it had become apparent that selling a Tyson fight would now require some creativity, and that meant, perhaps, taking the show on the road, where Tyson was still considered something of a novelty. Beijing was mentioned as a possibility, as were sites in England, Israel, and Indonesia. So, too, was Japan, where Tyson was enormously popular, a fact that had been made abundantly clear in March 1988, when he defended his title by knocking out Tony Tubbs in Tokyo.

More effort, it seemed, was poured into the selection of a venue than the selection of an opponent. But maybe that was no great surprise. All that was needed, really, was a warm body on the opposite side of the ring. Someone smart and good-natured enough to accommodate the foreign press. Someone who could be counted on to look mildly inspiring (and inspired) for a round or two, throw a few heavy punches, and then hit the canvas. Someone with boxing skills, a superficially impressive résumé, and a reliably faint heart.

Someone who would be happy to take the money (and relatively little of it) and run.

5

John Russell came straight out of central casting, a self-proclaimed gym rat and boxing vagabond who had spent most of his forty-one years in and around the ring. Though he called Akron, Ohio, home, it wasn't unusual for Russell to take off for weeks or months at a time, living out of a suitcase or a duffel bag, sleeping in hotels of varying degrees of decrepitude. Slightly disheveled, with a shock of sandy brown hair, a mustache in need of trimming, and a voice punctuated by flattened Midwestern vowels, Russell was a persnickety, old-school trainer whose gyms were bullshit-free zones, peopled by fighters who took their work seriously. In return, he provided structure and teaching, and the periodic pat on the back.

In truth, Russell was an emotional man prone to becoming attached to his fighters, both amateurs and professionals, but never at the expense of cutting them any slack when it came to training and conditioning. Boxing was his life. There was no wife; there were no children; there were no hobbies to speak of. In short, there were no distractions, nothing to prevent him from accepting a job on short notice. More times than he could remember Russell had taken a phone call, quickly assembled his gear, tossed it into the back of a dilapidated Volkswagen bus, and crossed two or three time zones to work a fight. Sometimes he'd run the show from the opening of training camp until fight night; other times he'd be brought in at the last minute when a fighter needed an expert cut man, or just an additional body in the corner, someone who might have a few words of wisdom when the battle heated up. It didn't matter to Russell. He could do just about anything and considered almost no job beneath him (so long as he respected those with whom he'd be working). A fight was a fight, after all, and what better place to be if you were a trainer than in a gym or a club on fight night, wrestling with a spit bucket, soaking up the smell of liniment and sweat, your hands encrusted in mucous and blood and Vaseline? If it wasn't an elegant life, it was a simple and gratifying life, and it suited Russell well.

There had been fleeting moments of greatness in the trainer's career, brushes with fame and fortune that threatened to elevate him on at least a temporary basis to boxing's upper echelon. Russell had worked for a while with Ernie Shavers, a hard-punching (and hard-headed, in the best sense of the word) heavyweight contender who had the misfortune to be active during a period (the 1970s) when the heavyweight division was simply too thick with talent. Russell also had trained lightweight champion Harry Arroyo to a pair of title defenses in 1984; in 1985 he teamed up with Columbus welterweight Jerry Page, who had won a gold medal at the 1984 Olympics in Los Angeles, in what might have represented a career-making opportunity. As a professional, however, Page was a disappointment, winning eight consecutive fights before losing four of his next seven and fading into retirement in 1990, at the age of twenty-nine.

Russell never stopped working during that period. His reputation for craftsmanship and attention to detail, while unnoticed by the layperson, was admired and respected within boxing circles. In the parlance of the game, Russell was considered a *pro,* in many ways every bit as knowledgeable and reliable as Angelo Dundee or Eddie Futch, or any of the other trainers fortunate enough to have become household names. Russell understood the vagaries of boxing; a trainer, after all, is only as good as the talent in his gym or his corner.

If wealth and notoriety had proved elusive, success had not. He was a working trainer, and that wasn't such a bad thing.

When Russell received an invitation to join the crew charged with preparing James Douglas for his unlikely rendezvous with Mike Tyson, his natural enthusiasm was tempered by a tendency to view life—and boxing—pragmatically. Russell had known Bill Douglas rather well, and in fact considered the fighter to be a friend. Though Russell and Dynamite had never teamed up professionally, Russell had worked the corner of Paul Ramos when Ramos met Douglas in the last fight of Dynamite's career.

"Billy was forty or forty-one years old at the time," Russell recalled with a laugh, "and still just as tough as ever. He never let me forget that, either."

In later years, as Russell grew closer to James Douglas, Bill would occasionally tease the trainer, waving a finger at him as he shook his head in admonishment: "I remember you over there . . . on the *other* side."

Russell would just grin and let it pass. More than most people, he understood what drove Bill Douglas, what sparked his mood swings; in Buster, Russell saw the good side of the old man, the tender, caring side. He also sensed that somewhere within James Douglas was a championship fighter. Whether that fighter had any desire to reveal himself was an altogether different matter. Russell was not completely unfamiliar with Buster's checkered past, having worked his corner for a 1987 knockout of Donnie Long. That was Douglas's first fight after the ignominious collapse against Tony Tucker, and if it wasn't exactly a complete turnaround (Long was a far less formidable opponent than Tucker), at least it presented the possibility that Douglas's career could be resuscitated.

"I wasn't friends with James at the time, but I certainly knew of him," Russell said. "I always thought he had a ton of talent. It just needed to be brought out of him."

Two years passed between the Long fight and the invitation for Russell to return to Douglas's corner. In that time Douglas registered five consecutive victories against opponents of increasingly substantial pedigree. The first three of those victories were by knockout, but more impressive, if less dramatic, were ten-round decisions over Trevor Berbick (on February 25, 1989) and Oliver McCall (July 21, 1989), for these were performances that evinced courage and stamina (the very traits Buster purportedly lacked), achieved against legitimate heavyweight contenders.

Even more telling was the evidence that Douglas, who had long demonstrated reluctance, if not an inability, to fight effectively when things got messy in his life, suddenly seemed capable of that rarest and most ethereal of athletic qualities: focus.

There had been whispers after the victory over Berbick (achieved on the undercard of the Tyson-Bruno fight) that Douglas had made the short list of boxers deemed suitable for slaying at the hands of Mike Tyson. As summer drew near, the whispers grew louder. The Douglas-McCall fight was placed on the undercard of Tyson's title defense against Carl Williams in Atlantic City. A creditable performance—i.e., one in which Douglas looked good, emerged victorious, but did not appear to be a serious threat to Tyson (then again, no one, save Holyfield, was considered a threat to Tyson at this time)—would likely result in Douglas being rewarded with the most significant opportunity of his career: a shot at Tyson and the heavyweight championship. For Buster this would be bigger than the Tucker fight, of course, since Tyson was infinitely more compelling than Tucker, and any man willing to stand in the ring against him typically received a paycheck bearing more zeros than he had ever seen before.

As if that weren't enough pressure, Douglas entered the ring against McCall as a man whose personal life was fraying at the edges: his two-year marriage to Bertha was already in a state of decay; Doris Jefferson, the mother of his son, Lamar, was suffering from leukemia and kidney failure, and now Lamar needed his father more than ever, from both a financial and an emotional standpoint. Lula Pearl Douglas, James's mother, was sick, too, having experienced a series of unexplained seizures. The lucrative payday that a Tyson fight promised would not solve all of Buster's problems, but it would surely ease some of the anxiety associated with not being able to protect those he loved from life's assorted miseries.

The almost inexplicable calm and the sense of resolve Douglas exhibited in the ring against McCall can be attributed, at least in part, to a profound philosophical shift in his outlook on life. It happened, he said, in a dark hotel room on the morning of the McCall fight. As Douglas tossed fitfully, trying to relax, his mind raced. The world seemed to be closing in on him. How could he possibly fight that evening? When two friends entered the hotel room to check on him, they sensed Buster's nervousness and apprehension, and urged him to find strength. "Accept God into your heart," they said. "He'll take all the burdens off your shoulders."

Buster began crying. Weeping like a baby boy. "I accept him," he said.

Douglas is not one to invoke this transformation casually, but neither does he deny its importance. For whatever reason, from whatever source, he summoned the will to fight and defeat McCall, despite the fact that at 242 pounds he was at least ten pounds above his optimal fighting weight. And just like that, the pieces of the puzzle began to fall into place.

In the middle of August, following a meeting with Don King, John Johnson announced that a tentative agreement had been reached for a fight between Tyson and Douglas. The venue had not been determined (maybe Las Vegas); nor had the date (probably sometime in the fall, after the World Series). But Johnson was confident that the deal was solid and that hammering out final details would present no great challenge. In a statement of almost incomprehensible irony, given what would take place in the months to follow, Johnson said, "We didn't get everything we wanted, but Don King is the reason boxers make the money they make today. He's been fair with us."

With a record of 28-4-1, and a No. 2 ranking by the IBF, Douglas seemed an almost ideal opponent for Tyson. No one could argue persuasively that Douglas hadn't earned consideration for a shot at the title; at the same time, neither his record nor his reputation indicated that Douglas was the man likely to interrupt Tyson's evisceration of the heavyweight division. The unstated expectation was that Buster would accept his assignment with a smile and a handshake, and then acquiesce without regret when it came time for Tyson to end the show. It would be short and sweet—just another public display of Tyson's invincibility. Really, that was all King had left to sell at this point, and he pitched with his usual gusto.

"It ain't about if [Tyson] knocks a guy out," the promoter brayed. "It's about how he knocks a guy out. It's the style, the improvisation."

Boxing being boxing, it came as no great surprise that just as Douglas began preparing in earnest for his encounter with Tyson, he discovered that another fighter had taken his place—or, at the very least, cut in line ahead of him. Instead of next facing Douglas, King announced that Tyson would defend his title against Canadian Donovan "Razor" Ruddock on November 18 in Edmonton, Alberta. As for Douglas, well, he'd have to wait. Maybe there would be a title fight somewhere down the road, sandwiched between Tyson's presumed dispatching of Ruddock and his showdown with Holyfield; then again, maybe not.

In the meantime, Douglas continued to train, not only because he wanted to be prepared for any opportunity that might come his way, but also because the training was therapeutic, providing an outlet for the mounting stress in his life. Not long after the McCall fight, Bertha Douglas walked out on James, leaving him alone with his two dogs, Aspen and Shakespeare. Sometimes James eased the pain of loneliness with alcohol, which led to his being arrested and charged with driving while intoxicated. Douglas did not deny the charges; he pleaded guilty, agreed to take a course on alcohol abuse awareness, and retreated to the security of the gym.

"That was a tough time for me, personally," Douglas recalled. "I was going through a lot of things at home. Boxing was a release. I was able to vent and deal with what was going on in my life."

James and Bertha had met in 1982, not long after he had returned to Columbus and resumed boxing. He was a local hero, a star basketball player and the son of a well-known fighter. Bertha was an athlete, too, having been a sprinter on her high school track team. A native of Chesapeake, Virginia, she had attended boarding school in Pennsylvania before finally settling in Ohio. Upon arriving in Columbus she took a job as a hostess at a local restaurant and soon forged an easy friendship with one of the cooks, a spirited woman named Lula Pearl Douglas.

As mothers are wont to do, Lula Pearl bragged endlessly about her family, especially her firstborn, James. What a lovely young man he was, Lula Pearl said, big and strong and funny. Good-looking, too. One day she showed Bertha a picture of James, clipped from the local newspaper. *Not bad,* Bertha thought. At the same time, unbeknown to Bertha, Lula Pearl was vigorously working the matchmaker angle with her son as well. James was unimpressed.

Bertha? You're trying to fix me up with someone named Bertha? Thanks, anyway, Mom, but I can find my own women.

Lula Pearl was nothing if not persistent, and eventually James showed up one night at the restaurant.

"I thought he was just a patron who wanted to be seated," Bertha recalled. "But I guess he was watching me for a while. He was just standing there when I came up to the hostess station, and we started talking. I didn't know at the time that his mother had set the whole thing up. But she had."

They married on January 2, 1987. Within a couple years they had begun to drift apart, the relationship wounded by transgressions small and large, but mostly, according to both James and Bertha, a victim of immaturity and selfishness. As James climbed through the boxing rankings, his circle of friends and acquaintances expanded, a development that did not entirely please his wife.

"A lot of strangers came into our lives, and James's career pretty much started to become their agenda," Bertha recalled. "Instead of me being mature and realizing this was our life, and that we had control over it . . . Well, you really don't understand that in the beginning. You get married and it's like, Okay, now what? It's not like you have a manual. You come to those bumpy roads and you try to get through it. But in retrospect you say, It would have been better if I'd done this. You learn . . . and we learned that we had to be strong, to be there for each other. To believe in each other, because there will always be other people who will come in and try to destroy what you have, just because they don't have it.

"Mainly, I think, it was just a matter of us being young, learning how to deal with problems on a day-to-day basis. Me, I figured, I don't know those knuckleheads, I don't have to be around them. I'll just wait till it all settles and then we'll do our thing . . . and that's exactly what happened. You know how that is—people want to be around you when you're the man. They want to be associated with the limelight, but when the limelight is gone, they're gone, too."

Whatever limelight Douglas had known, it paled in comparison to that which he experienced beginning in the fall of 1989. First, in late October, came word that Tyson's bout with Razor Ruddock had been postponed due to an unspecified injury or illness. Published reports, some filtered through Don King's publicity machine, described the champion's ailment as an inflammation of the rib cage, attributed to either an upper respiratory infection, such as pleurisy, or perhaps an injury, such as a pulled muscle or torn cartilage. More skeptical observers suggested that Tyson's fondness for late-night activity had left him in something less than peak physical condition and thus provoked King to back out of the fight.

Regardless, with Ruddock out of the way King swiftly went about the business of arranging a new agenda for his fighter. On November 15 Home Box Office announced that it would broadcast Tyson's next fight sometime in February. An opponent was not named, but rumors were circulating at the time that the challenger would be James Douglas and the site would be Tokyo. Sure enough, two days later HBO formally announced its intention to broadcast from Tokyo, Japan, on February 12 (the fight would actually be held on February 11, February 10 in the United States;), a heavyweight championship fight between Mike Tyson and James Douglas. Tyson, it was later revealed, would receive $6 million for the fight; Douglas would receive $1.3 million, a princely fee when weighed against his previous paychecks, but a relative pittance compared to what other Tyson challengers were asking.

Indeed, it was a willingness on the part of Douglas and Johnson to accept less money (far undercutting the $3 million sought by another top contender, Michael Dokes) that pushed Douglas again to the front of the pack.

"John [Johnson] wasn't very happy with the money," Douglas said. "But I thought, It's just an opportunity, and you have to make the most of it."

It's axiomatic that every boxer believes he can win every fight; otherwise, how could he possibly step into the ring and face the ensuing carnage? Certainly, from the beginning, Douglas expressed nothing but confidence—to anyone who was willing to listen. But there was something in his demeanor, in his voice, that reflected a sense of purpose. Let others think of him as a sacrificial lamb; Douglas had something else in mind.

"Actually, some fighters don't bother to convince themselves," observed boxing writer Richard Hoffer, who covered the Tyson-Douglas fight for *Sports Illustrated*. "They're just trying to make a living. Buster was different; he honestly thought he could win."

Even the best of alliances, the ones that produce great and memorable accomplishments, sometimes go sour. And so it would be with the team that guided James Douglas to the heavyweight championship of the world in February 1990. Douglas and John Russell remain close, perhaps closer than ever; however, neither man considers John Johnson or J. D. McCauley to be a friend, thanks largely to events that unfolded in the wake of the Tyson fight. The rift, particularly between Russell and Johnson, is most evident when the two men reflect on their time together in Columbus, helping Douglas to prepare for his trip to Tokyo.

Revisionist history is a tricky thing, and in Johnson's version of the story Russell was a minor player, a seasoned cut man brought in shortly before the team broke camp and headed overseas. McCauley was the trainer, Johnson the manager, Douglas the fighter. Russell provided a service and did so with professionalism, but according to Johnson his role, viewed through the prism of time, has somehow become distorted and inflated. Russell is sometimes referred to as a cut man or cornerman in books and articles and documentaries about the Tyson-Douglas fight; just as often, however, he is referred to as a "cotrainer," or even simply, "trainer," conferring upon him a status that Johnson feels is unearned.

"I honestly resent the fact that he takes credit for being Buster's trainer for the Tyson fight," Johnson said. "He wasn't. He was brought in as a cut man, and he did a great job. We didn't have any cuts or anything, but he did a great job with us going into that fight."

According to Johnson, there were others in line for the job ahead of Russell, but the manager pushed for Russell's inclusion.

"I went back to James and said, 'Hey, man, let's give this guy a chance. At that time he wasn't working with anybody or anything, and James said, 'Well, okay, if that's what you want to do.' John was brought in probably two weeks before we left to go to Tokyo . . . and he played his role. But J.D. is the one who for years had done [the training]. And, honestly, there were times in the gym when I would make James so mad he'd throw chairs—just because I'd say you have to do this or that. That's one reason I kind of resent what John has said. J.D. is the one who would go over there and make James run. Sometimes it would take an hour to get him going. We trained for that fight for months before John Russell was even brought in. And he was not brought in [to serve] in a training capacity. At all. He was brought in as a cut man."

When pressed on whether Russell's role expanded after his arrival, Johnson hesitated for just a moment before responding. "I think he helped, yes."

Russell, naturally, has a different recollection of the time he spent in Columbus.

"They called me to come in and be the cut man," he said. "That was probably about two or three months before the Tyson fight. I went to Columbus and started working with Buster. They saw that I knew what I was talking about and so they made me the cotrainer, and that led to me being the chief second in Tokyo.

"I was brought down to be the cut man, and the cut man really doesn't do anything but go to the fight and work the corner, but I got [to Columbus] and I was basically training the guy. Buster seemed to enjoy it, and the people with him seemed to [realize] that I knew what I was doing, so I became the cotrainer."

Russell insists, however, that he had no intention of usurping the authority of Johnson or McCauley; nor did he force himself into the role of trainer.

"It was just there," Russell said. "Nobody was really doing it. It was kind of odd, considering the magnitude of the fight, but [James] wasn't training like a professional athlete training for the fight of his life. So I started doing things that I knew. He wasn't being taken care of like a professional, like I knew how to do—the rounds he should have been sparring, working the mitts, the running . . . different things like that. To me, it just wasn't being done . . . *correctly.* So I started doing those types of things for him, and he's looking to me, like, Wow, I never had this before; I've never been treated like this before."

When informed of Johnson's claim that Russell spent only a few weeks in the Douglas camp, Russell's veneer of civility and diplomacy fell, revealing a mixture of incredulity and anger: "Oh, bullshit! That's a lie. I was down there for at least two months. We left [for Tokyo] at the end of January; I think I went down [to Columbus] in October or something. The end of October."

To break the tie (and facilitate the resumption of the story), it might be best to turn to Douglas, who was, after all, the object of all this attention.

"We brought [John Russell] in as a cut man, but he ended up being more of a trainer," Douglas explained. "My uncle, J.D., was like the head trainer, and John Johnson was the manager. But then John [Russell] was getting more and more involved, running with me and stuff. And working with me in the gym. We kind of really bonded."

So . . . two weeks? Or two months? Or more?

Douglas laughed at the question. "John [Russell] was there at least two months before we left," he said. "That guy [Johnson], man . . . that's just bullshit. Two weeks . . . That's ridiculous.

"It went just like this: J.D. and I ran every morning, talked about the future, and then we'd go to the gym, meet up with Johnny [Johnson], talk about what's on the table, and then John Russell was the chief trainer in the gym. He wrapped me up, warmed me up, told the sparring partners to be ready. He controlled the gym. John Johnson was there, just there."

Disputed time lines and job descriptions notwithstanding, there was, at least for a while, harmony in the Douglas camp, at a time when harmony was precisely what Buster needed most. The challenger embraced the discipline of training with a fervor he'd never expressed in the past. He did roadwork without complaint (well, mostly); he absorbed suggestions in the gym. Like most people who came to know the fighter, Russell found Douglas enormously likable. Smart, too. But the trainer also sensed something different in Douglas, something that hadn't been there in '87, when Russell worked

Douglas's corner for the fight against Donnie Long, and something few people had seen in Douglas over the years.

This version of Buster was attentive and serious. He followed instructions to the letter. He *listened*. In sparring sessions, if Douglas got careless or headstrong—if he chose brawling over boxing—Russell would quickly set him straight. There was a strategy to beating Tyson, and it hinged on neither leading with one's chin nor fleeing in fear.

"If you're standing on the railroad tracks, James, and the train is coming at you, what do you do?" Russell would say.

"Step off."

"Exactly. That's what you do to this guy: You step to the side. You don't back up, right, because the train runs right over you. If you back up against Tyson, he's going to run right over you. Just keep moving to the side . . . Don't let him get set."

"Okay," Douglas would say. Then he'd tap his gloves and go back to work.

Almost from the day the fight was announced, John Johnson predicted victory for his fighter. Whether he really believed his own pronouncements or whether, in the great tradition of boxing management, he was merely trying to fan the flame of interest, is impossible to say. (To this day, Johnson insists he never doubted that Douglas would upset Tyson.)

For his part, Russell took a more measured approach. As he watched Douglas hit the road with McCauley each morning, as he saw the fighter's progress in sparring sessions, and, especially, as they chatted for hours on end, a certain confidence swept over the trainer. Russell had always dreamed of training a heavyweight champion and now it seemed at least possible that the dream was within reach. Then again, talent and technique had never been an issue for Douglas. He had athleticism to spare. Certainly he was more athletic than any other fighter in the heavyweight division, including Tyson. Of greater concern whenever Douglas fought were conditioning and attitude. The former no longer appeared to be a problem. A long and rigorous training camp had trimmed most of the excess weight from Douglas's frame, to the point that he now appeared almost to be cut and defined. Not since his days as a basketball player had Buster been so lean. Whether lean meant "hungry" was another matter entirely. What Russell did not know, and could not measure, was the size of Buster's heart, which had long been subject to fluctuation. He had quit in the past. Maybe he'd quit again.

One day Russell sat down with Douglas and began talking about the fight, as he often did. This time, though, the trainer did not invoke strategy or philosophy; rather, he addressed the issue on a primal level. For too long Douglas had been known as something of a gentle giant. It was time for a different persona.

"James, this guy is about five foot ten, five eleven at the most," Russell said. "You're six foot four." The trainer paused to let those numbers sink in. "I'm five ten, and I'm going to tell you something right now: There's no guy five six who's going to kick my ass. Seriously. So if Tyson kicks your ass, shame on you!"

Douglas said nothing, just stared at the trainer.

"I could see it in his face," Russell recalled. "I could tell what he was thinking: *This guy ain't kicking my ass!*"

Not that anyone outside the Douglas camp took notice. Even in Columbus, few people seemed to view the Tyson-Douglas fight as anything more than a minor diversion. This was a contest for the undisputed heavyweight championship of the world, and yet Douglas was hardly treated like an athlete attempting to summit one of sport's highest peaks. At best, polite indifference was the order of the day. Newspaper and television coverage was sporadic, befitting the seemingly quixotic nature of Douglas's quest. The great majority of Douglas's workouts at the Fitness Trend, a Columbus health club, were open to the public. To say that crowd control wasn't an issue would be an understatement.

Beyond the environs of the polite Midwest, naturally, courtesy was meted out less generously. The impending execution of James "Buster" Douglas (and wasn't the name just begging to be used as a punch line, so to speak?) became fodder for stand-up comics, late-night talk show hosts and journalistic pundits. *Sports Illustrated* quipped that Tyson would go through Douglas "faster than a plate of tuna in a sushi bar."

The Tyson camp, notably Don King, proceeded with the business of advancing the champion's career without giving due consideration to the possibility that Douglas might somehow interrupt the inexorable march to boxing immortality. In early January, just as promotion for the Douglas fight should have been heating up, King and Tyson appeared at a satellite news conference from Beverly Hills, at which it was announced that Tyson would defend his title in a long-awaited showdown against Evander Holyfield.

Las Vegas oddsmakers famously installed the champion as a 42-to-1 favorite (although the Mirage was the only casino that claimed afterward to have accepted wagers on the fight), an outrageous margin even by Tyson's standards. And yet even those odds were generally considered insufficient.

"Everybody quotes the forty-two-to-one odds," said Bert Sugar. "But try to find a single house in Vegas that actually had it up and anybody who bet on [Douglas]. No one thought he had a chance."

Well, with a few exceptions, anyway. Douglas believed in himself all along, he insists. And not because he had any indication that Tyson might show up in Tokyo as something less than the barbarously effective fighter he'd always been. Douglas simply looked at Tyson, short, wide, nasty . . . all snarls and scowls and sinew . . . and saw not so much a perfect fighting machine as a bully. And a beatable one at that.

"I never had any doubt in my mind," insisted Douglas. "And it wasn't like I thought, *Oh, good, he's not ready; maybe I'll have a chance.* I was just ready. John [Russell] kept telling me, 'Keep him turning, keep moving, use the jab. Don't stand in front of him. Don't let him take a picture. Don't run, but don't be stationary. *Bang-bang-bang,* move to the left! *Bang-bang-bang,* move to the right! *Bam-bam!*'"

Douglas paused to let that image sink in, and it is an effective one, refuting, as it does, the notion that dumb luck carried Douglas that night in Tokyo. More likely, the upset was provoked by a constellation of factors, and among the most important was the challenger's preparation.

"Tyson has to be planted," Russell would tell Douglas. "Then he jabs. Then he throws a barrage of punches. Just keep moving, keep punching."

A similar message was communicated to James by his father. While the relationship between the two men had been strained by their professional differences, they had never really become estranged (as has been suggested over the years). James continued to communicate with Bill Douglas and in fact would talk to him almost every night by telephone while he was in Tokyo. Before leaving Columbus, James visited his father. They talked quietly, casually, about all sorts of things. Eventually the conversation turned to Tyson.

This was the fight Dynamite never got, the opportunity that never came his way. Surely it pained him to be on the sideline now, outside looking in, saying goodbye to the fighter he had helped create. James, after all, was his son, his flesh and blood. And now other people were getting all the credit for molding him into a contender. Was that fair? Was that just? If there was resentment, it lay dormant during this visit. For now they were just father and son, talking about work. It started quietly enough, the two of them dancing around the topic, avoiding the meat of the subject, the importance of the fight and what it meant to both of them. Suddenly, Bill's voice grew louder. He rose from his seat and began moving around the living room, shadowboxing, rolling his shoulders, snorting and snapping off jabs at imaginary opponents, as if Tyson were there now, directly in front of him.

You gotta go through me to get to my son!

"My dad. . . . Man, he was so intense," Buster reflected with a laugh. "Off the fucking charts."

It went on like that for a while, Bill bobbing and weaving, barking out commentary and instructions.

"You just gotta work him! You gotta rip him!"

Assisting in Buster's cause was a healthy dose of personal animosity directed at the champion. Boxing is a brutal and unnatural act, and fighters typically consider it beneficial to summon a certain amount of hostility toward their opponent, if only temporarily; Douglas did not have to reach deep into the well to find something unappealing about Tyson.

"I remember when he first came on the scene, and you started hearing about him," Douglas said. "I was ranked, like, number four at the time, and he wasn't even in the top twenty. And all of a sudden it was like, Oh, my God! Mike Tyson this, Mike Tyson that. Well, you know what? Fuck Mike Tyson! I'm the contender, man! But everybody was looking at it like he was the one to contend and I was just coming up through the ranks. It was just a blitz.

"They did a hell of a marketing job with him. And he was killing people. But I always thought he could be beat. I looked at him personally and it was like, Oh, man . . . the way he dressed, the way he talked . . . his mannerisms and stuff. He was . . . goofy."

True, but Tyson was still an adolescent when he began shredding the heavyweight division. Even now he was barely an adult, a distinction that warranted little consideration from Douglas.

"I don't give a shit about that," Douglas said. "The guy had no class, no style. I mean . . . hell. He was all right, but he wasn't too smooth."

To most eyes, it was precisely that roughness around the edges that made Tyson such a menacing presence. The street fight with Mitch Green, the cavalier dismissal of his trainer (and the attempted dismissal of his manager), the numerous traffic infractions, the accusations of spousal abuse—all of these things, while personally unattractive and undeniably damaging to Tyson's marketability outside the ring, only served to accentuate his malevolence. He wasn't just a boxer. He was a monster. And that characterization contributed to the likelihood that anyone who found himself staring across the ring at Tyson would be scared shitless.

Douglas, apparently, had a different outlook. The sight of Tyson filled him not with fear, but rather contempt.

"Most of the guys who fought Tyson lost before they got into the ring," said John Russell. "They lost in the gym . . . or going up the steps into the ring. They were scared to death of the guy. [Tyson] had a mystique about him—the way he came into the ring, the way he acted, the way he dressed, the power he had, his actions, jerking around. I can understand some of that. But James had no fear of him. None whatsoever. And believe me, I was looking for it."

Russell wasn't alone.

At a New Year's Eve party less than a month before he would leave for Tokyo, Douglas was hanging out, talking with some friends, when an attractive young woman caught his eye from across the room. They smiled at each other. The woman began walking in

Douglas's direction. Douglas and Bertha had not yet reconciled, although they were working on it, so technically he was a free agent.

"She was pretty," Buster remembered with a laugh, "and I thought maybe she was interested in me."

Not really. Turned out she was merely curious.

"You're fighting Mike Tyson?" the woman asked, almost in disbelief.

Buster took a gladiator's stance: head high, shoulders straight, back erect. He nodded coolly. "Uh-huh."

"Wow!" the woman exclaimed. "You must really be desperate for money."

A short time later, Douglas noticed a crowd gathering in front of a television set. The image of a comedian ("One of the Wayans brothers, I think") impersonating Mike Tyson flickered across the screen.

"The laughs got really loud when I walked into the room," Douglas remembered. "Because they're on TV, talking about guys fighting Mike Tyson, and how pitiful it is . . . Guys peeing on themselves, they're so scared. It was hilarious. And I was next."

A few days later Douglas got a call from his mother. Lula Pearl had been sick for months, her condition ebbing and flowing as doctors tried with varying degrees of success to treat her extreme hypertension. James worried about her, wanted her to rest as much as possible, but now Lula Pearl was on the phone, saying she needed to speak with him—in person. Right away.

The urgency, it turned out, stemmed from a long night of reading, during which Lula Pearl had consumed a heaping portion of *Fire and Fear*, Jose Torres's biography of Tyson. The marathon session, punctuated by graphic exposure to more intimate details of Tyson's life than Lula Pearl cared to know, had left her shaken.

This was the man her son would be fighting? Maybe there was time to stop him, to shake some sense into her little boy. End the charade. He wasn't really a fighter, right? He was the gentlest of her children. The nicest.

"Are you going to be okay?" Lula Pearl asked when James arrived.

"Mama, don't worry about nothing. I feel good."

"Aren't you afraid?"

"How could I be afraid?" Buster said. "I'm the son of Lula and Bill Douglas."

"I don't know, baby . . ."

With that, James lost his cool. He threw his hands into the air and began screaming at his mother.

"Mama, I ain't worried about that punk! I'm a killer!"

The room fell silent. Lula Pearl stared at her son. A smile, or something like it, came to her face. And then tears. "Oooh," she whispered. "You're so mean."

After that, Lula Pearl ran all around town bragging on her son, telling anyone willing to listen that James was going to kick Mike Tyson's ass! That's just the way she put it, too. No delicate phrasing, no hedging her bets.

"*My baby's gonna kick . . . his . . . ass!*"

"See, I think she just needed to see it herself," James said of his outburst. "I guess she'd heard so much [about Tyson], and all of her girlfriends were saying, 'Oh, my gosh, Lula, your baby is fighting *this* guy?' It was like everybody forgot where I came from. They used to talk about my dad and what a great fighter he was, and how tough he was. And I'm his son! Now I'm fighting this guy and it's like, 'He's too soft!' "

Three days later, shortly before daybreak on the morning of January 18, 1990, the phone rang in James's apartment. He knew right away something bad had happened. Who delivers good news at 4:00 A.M.? James threw on some clothes and drove frantically through the ghostly gray of dawn. By the time he arrived at his mother's house, Lula Pearl was already gone. She'd suffered a massive stroke, James was told. She was forty-seven years old.

At the funeral James knelt at his mother's casket and wept, and with that outpouring of grief came something totally unexpected: tranquillity. There was no shortage of people who wondered how Douglas might respond to Lula Pearl's passing. Heaped on top of the other anguish in his life—the absence of his wife, the escalating health problems of Lamar's mother (who had recently been hospitalized)—it wasn't unreasonable to think Buster might be near the breaking point.

At the very least, he'd been dealt an easy exit. What cold, heartless bastard would ask a man who had just lost his mother to fight Mike Tyson?

Certainly not John Johnson, John Russell, or J. D. McCauley, each of whom approached Douglas, separately and privately, and offered the fighter a chance to back out. James assured each of them that he would be fine.

"Yeah, I had an out," Douglas recalled. "But I was already determined to do my thing. After my mother passed, that just escalated, because I knew that would be the worst thing for her; it was the last thing she would have wanted. She would have wanted me to stay strong."

6

As darkness lifted on the morning of January 26, 1990, James Douglas and his entourage slowly made their way through Port Columbus International Airport. There were more than two dozen of them—friends, family members, support staff—all decked out in black nylon warm-up jackets, expressing quiet solidarity for the team. Some would soon be boarding a short flight bound for Chicago, followed by a fourteen-hour nonstop flight to Tokyo. Most, however, would be staying behind, tracking the news of Douglas's journey through the media or by telephone, and waiting anxiously for what they hoped would be a triumphant return.

If there was a quaint and subtle confidence emanating from the group, it went mostly unnoticed by the small pockets of sleepy-eyed road warriors in business suits, most of whom glumly sipped coffee or remained immersed in their morning newspapers, even as a pair of local television crews pressed the fighter and his camp for a few parting thoughts. There was no band, no crowd, no pageantry, no hero's sendoff. In what amounted to an unofficial farewell party, Douglas had signed autographs for a couple of hundred fans the previous night at a Columbus auto dealership. But even that had turned out to be something substantially less than a true civic celebration.

"The mayor was supposed to be there," John Russell remembered with a laugh. "He didn't even show up. But Buster didn't care. He was cool with it. I looked at him, he looked at me, and I said, 'You know what, James? If we go over there and kick Tyson's ass, when we come back they're going to put up a monument to you downtown. It doesn't matter now whether these people come or not. It has no bearing on whether you can beat Mike Tyson.'"

That Tyson might indeed be beatable was a possibility left largely unexplored as the Douglas fight drew near. If there were chinks in the proverbial armor, they seemed insufficient to cause concern, particularly given the nature of Tyson's opponent. True, many observers had duly noted Tyson's apparent rustiness during his few forays into the ring over the course of the prior year, and a handful of boxing analysts had suggested that the champion might have trouble with a certain type of fighter—a fighter who was tall and strong, with a substantial reach advantage, a withering jab, and, most important of all, the incentive to put these tools to proper use. Whether that fighter even existed at the time was open to considerable debate; not open to debate (at least, not outside the challenger's camp) was whether Douglas was that fighter. He simply wasn't.

"There was very little indication, even in the boxing world [that Tyson had slipped]," said HBO's Ross Greenburg, who produced the network's broadcast of the fight from Tokyo. "He was defensively a genius, maybe possessed the quickest hand speed of any heavyweight, post-Ali, that any of us had ever seen. He threw vicious combinations to the body and uppercuts to the head . . . that I think Frank Bruno can talk about. He was a machine. The only difficulty he ever had was with bigger fighters. And if fighters didn't want to come to him, and didn't want to fight, he had difficulty at times catching them. So there were a couple of lackluster fights. But no one attached those to Mike Tyson; they blamed his opponents, because then he would follow up [those performances] with spectacular knockouts."

If there resided in the nooks and crannies of the arcane boxing universe an observer prescient enough to forecast imminent disaster for Tyson, he kept his thoughts mostly to himself. Ostensibly impartial observers who gave Douglas even the remotest chance did so primarily for sentimental reasons. Here was a real-life "Rocky," the longest of long shots, a genuinely decent and likable man fighting for his family, invoking the memory of his recently deceased mother. What a wonderful story. How nice to think it might have a happy ending.

And so there was the odd pundit (most notably Tim May, columnist and reporter for Douglas's hometown paper, *The Columbus Dispatch*), moved by the challenger's story, creeping out on a limb and predicting, against all reason, the upset of the century.

While the champion routinely took a public beating for his perceived ethical and behavioral transgressions, there remained no shortage of Tyson apologists—meaning those unwilling, or disinclined, to interpret his failings, inside or outside the gym, as symptomatic of an erosion of his skills and thus a harbinger of defeat.

Tyson had arrived in Tokyo eleven days earlier than Douglas, giving him more than three weeks to become acclimated to the time difference and acquire a degree of comfort with his surroundings. The Japanese were fascinated by Tyson, the media having enthusiastically chronicled his every move during a previous visit to Japan, when he had knocked out Tony Tubbs. Tyson had generally responded to the attention on that trip with a cheerful sense of amusement. Guided, and kept in line, by his original supporting cast (Rooney, Baranski, Lott), he had sparred verbally with the press, smiled for the cameras, but conducted his business professionally and with purpose. This time, however, Tyson appeared less focused in the gym, less genial with his Japanese hosts and Western visitors. There were myriad explanations and excuses for this transformation: the dissolution of Tyson's marriage; the impending birth of his first child (by a woman who remained home in the United States); ongoing legal and financial concerns resulting from his divorce from Givens; and his estrangement from Cayton.

Together these factors (and countless others) combined to produce a fighter who was already well on his way to becoming something less than he had been on his previous trip to Tokyo; a fighter whose interest, if not his ability, was on the wane.

"Mike basically had to be dragged onto the plane for that fight," said Jay Bright, Tyson's cotrainer. "He didn't want to be there. He had too many distractions."

Among the primary distractions, if the stories are to be believed, were frequent and energetic trysts with the working women of Tokyo. (Western media routinely, and perhaps sloppily, referred to Tyson's fondness for "geisha girls;" given the nuanced art of the true geisha and her respected role in traditional Japanese society, this seems to be more of a euphemism than a statement of fact, attributable not only to a cultural misunderstanding but a thriving Tokyo sex trade in which prostitutes are often casually characterized by, and marketed to, Western visitors as geishas, resulting in a general cheapening of the term.) The Douglas camp naturally finds these rumors to be nettlesome, for they imply a certain lack of seriousness and commitment on Tyson's part and thus detract in some way from the magnitude of Douglas's accomplishment. But given Tyson's indelicate history of "ravenous heterosexuality," as former *Times of London* boxing writer Neil Allen so gleefully observed, it seems reasonable to believe that the stories have at least some basis in truth.

"I didn't see anything, but I did hear Mike talk," recalled Paul Antonelli, who covered the Tyson-Douglas fight for the Catskill *Daily Mail.* "He boasted about it, the fact that he was with all these women, and how one night he had two or three women. This was not something where it was talking in confidence; this was boasting. And afterward he acknowledged it: 'I didn't train right for the fight. I was with women, and this and that.' One of Cus's philosophies was, Train in a secluded environment. That's why he wanted Mike to stay in Catskill, to stay at Camille's. Because he thought that's where fights are won and lost: in training. Mike shied away from that, started partying, not working."

The most glaring indication of Tyson's creeping vulnerability occurred on January 23, several days before Douglas had even left Columbus, during a sparring session at a Tokyo gym. In what should have been nothing more than a routine workout with heavyweight Greg Page, Tyson was knocked down. For a fighter who had never been off his feet in a professional fight, the knockdown represented not only cause for concern in the Tyson camp, but earthshaking news to the Japanese media, and it was duly reported as such:

TYSON SINKS!

SHOCKS THE WORLD!

FIRST DOWN IN HIS CAREER!

These were among the phrases used in headlines of Japanese newspapers the following day, accompanied by photos of the heretofore invincible champion sprawled on his back. Damage control predictably followed, including comments from gym employees who insisted that Tyson had not been knocked down in the traditional or literal sense of the term, but rather had merely lost his footing after slipping or being pushed.

As videotape of the sparring session surfaced, however, it became evident that Page had indeed clipped Tyson with a solid right hand to the head, a short hook or overhand right at close range that buckled the champion's knees. Tyson hit the canvas, perhaps out of surprise as much as anything else, and quickly scrambled to his feet. Then he turned to cotrainer Aaron Snowell for advice—and perhaps a reprieve.

What he found instead was an unsympathetic ear. Page was a former heavyweight champion who had been humiliated by Tyson during a sparring session several months earlier, prior to Tyson's fight against Carl Williams. In front of a crowd of onlookers that included Donald Trump (and Aaron Snowell), Page had absorbed quite a beating that day in Atlantic City, getting pushed all over, and eventually nearly out of the ring by Tyson. Since then Page had trained diligently to get back in shape, surmising logically that his best opportunity for a steady paycheck was to provide Tyson with a good workout in the gym. Maybe, if he looked sharp enough, he'd get another shot at a title one day.

Stranger things had happened.

"Greg was ready for Mike," Snowell recalled. "He was working hard in order to get back at Mike for the total embarrassment that was given to him by Mike in Atlantic City. Greg Page was waking up every morning, running and training real hard in Tokyo. And Mike really wasn't into it. His mood . . . You could just tell. And Greg pulled it off. Maybe it was a partial slip or whatever, but he did hit Mike. It was like a right hand over the top—the same type of shot buster Douglas [would] hit him with."

As luck, or fate, would have it, the knockdown occurred during a session open to the media.

"So it was like fireworks going off," Snowell added. "The cameras going *click-click-click*. It was unbelievable. But it's funny—You're going to pay your dues in this game. I don't care what fighter you are, what fighter you've got, one day you're going to hit the deck. It's part of the game, the nature of this business. Eventually it catches up. That's what happened. Mike got knocked down, got up, looked at me like [he was thinking], *Take [the gloves] off*. I said no, wiped off his gloves, said, 'Time! Now get back in there.' See, when you're training, the boxing gym is school. And how you handle yourself in the gym when things like this happen, it prepares you for fight situations."

Depending on how one chose to spin the story, Page's knockdown of Tyson represented either an ominous and unmistakable indication of the champion's fading brilliance (the piper being paid, so to speak) . . . or nothing of the sort. As the Japanese media indulged in breathless hyperbole, calls went out stateside to those who might offer a less hysterical point of view. Bill Cayton was quick to remind anyone willing to listen that while Tyson had never been knocked down in a professional fight, he had in fact tasted the canvas on more than one occasion during training. Oliver McCall and Mike Williams (both of whom, it is worth noting, were tall, strong fighters with a substantial reach advantage over Tyson, not unlike Douglas) had uprooted Tyson during sparring sessions. Neither incident provoked great distress in the Tyson camp; indeed, the knockdown by McCall—on a body shot, no less—had occurred during Tyson's preparation for his title defense against Michael Spinks, which turned out to be arguably the greatest performance of Tyson's career.

Gauging the precise weight of Page's knockdown, then, proved to be a far more complex task than it might have appeared. Maybe it meant something . . . maybe not. Cayton, ever the shrewd observer, looked at the knockdown and shrugged it off. A more important consideration, he suggested, was the condition and preparedness of Tyson's opponent, who possessed "a very good straight left and a style that could bother Mike for a few rounds. Douglas has a reputation for never having trained very hard, but a well-trained Douglas could well be a different opponent."

Following a 6,000-mile flight, the challenger arrived in Tokyo on the afternoon of Saturday, January 27, and was taken by limousine to his hotel, the Grand Palace, where he faced the first of his publicity obligations: a brief press conference attended almost exclusively by the Japanese media. The great majority of Western news outlets had yet to dispatch reporters to Tokyo. Indeed, many would choose (prudently, it seemed) to skip the event altogether, a decision that would prove to be among the biggest blunders in the history of sports journalism.

Coverage of Douglas's arrival in Tokyo, such as it was, belonged to the Japanese, and information was passed along to Western news organizations via wire service reports or telephone interviews.

"The first press conference was funny," Douglas recalled. "It was me, J.D, Johnny, and John Russell, all sitting up on the podium. And Don King was there doing his little spiel: 'Hey, how you all doing? Happy to have you here in Tokyo for the Tyson-Douglas fight!' There must have been fifty chairs in the audience, and probably six or seven reporters. Mike had his first press conference prior to mine, and it was wall to wall [reporters]. My press conference there was nobody. Reporters were sitting there scratching their heads, tapping their pens, asking questions like, 'Uh, what's your favorite food?' I was, like, *Oh, boy* . . ."

The fight itself would be sparsely covered by Western media, with only a fraction of major U.S. news outlets deeming the event (which would surely be nothing more than another Tyson walkover) worthy of the inordinate expense that would be incurred by sending a reporter to Tokyo.

Among those in attendance on fight night: boxing writers from

Sports Illustrated, the Associated Press, *The Boston Globe,* the *New York Post,* the *Philadelphia Daily News,* the *Los Angeles Times,* the New York *Daily News,* and *The National,* an ambitious (and short-lived) daily tabloid devoted entirely to sports coverage, as well as representatives of the fighters' hometown newspapers, *The Columbus Dispatch* and the Catskill *Daily Mail.* Among those publications that had devoted rivers of newsprint to Tyson reportage in previous years, yet chose not to assign a sportswriter to the Douglas fight: *USA Today,* the *Chicago Tribune, Newsday . . .* and just about every other major metropolitan daily.

The *New York Times* determined that the event required coverage, but did not warrant the cost of sending a reporter from the States. So, instead of assigning its highly respected and experienced boxing writer, Phil Berger, the *Times* reached out to James Sterngold, a correspondent based in the newspaper's Tokyo bureau. (*The Washington Post* exercised a similar strategy, assigning coverage of the fight to Fred Hiatt, who was then the paper's Northeast Asia co-bureau chief; Hiatt had also covered Tyson's previous fight in Japan.) Much of Sterngold's time in Tokyo had been devoted to the coverage of complex business matters, trade wars between Japan and the United States, for example. Although he was not unfamiliar with the world of sports, having been an athlete himself and having written the occasional outdoor travel piece for the *Times,* Sterngold was undeniably a boxing neophyte: Not only had he never covered a fight, he had never even *attended* a fight.

When the call came from *Times* sports editor Neil Amdur, however, Sterngold enthusiastically accepted the assignment, which, if nothing else, promised a welcome respite from the tedium of business coverage.

"Neil called me out of the blue one day in Tokyo," recalled Sterngold. "He was very apologetic, and said, 'I have a favor to ask. I know it's going to be a pain, but it would really be helping me out.' I said, 'Sure, what can I do?' He said, 'Tyson is coming to Tokyo, he's going to fight this journeyman guy named Douglas, who's going to lose in ninety seconds, and I cannot frankly justify sending my boxing guy halfway around the world for ninety seconds. Would you mind covering it?' Needless to say, I was thrilled. I said, 'Sure, I'd love to.'"

As it was for most of the writers who covered the Tyson–Douglas fight, the assignment would be among the most memorable of Sterngold's career.

"It was one of the most thrilling, exhausting, exciting, stimulating, appalling experiences of my life," he said. "I was covering at the time basically a boxing match between the two most powerful countries on earth: Japan and the United States. And it was all layer after layer of head fakes and feints, with no punches actually thrown or landed. And no resolution. I was in this world where the stakes were presumably high, but it was all talk and innuendo and psych-out. And now I was in a world where . . . there are these two guys and there is nothing between them except a pair of shoes and shorts and gloves."

Most reporters found access to Tyson limited in Tokyo, due in large part to the fighter's oddly ambivalent attitude toward Eastern culture. The Japanese fascination with American boxers, particularly those in the heavyweight division, has often been credited to Muhammad Ali, who met Mac Foster in a nontitle bout in Tokyo in 1972, and then, in 1976, somewhat infamously, tangled with Japanese wrestling champion Antonio Inoki in a hybrid match that earned millions for both men, but did little to enhance the reputation of either (Inoko spent nearly the entire fifteen-round match supine, kicking at the legs of a dancing, frustrated Ali). In reality, Western heavyweights had long been held in high regard by the Japanese, dating back some sixty years or more to an exhibition by Gene Tunney, who was greeted regally by throngs of fans in the streets of Tokyo; similar responses were later generated by Joe Louis and Rocky Marciano when they visited Japan. In 1973 George Foreman demolished Joe "King" Roman in the first heavyweight championship bout held in Japan.

Whatever affection the Japanese had for any of these fighters, though, it seemed minimal compared to what they felt for Tyson. While his popularity had begun to wane in the United States, Tyson remained a symbol of the warrior spirit held in such high esteem by the Japanese, and as such he was adored by Japanese boxing fans. Reciprocally, Tyson considered himself, at least on some level, an admirer of Eastern culture. While his taste, admittedly, tended toward the lowbrow—for example, the simplistic mayhem of Asian grindhouse cinema (kung fu splatter and samurai-inspired revenge flicks being particular favorites)—Tyson did feel something of a kinship with his Asian hosts. But on this particular trip to Japan, the champion found it difficult to muster any enthusiasm for interaction with the Japanese themselves.

The first time James Sterngold visited Tyson in his hotel room, for example, "He was on a couch watching kung fu movies, and there were a few people wandering around. It was a pretty desultory scene. Tyson was kind of wrapped up in a blanket—this was daytime—and he was not terribly responsive. Just kind of giggly, and clearly not thrilled about being in Japan. He made fun of the Japanese, how they would rush up to him and speak to him in a language that to him sounded like gibberish."

To avoid these encounters, Tyson rarely left the hotel during his nearly month-long stay in Tokyo (the partying came to him); when he did venture forth, the results were nothing if not unpredictable. A highly publicized meeting with a well-known Japanese martial arts practitioner named Gozo Shioda went well, with Tyson offering wide-eyed praise and respect for the seventy-eight-year-old master. A visit to the Ueno Park zoo prompted a different response, as Tyson scooped up a pigeon with his bare hands and explained to a mesmerized crowd that he had once tried to kill a rooster by twisting its neck off. Smiling, he added, "You can break a chicken's neck, but you can't get the head off."

There was a pause as Tyson—whose contradictory personality included a sensitivity reflected in his affection for pigeons, dating back to his adolescence in Brooklyn—cradled the bird in his hand, a moment when everyone wondered what he might do next. Then he casually spread his fingers, allowing the bird to flutter away, and the crowd let out a collective sigh of relief.

"That was kind of interesting," recalled Vic Ziegel, who covered the fight for the *Daily News*. "You always had that element of danger with Tyson."

Volatility and unpredictability notwithstanding, there seemed to be little chance that any of Tyson's increasingly quirky behavior would spill over into the ring and result in a close or otherwise memorable encounter with Douglas. Certainly the Japanese were expressing something less than wholehearted support for the fight. Perhaps their reluctance stemmed from the memory of Tyson's too-brief tussle with Tony Tubbs or the fact that ticket prices for the Douglas fight ranged from $35 to $1,035 (ringside), a roughly 50 percent increase from the Tubbs fight. Given the likelihood that Douglas would provide even less of a challenge than Tubbs, the fight hardly seemed like a worthwhile investment. As a result, ticket sales were slow; indeed, of the approximately 63,000 seats available at Korakuen Stadium (also known as the Tokyo Dome, or, more colloquially, the Big Egg), only about 40,000 seats would be occupied on the day of the fight. By contrast, a crowd of 51,000 had watched Tyson defeat Tubbs.

None of which meant a thing to Douglas, who went about his business with professionalism and an acute sense of purpose, for the most part oblivious to the attention being heaped on Tyson, and unfazed by the utter disregard both the champion and the media seemed to have for the challenger. (King rather obviously fell into this category as well. On the promotional contract prepared for Douglas, King had crossed out the number 25, signifying the allotment of free tickets issued to the challenger, and replaced it with zero.)

"I just kept thinking, Oh, man, are they going to be surprised," Douglas said. "I never had any doubt in my mind."

John Russell was slightly more analytical in his assessment of the upcoming bout. The trainer was impressed with Douglas's work ethic and skill. Nevertheless, Russell tried to temper his enthusiasm and excitement with a bit of clear-eyed practicality. Sure, Douglas looked great in the gym, and he did seem to possess a newfound devotion to the sport and the training required to be a champion.

And yet . . .

There was the opposition to consider. Douglas was not the first man to proclaim fearlessness and predict victory on the eve of a fight with Tyson. The truth was inescapable, the evidence incontrovertible: Every one of those men had left the ring a loser; the vast majority had been knocked silly. Yes, Douglas had the size and strength and speed to give Tyson trouble, but he wasn't the first fighter to make that claim. Based on careful observation, Russell came to the conclusion that Douglas had the *potential* to upset Tyson. He believed in his fighter, admired what Douglas had endured and overcome. If the stars were properly aligned on February 11—if Douglas followed the game plan (*jab, move, jab, move*) and somehow managed to channel the fear that would inevitably accompany his appointment with the champion—then he might have a chance. If, like so many others, he became lost in the fog of battle and simply led with his chin . . . well, then Douglas would be on the first flight back to obscurity.

Russell left the public bravado to others. While Douglas quietly promised to "make history," and John Johnson shouted from the rooftops that his fighter would leave Tokyo as the heavyweight champion, Russell bit his tongue. He had seen too many fights and worked too many rounds to arrogantly predict victory against any opponent, let alone a fighter with Tyson's pedigree.

"My whole thing was, we had to get by the first two rounds, and then anything could happen," Russell said. "We could lick Tyson. To be honest, though, I thought there was a chance we might not get by two rounds. And I told James that. I said, 'It's all in what you do.'"

Admittedly, there were times when Russell found it difficult to hide his excitement, as, for example, the day that Douglas cut a murderous swath through his camp's stable of sparring partners. One day earlier Douglas had momentarily reverted to form, evincing the sort of lackadaisical attitude and effort that had typified his career, resulting in a near knockout at the hands of James Pritchard.

"Pritchard rocked him with a left hook, and Buster was out on his feet," Russell recalled. "I think I was the only person who saw it, so I kind of called time and pulled him aside."

Later, in the dressing room, the trainer admonished his fighter.

"He [hurt] you, huh?" Russell said.

Buster nodded. "Yeah, I just got a little lazy."

"That's right. And you can't let that happen with this guy [Tyson], or he'll kill you."

Douglas said nothing for a moment, just sat there motionless.

"You know that, right?" Russell said.

"Yeah, I know."

So there was Douglas one day later (just five days before the fight, the same day his eleven-year-old son, Lamar, arrived in Japan with a small group of friends and relatives), beating the piss out of one sparring partner after another, until finally it was Pritchard's turn in the ring. Short and bullish (like Tyson), with a propensity for talk-ing trash, Pritchard went at Douglas with the fervor expected of one who had recently gotten the better of his boss. Douglas said nothing, even as Pritchard kept punching and yapping, teasing and taunting, like a dog nipping at his heels. Finally, Douglas unloaded on Pritchard, using a combination of punches to drive the smaller fighter into vir-tual submission.

When Russell encountered Pritchard a short time later, he couldn't resist a subtle jab.

"You looked like you were on roller skates, my man."

Pritchard laughed. "Hey, you try getting in there with that big motherfucker!"

No thanks.

Examples of Douglas's athleticism and newfound taste for condi-tioning abounded in Tokyo—for anyone who was willing to look. J. D. McCauley, who had, over the years, expended enormous energy coaxing and coercing Buster to do roadwork, found the fighter sud-denly and inexplicably self-motivated. Back in Ohio the day's train-ing typically had begun with a five-mile jog through Sharon Woods Metro Park in the Columbus suburb of Westerville. It was an impor-tant and fundamental part of Douglas's regimen, and one he wanted to maintain in Tokyo, so shortly after arriving he mapped out a loop around the Imperial Palace. The daily jog was a little more than four miles in length, and Douglas traversed it with increasing ease, until eventually he turned to McCauley and promised, "You know, one day I'm going to come out here, and we're going to run this thing twice."

McCauley, impressed by his nephew's ambition, nodded his ap-proval.

"And when I run it twice, that's when I'm going to kill this guy."

Two days later McCauley found himself standing outside the Im-perial Palace, waiting for Douglas and his running partner, Terry Ste-gall, to finish their usual jog so that they could all get on with the rest of the day's work. But a strange thing happened: As Douglas and Ste-gall came into view, they didn't appear to be slowing down. Not in the least. As the duo passed McCauley, Douglas smiled and waved . . . and kept right on running.

Now where the hell are they going?

The answer came a short time later, as the pair completed a second lap. Buster sprinted across the finish line—eight and a half miles in the bank!—and began dancing around, throwing jabs at the air and hoisting his arms in triumph.

"Just like in that movie . . . *Rocky,*" McCauley said. Except this time there was no sound track, no soaring Bill Conti fanfare. Just the sound of Buster screaming wildly, madly into the Tokyo morning:

"I'm gonna kill him! I'm gonna kill him!"

McCauley wasn't the only one impressed by Douglas's affinity for roadwork, which may or may not have foreshadowed an upset, but at the very least reflected a serious commitment to conditioning, to taking the fight, and himself, seriously. In contrast, Tyson had adopted a distinctly cavalier attitude toward some of the more mundane aspects of training—like roadwork—a development that caused quiet concern, and consternation, among his trainers.

"What makes a great fighter is a great work ethic," said Aaron Snowell. "You've gotta work hard to stay on top, and when you stop wanting to work hard, you just become average. That happens to anyone. Training? You could see Mike didn't really want to do it. There were days that he wouldn't show up. When he was there, he didn't want to put 100 percent effort into it. We used to get him and run with him—that's how I got him to lose a lot of weight. I'd wake him up in the morning, run with him, and things like that, help carry through his exercise. But when we got over to Tokyo, Mike told everyone, 'If the trainers come around me in the morning, I'm not fighting.' He didn't want anyone to wake him up and run with him. He said, 'I'll run by myself.'"

That rarely happened, according to Snowell, whose job description was "cotrainer," but who clearly took his orders from the fighter. "You do your job the best that you can do it being handcuffed," Snowell said. "I had talked to Mike about it, and I had told him, 'The best that I know in this game, you're heading for a butt-whooping if you don't straighten up and do the right things.' But Mike knew that. He knows the game. He's a historian of the game."

What he wasn't, at least in Tokyo, was a dedicated practitioner of the game. On the few occasions that he has discussed the Douglas fight, Tyson has been quick to give credit to his opponent; he also unfailingly points out that his own preparation left something to be desired. Tyson was unimpressed by his opponent, and certain to the point of arrogance that Douglas would take the first available opportunity to hit the canvas and call it a night.

"Look, I thought he was going to quit, just like everyone else," Tyson said.

Because of Douglas's reputation for being softhearted?

"No, because that's who I was. It wasn't about who Buster was. It was about my little fucking, sick, demented megalomania mind. It was about *me*. It wasn't about *him*."

In point of fact, it was about both of them. As Tyson settled for a cavalier approach to a sport that demands nothing so much as seriousness and discipline, Douglas trained with purpose. That a constellation of factors might be in place was never more apparent to Snowell than while he was out jogging with several members of the Tyson camp (notably absent, however, was the fighter himself) near the Imperial Palace one morning. Ahead of the group, jogging in the distance, was a solitary figure, dark-skinned, tall, and thick-muscled.

Buster.

Snowell had known Douglas for some time, dating back to the mid-1980s, when James had been invited to Don King's training center in Ohio to work as a sparring partner for heavyweight contender Tim Witherspoon, who was then trained by Snowell. Funny thing about Douglas, Snowell recalled: He had so much talent, so much athleticism. But something was lacking. Snowell's enduring image of Douglas was of the fighter sneaking out a back door and trying to run across a field after getting knocked down by Witherspoon in a particularly brutal sparring session.

A quitter to the core.

In the back of his mind Snowell had always wondered what type of fighter Douglas might be . . . if only he committed himself to the sport. Snowell knew precisely what Bill Cayton meant: A well-trained Buster Douglas might be dangerous.

Pick up the pace, Snowell thought as he watched Douglas's hulking figure lumbering around the Imperial Palace. *Let's see what he's got.*

The answer came soon enough; speaking literally and metaphorically, it left the trainer breathless. As the pack closed in on Douglas, he sensed their presence; with seemingly little effort the challenger shifted into another gear and disappeared down the road. Not once did he look back.

"I started putting pressure on him to see if he could run, to see what kind of shape he was in," Snowell said. "But he just took off. I mean, sprinting! There were a bunch of us all running together, and we all looked at each other. And we knew: he was in great shape."

By this point more than a small amount of anxiety had crept into Tyson's inner circle, though it had yet to permeate the psyche of the champion himself. Snowell approached Tyson repeatedly, tried to discuss with him the potential for the fight to be something unexpectedly rigorous and potentially disastrous. But Tyson ignored his overtures.

"We talked a lot," Snowell recalled. "I said, 'Mike, if you don't listen and buckle up, man . . . My life, my career, my family, and my name are on the line with you. Know what I mean? You've got to straighten up and apply the science of the sport the way it's supposed to be applied, so you can go in and perform on that level. You're not Superman.'"

"Don't worry about it," Tyson said. "If I get my butt whipped, I'll take the blame."

"Well, then," Snowell cautioned, "get ready to take the blame."

While responsibility for the loss would ultimately rest with Tyson, events would unfold at the Tokyo Dome in such a catastrophic way as to cast his cotrainers in a dramatically unflattering light.

Criticism of Snowell and Bright had begun months earlier, as boxing observers openly questioned the wisdom of jettisoning seasoned professionals (and proven winners) such as Rooney, Lott, and Baranski in favor of two men who seemed, at least on the surface, to lack the requisite credentials—aside from their connection to Don King or Tyson and their apparent willingness to turn the trainer-boxer dynamic on its ear—to permit the fighter to dictate the terms of the training.

The selection of Snowell and Bright, observed HBO's Larry Merchant, "was a reflection of how the people around him were taking things for granted and were not professional, and somehow that is always communicated to the fighter: *Okay, this is just another setup, another trip, another few million dollars.* This is a trope I've used on many occasions: If you don't take an opponent seriously, you turn him into a serious opponent, or you run the risk of turning him into a serious opponent. I think in part that's certainly what happened that night. When people asked me about it afterward, I said, Look, that's Tyson's responsibility. He wanted amateurs in his corner. He didn't want to be around people who would tell him stuff. He wanted people around him who would be subordinate to him, to treat him not as a fighter, but as a king. As a celebrity or whatever. So he had guys around him who just . . . They were not the Emmanuel Stewards, the [Eddie] Futches, the top trainers who, when you're in the gym, you're not a star, you're just a fighter. He wanted people who would treat him as a star.

"Something can always go wrong. The way I put it after the fight was, 'You don't go and find a twelve-year-old girl in the park to sit on the back of Secretariat; you get the best jockey in the world—just in case something happens.' "

If not exactly a Hall of Fame trainer, neither was Snowell (in particular) nor Bright the hapless buffoon so often depicted in the media. Originally from Pottsville, Pennsylvania, Snowell grew up not far from Muhammad Ali's Deer Lake training camp. Injuries sustained in an automobile accident when he was just a boy limited Snowell's competitive athletic pursuits, but he harbored a fascination with boxing from his earliest days and eventually apprenticed under "Slim" Jim Robinson, a respected Philadelphia boxer and trainer whose fighters included, most famously, Mike Rossman, a light heavyweight champion in the 1970s.

Snowell worked steadily throughout the 1980s, primarily under the auspices of Don King. In addition to having assisted Robinson in training Witherspoon (a job he later assumed in full), Snowell had worked with WBA junior middleweight Julian Jackson and would later guide world champion Frankie Randall to a number of impressive victories, including a 1994 upset of Julio Caesar Chavez in the first loss of Chavez's career. Additionally, Snowell had worked with a pair of Tyson victims, Mitch Green and Alfonso Ratliff. Snowell was in Ohio in the fall of 1988, training Jackson, when Tyson showed up at King's camp to begin preparing for his next opponent (who would

turn out to be Frank Bruno). The champ was separated from his
wife, estranged from his manager, and in the process of ditching his
entire support team. As Snowell remembers it, he also had the swollen
look of a man who had spent far too much time indulging his various
appetites: "He must have weighed close to 300 pounds."

Tyson and Snowell had met several times previously, although it
would be inaccurate to suggest they were friends. As Snowell helped
the champion shed weight and get back in shape, they grew comfortable with one another, and eventually Snowell received an invitation
from King to begin working with Tyson in a more official capacity.
By February 1989, when Tyson entered the ring against Bruno,
Snowell was chiefly responsible for preparing and training the heavyweight champion of the world—just as Tyson was beginning to slip
from the exalted position he had once held.

"As a trainer, if you're going to take the wins, then you have to
take the losses, too," Snowell said. "I don't have any problem with
that. The problem I have is the lies that have been told to discredit
someone. The things that they said about me—that I was never in
boxing, I don't know what I'm doing. People like Teddy Atlas, Kevin
Rooney—I would match my credentials against theirs anytime."

Dismissed with greater ease (by those inclined to do so) was Jay
Bright, whose friendship with Tyson stretched back nearly a decade.
Like Tyson, Bright was a New Yorker who had been taken in as a
youngster by Cus D'Amato and Camille Ewald. Bright's mother had
died when he was just eleven; his father passed a year later. Through
Jimmy Jacobs, a family friend, Bright had gotten to know D'Amato.
After his parents died, Bright began spending vacations at the home
D'Amato shared with Ewald. Sometimes he'd stay for a few days or
weeks; sometimes the weeks would stretch into months, until eventually Bright became a full-time Catskill resident.

Unlike Tyson, Bright was hardly a physical specimen who inspired
dreams of boxing greatness in D'Amato. Rather, he was something of
an outcast, dangerously overweight at more than 385 pounds, with a
fifty-six-inch waist and a fondness for spending time in the kitchen. But
the boy had attributes. He was smart and thoughtful and well-spoken;
he loved boxing, so much so that he was willing to train diligently in

D'Amato's gym (where, he says, he eventually lost more than 200 pounds). If he never became a real fighter himself, well, that was okay. At least he had a home. And a mentor.

Bright was twenty years old when he first met Tyson, and like everyone else he was immediately struck by the young man's physical gifts. Despite their age difference, he and Tyson became friends. As Tyson rapidly rose through the heavyweight division, Bright was a fixture at ringside, often sitting beside Jacobs. Later, when Tyson's allegiance shifted from Cayton to King, and a new training team was put in place, Bright was invited to be part of the transition, not merely because his friendship with Tyson had withstood the turmoil of the preceding months, but, more practically, because he provided a spiritual and emotional link to D'Amato. Bright by this time had studied theater at Bard College and worked as a teacher and chef. He'd also helped train would-be fighters in a boxing program at a correctional facility in Greene County, near Catskill.

"I think that Cus's ideology and style were so alien to them that they needed somebody else there," Bright said. "They sensed that Mike wasn't comfortable."

That Bright's job would consist primarily of reminding Tyson of the things they had both been taught by D'Amato made sense; that he was capable of anything beyond rudimentary parroting of the late trainer's directions was, to some observers, patently ridiculous. Among the loudest voices in this latter group were members of the original Team Tyson, each of whom revered D'Amato and found it incomprehensible that Bright was now channeling the trainer's wisdom.

"Jay Bright," Matt Baranski said flatly, "didn't know his ass from his elbow."

Over the years, Rooney has been equally derisive, a fact that neither surprises nor particularly pains Bright, who is nothing if not philosophical.

"When you hear things like that, you have to look at the source," he said. "There's an old saying: You have to consider the well from which the water was drawn. [My job] was to tell Mike the truth. That's it. Whether he was in the ring and looked a certain way, or doing something outside the ring that wasn't proper. I believe he respected me for that, because we came from the same roots; we were raised by the same people."

Bright, like Snowell, saw in Tokyo a fighter who had neither trained properly nor accorded his opponent the proper level of respect. Bright argued repeatedly with Tyson over the fighter's ambivalence, which manifested itself in ways large and small: refusal to do roadwork, abruptly shortened training sessions, an unwillingness to take directions of any kind. There had been turmoil in the Tyson camp in the past, but never had the collateral damage spilled into the ring. This time Bright was worried.

"I have total respect for Buster Douglas and what he did," Bright said. "Even before this fight I had told Mike, 'Don't underestimate anybody. When you walk into the ring, that person in front of you, in your mind, has to be the best fighter you've ever fought in your life.' That's the ideology he should have had. But I could tell he just didn't want to be there."

That much was glaringly obvious at the final prefight press conference, on February 8, when Tyson arrived thirty minutes late (an act of inconsideration that visibly riled John Johnson but had no apparent effect on Douglas) and proceeded to project an aura of profound indifference, alternately bobbing to the music pumped into his earphones and dropping his head onto a table out of abject boredom.

"Tyson was really [messing] with Douglas's head," recalled James Sterngold. "Douglas was there early, he was dressed in a suit, he clearly was really taking this very seriously. Tyson was late, wearing a T-shirt and jeans, going out of his way to let Douglas know that to him this was not a serious event, and he was going to swat Douglas away like a fly. And he was extremely cocky, just very lackadaisical— he had a smirk on his face most of the time. Now, I had not covered boxing, but I was a pretty experienced reporter. While I didn't know [much] about fighters, I did know a few things about human nature, and it struck me that this was a major psych-out, and probably somewhat effective. But Douglas seemed incredibly sharp and focused. He was trying to look professional; he wanted to come across as a pro's pro. And he was surrounded by people who were in the same mind-set. Whether he was going to win or lose, [Douglas] wanted to come across as a class act, and he was trying to psych himself up. And he had a very successful entourage around him. These people were on message."

The message was this: Tyson could be beaten, and Douglas was going to prove it. By and large, the message fell on deaf ears, as did Tyson's perfunctory response: "There's no way I can lose." Western reporters, who had witnessed this dance so many times before, scrawled and yawned, checked their watches, and calculated their frequent-flier mileage. Only when the interrogation turned to the issue of Tyson's questionable emotional state and mental preparation did the press conference generate any electricity. Specifically, Tyson was asked to validate or refute rumors that he had been undergoing psychiatric counseling.

The subject of Tyson's mental fitness had naturally become a point of increasing interest, propelled in part by his repeated public meltdowns. Over the years it has been widely reported that Tyson's moodiness, at least on occasion, has been chemically treated. (Tyson himself would acknowledge the use of antidepressant medication much later in his career.) Both Jay Bright and Aaron Snowell, however, insist they never saw evidence of such treatment in Japan and that, to their knowledge, Tyson was taking no prescribed medication at or around the time of the Douglas fight. As for psychiatric counseling . . . well, that was actually a reference to a New York hypnotherapist named John L. Halpin, who had been introduced to Tyson by D'Amato when the fighter was only sixteen years old. Halpin had been on the payroll for years, his value evident in the manner in which he smoothly transitioned from one regime (D'Amato/Cayton) to another (Don King).

"Part of my task is to build Mike into a state of controlled, confident violence, ready to 'fight fear with fear' as old D'Amato himself used to preach," Halpin explained.

Halpin was not named at the press conference, the subtle nuance of his relationship with the fighter left unexplored. Instead, Tyson merely glowered at the questioner and offered with colorful disdain, "If you can't fight, you're fucked."

Western reporters (and anyone else who spoke English) got the point; all others were left to chew on the meatless translation offered by a Japanese interpreter: "It is very difficult to fight a person if you do not have the skill."

The day before the fight Ross Greenburg, accompanied by HBO color commentator Sugar Ray Leonard, visited Tyson in his hotel room. To a degree, this was business as usual for Greenburg—a fundamental part of any of the network's boxing broadcasts is a lengthy prefight interview with each of the combatants. A couple of things separated this particular interview from the norm. First, analyst Larry Merchant was absent, having been banned from the proceedings by Tyson, who had reached a state of perpetual irritation at Merchant's penchant for asking challenging, probing questions. Second, Tyson was alone in his room (not even John Horne and Rory Holloway, typically attached to Tyson's hip, were in attendance), deeply amused by something flashing across his television screen.

"Hey, guys, come here," Tyson said with a smile as Greenburg and Leonard walked into the room. "You've gotta see this."

Greenburg glanced at Leonard, wondering what it was that so fascinated Tyson, but figuring it was likely just another of the martial arts films Tyson so famously favored. As the pair made their way into the room, however, they could see something else on the screen—something quite different, indeed.

"Check this out, man," Tyson said. "They're actually dying here. It's a real death tape!"

The object of Tyson's fascination was a volume from *The Faces of Death* catalogue (or one of its innumerable grisly imitators), a less profane but nonetheless sickening cousin of the snuff film, in which gruesome scenes of unfortunate victims meeting their demise in a variety of horrific ways are captured on videotape and served up, reality style, to a ghoulish audience.

Having worked with the fighter on several occasions in the past, and having known him for years, Greenburg was not easily shocked by Tyson's behavior; however, as the images of bloody car crashes and oozing gunshot wounds flickered luridly across the screen, the producer found himself virtually tongue-tied.

"Ray and I looked at each other like, *Are you kidding me?*" Greenburg recalled. "*This is what he does in his spare time?* And as I'm sitting there, watching this, I'm starting to fear for Buster Douglas's life."

The producer's concern intensified a short time later when he and Leonard, along with Merchant and play-by-play announcer Jim Lampley, visited Douglas in his hotel room for the second phase of prefight interviews. Befitting the challenger's status, Douglas's room was far smaller and less luxurious than Tyson's two-bedroom suite. But that wasn't what struck the broadcasting crew; what they noticed, almost immediately, was the labored breathing of the challenger and the rattle in his voice.

"About thirty seconds in, I start to realize that this guy has one of the worst head colds I'd ever heard in my life," Greenburg recalled. "I mean, just a horrendous head cold. And I'm kind of thinking, *What? How is he going to get in the ring? This is insanity!* His voice sounded like he had a head full of congestion."

Douglas had been suffering from a severe cold and sinus infection for a couple of days, and had already received an injection of penicillin and decongestant tablets from a Japanese physician in an effort to combat the ailment or, at the very least, alleviate some of the symptoms. He was tired and sick, yet apparently unshaken by the possibility that his weakened condition might have a deleterious effect on the next day's activities. After all, few people gave a healthy Buster Douglas much chance of withstanding a Tyson onslaught. What chance did he have if he entered the ring with a fever and an upper respiratory infection?

About the same, according to Douglas; and, frankly, he liked the odds.

"Douglas had a lot of conviction about not being afraid of Mike Tyson," Greenburg said. "I don't remember if he said he was going to use his jab to neutralize him, but he was certainly saying the very self-confident things you would expect a fighter to say. But we had been in so many of those meetings with so many opponents of Tyson who had talked the talk, but once they got in the ring, they froze. So we left that room and I remember turning to Larry and Sugar Ray and Jim at the time and saying, 'Okay, this will be over in about ninety seconds.'"

That the outcome was preordained was a message communicated openly to the Douglas camp at the official weigh-in the day before the fight. The weigh-in itself, an event typically long on ceremony and short on substance, provided little excitement, aside from an unusual request by John Johnson. The manager, after seeing Tyson's well-sculpted physique, and hearing his announced weight of 220½ pounds, suggested that Tyson receive a postfight drug test for steroids. As Johnson saw it, the champion, who had arrived in Tokyo looking soft and unfit, could not possibly have reached fighting weight without illicit help.

"The way he acts, the way he can go from being fat to in great shape in a matter of weeks, it is unbelievable," Johnson said.

Johnson's theory received little support, especially from the Tyson camp. Carl King, the son of Don King, said simply and pointedly, "Steroids? Buster better be worried about that left hook."

Jose Sulaiman, chairman of the World Boxing Council (and a friend of Don King's, conflict of interest notwithstanding), was equally dismissive, if less biting: "Mike Tyson has been doing this [cutting weight] for years. It is no surprise to us. There is no reason to be suspicious."

Douglas weighed 232 pounds and appeared fit and relaxed at the weigh-in, just as he had during his entire time in Tokyo. Nothing about the final day's events, however, did anything to dissuade even neutral observers that the outcome of the fight was preordained. At one point during the weigh-in, John Russell, who had been trying to keep a tight leash on his own confidence, sidled up to Larry Merchant and casually asked the commentator for his opinion on the fight. Russell had admired Merchant's erudite approach to broadcasting, as well as his boxing acumen, and was stunned when Merchant declared the bout a complete mismatch.

"He said, 'Oh, my God, does it really matter if [Tyson] knocks him out in the first round or the second round?' Russell recalled. "I will never forget that statement until the day I die. I was a younger guy at the time, all pumped up, been in boxing all my life, and here I am with Larry Merchant, the so-called expert of boxing, a big TV guy, and he makes a statement like that!? That hurt. And it pissed me off. I just looked at him and thought, *Well, we'll see.*"

Merchant has no recollection of the remark, but does not deny that he said it. "It may have just been a wisecrack," he said. And, really, who could blame him? "We had seen pockets where Tyson could be dealt with," Merchant added, "but we hadn't seen anybody who could put it all together. We had seen fragments where he wasn't the perfect fighting machine. But the positives far outweighed the negatives, and Buster Douglas had not given us a clue that he could put together the kind of performance that could hold Tyson off for an entire fight. He had shown that he would yield under pressure. And we had seen that Tyson was still young enough and excited enough that even when guys gave him problems, he would find a way to overcome it."

On the eve of the fight, both men reached out to their respective families. Camille Ewald, often referred to by Tyson as his adoptive mother, visited the champion in his hotel room. There she found a relaxed man, seemingly free of the conflict and doubt that often creeps into the mind of a fighter before he steps into the ring. Tyson even presented Ewald with an autographed poster of the fight, the last he would ever sign as an unbeaten champion of the world.

Douglas, of course, had to reach a bit deeper for parental support. A few days earlier, after a training session, John Russell had walked into the locker room to help Douglas cool down. It was part of their daily routine: the trainer unlacing the fighter's gloves, cutting the tape from his hands as the two of them privately discussed and dissected the workout. Sometimes they talked only about boxing; sometimes they talked about other things. On this day, as Russell entered the room, he could see that something was wrong. Douglas, normally upbeat and communicative, sat motionless on a bench, his head bowed, sweat pouring from his body. As Russell drew nearer, he could see that Douglas was crying.

The trainer didn't panic, didn't even ask for an explanation, since none was necessary. Douglas was halfway around the world, only a few short days separating him from an appointment with the most intimidating and dangerous fighter in the world. What would Lula Pearl have said? Would she have given him a warm embrace? A smack on the behind? Words of encouragement or caution? Coming from his mom, his best friend, any of those things would have sufficed. But there was only silence. And memories. So he grieved.

"I sat down and threw a towel over his head and said, 'It's okay, James,'" Russell recalled. "That was the first time I really saw him let it out. At first I was concerned, because this was a natural human emotion coming out, and we were trying to get ready to fight a killer. But we sat there for a while, with Buster sobbing, and then it was okay. He got himself together, cooled down, and I didn't let him out until he was right, because the press was waiting for him. By the time we left, I was more confident than ever."

As he had just about every day since leaving Columbus, Douglas called his father the night before the fight. Media reports around this time generally referred to James as being estranged from Bill Douglas, but that really wasn't the case. Their relationship remained complicated but strong at the core, the two of them bound by blood and love, but stepping delicately on the shifting terrain of their union. The son was out on his own now, doing things the father had only imagined, things he'd always wanted for both of them. That Bill was with James in spirit is doubtless true. It's also true that the distance probably helped. James could reach out when he needed advice or support; he could exercise control over the flow of information.

And so, with the fight just hours away, James picked up the phone. Pretty soon Bill was on the other end, morphing into Dynamite, tossing out advice, getting all worked up, urging Buster to stay busy, calling Tyson a "bully" and a "sissy."

"Let your hands go!" he exhorted, just as he had said so many times before. To Bill Douglas, there was no more egregious sin for a boxer to commit than to leave the ring without having thrown enough punches. "You can't be sitting back waiting. You have to attack this guy!"

James let the words wash over him, taking comfort in the familiarity of the voice . . . and the cool logic of its message. The conversation closed as it usually did, not with an overt expression of affection or an outpouring of emotion, or anything like that, but rather with Dynamite saying, simply, "I wish I could fight this guy."

The whole camp was with me in the locker room. We were all to-gether, and I was getting ready, putting on my stuff, putting on my boots. I had my tassels, you know? First time I ever wore those in a fight—just to give them an inkling, like, "Damn! This guy must be good. He must be serious!" I mean, you don't wear tassels when you're bullshittin'.

—James Douglas

At approximately 11:15, local time, on the morning of February 11, 1990, Ross Greenburg found himself sitting in a makeshift studio in the bowels of the Tokyo Dome, preparing for an-other day at the office. In forty-five minutes HBO's broadcast of the heavyweight championship fight between Mike Tyson and James Douglas was scheduled to begin. A series of switches would be thrown and a live feed would be transmitted around the world, per-mitting viewers on the densely populated East Coast of the United States to witness Tyson's deconstruction of another overmatched and frightened challenger at its customary time: approximately ten o'clock on a Saturday night.

Technically speaking, the production presented a fairly unique and specific set of challenges, each of which had been addressed by Greenburg and Mark Payton, the on-site director for the broadcast, during a series of meetings in the months prior to the event.

"It's obviously pretty painstaking to do a broadcast in Tokyo," Greenburg observed. "We did a couple of surveys for the Tokyo

Dome, and it was a quite a laborious and difficult negotiation with the Japanese broadcasters to even get the facilities and the kind of coverage that we needed at HBO to match our level of broadcast. You go to the arena and you sit with the Japanese broadcasters and you kind of negotiate how many cameras you need, and you figure out how to do side-by-side coverage of the event so that you can broadcast to the United States while they're doing an entire broadcast for Japan. It's a logistical nightmare."

Further complicating matters was the fact that the Tokyo Dome was scheduled to play host to a series of ten concerts by the Rolling Stones in the days following the Tyson-Douglas fight. "So we were sweating out whether we would have all of our facilities in place to broadcast that afternoon," Greenburg said. HBO support crews began setting up for the broadcast shortly after midnight on February 10. Work continued through the night, and by midmorning the Tokyo Dome had been transformed into a boxing arena.

As airtime approached, Greenburg and the rest of the HBO team settled into a comfortable routine of technical checks and rehearsals, preparing, as Larry Merchant noted, "to put on a show." Indeed, there is a rhythm to every broadcast, and while the setting and circumstances may vary (in this case rather dramatically), the preparation is consistent and systematic; from the prefight interviews and research conducted by on-air commentators and analysts to the plethora of technical issues addressed by producers and engineers, every broadcast travels a familiar route. As morning gave way to afternoon, there were no indications that this broadcast would be in any way memorable or unusual. Perhaps, then, it was some sort of portent that as Greenburg quietly and methodically guided his team through final prefight arrangements, the calm was broken by the sound of a control-room door opening and the frazzled appearance of a production manager named George Wensel.

"Ross, we've got a big problem," Wensel announced.

"And as he's saying this," Greenburg recalled, "we lose power completely—forty-five minutes prior to air. All the monitors went black in front of me, and all of the switchers—which is how you get yourself on air—they're usually all lit up, and they all went dark. And panic struck. I broke out in a cold sweat."

The outage, Wensel explained, could be traced to a fire that had ignited in a transformer, thus killing all power that would normally be fed to HBO's unit.

"And so, with that, the two of us rush over to this transformer, which is just outside the control room area," Greenburg said. "And I'm watching as smoke is billowing from this transformer, and George is shaking like a leaf. He had never been involved in this kind of potentially tragic [incident]. I'm actually losing it, too. My voice is starting to rise, because I know we're about to embark on a Mike Tyson heavyweight title fight, and we've got forty-five minutes to get ourselves on the air. And [Wensel] just started doing his magic. George is the type of person who could pull a rabbit out of his hat, and within about fifteen minutes, maybe half an hour to air, we started to get power back. When I say 'started,' I mean a certain amount of amperage coming back, certain monitors coming on, certain cameras starting to appear, and transmission was okay back to New York.

"We actually went on the broadcast with not a full complement of cameras and tape machines working, due to the power outage, but we had enough to get ourselves on the air. By the time we hit the fight we were fully loaded, but I like to remind people that if not for George Wensel and that power being restored, HBO Sports would have suffered the worst embarrassment in the history of American television: not being able to broadcast what became the most historic upset in heavyweight history."

Most athletes take solace in the rituals that precede competition; this is particularly true of those whose chosen sport involves a significant amount of pain. Performance anxiety is not uncommon among athletes, but it takes on a unique level of importance for the distance runner, rower, cyclist, wrestler, and, especially, the boxer, whose success or failure is determined not only by skill and preparation and ambition, but also by the degree to which he is able to endure the extraordinary discomfort that is part and parcel of training and competition.

Fear is normal in the ring, a lubricant that encourages a boxer's machinery to work smoothly and safely; the trick is to balance courage with the natural instinct for self-preservation. In his reign as champion Tyson had proved to be not only a terrific and disciplined tactician, but a master at the art of psychological warfare, a fighter whose very presence at the opposite side of the ring provoked a sort of temporary paralysis in even the most hardened and experienced of opponents. A single glance at Tyson, twitching and scowling and snorting as he paced in a tight circle, like a tiger waiting to be fed, was enough to tighten the sphincter of any challenger. You could see it in their eyes: men who stood six inches taller than Tyson, men who were bigger and stronger, withering in fear as prefight introductions echoed through the arena.

There was only so much a trainer could do to mitigate the aura of invincibility that Tyson brought to the ring. Sound preparation and diligent training were prerequisites, of course—one couldn't merely hope to get "lucky" against Tyson, after all—but there were mental tricks to be played as well. It was, for example, John Russell's opinion that while Tyson clearly deserved enormous respect, the success or failure of any reasonable fight plan hinged on the challenger's ability to view Tyson not as a beast, but rather as a human being, with foibles that might be exploited. Endless rounds of sparring against opponents of similar physical stature and style were hallmarks of the desensitization process, as were brainstorming sessions both formal and informal, and the reviewing of videotape. By the time Douglas entered the ring, Russell hoped, he would view Tyson as merely another opponent, albeit one who presented a unique and undeniably rigorous set of challenges.

Granted, there was always the chance that Douglas would simply unravel before the opening bell, just as so many others had done. But as the fight drew near, that seemed increasingly unlikely. Even on the eve of the bout, as Russell gently coaxed him through a favorite prefight routine, Douglas remained almost eerily calm and resolute.

"Usually on the day of a fight you have so much time to kill that it can drive a fighter out of his mind," Russell explained. "So I like to do this thing the night before. I make him put on his shoes, put on his trunks, and move around a little—even if it's just in the hotel.

With James, I didn't want people to know what I was doing, so rather than going downstairs, I took him to the area near the elevator on our floor, and I shadowboxed him a little. For like six, seven rounds. Got him nice and warm, and then put him to bed. I always do this with my fighters, and I always do it the night before; it keeps them loose, helps them sleep. I don't want them sitting around, thinking about the fight all night. And James was fine, just as sharp as a tack. He was just so confident."

The fourteen-hour time difference between Tokyo and New York theoretically provided Douglas with an advantage claimed by few of Tyson's opponents: Since the broadcast would begin at noon, local time, Douglas would be spared the aforementioned agony of sitting around his hotel room all afternoon, time easily and unadvisedly given over to playing mental highlight reels of Tyson's greatest knockouts. Rather, Douglas woke early and had a light breakfast at the hotel before departing for the Tokyo Dome at approximately nine o'clock. By ten he was in his dressing room, getting changed, chatting amiably and comfortably with his handlers—Russell, J. D. McCauley, John Johnson, and a handful of sparring partners—and continuing to exhibit little or none of the apprehension that one might have anticipated.

"As I sat him down and started wrapping his hands, I saw no sweat on him, no fear, and I thought, *Oh, shit, we've got this guy!* Russell remembered. "Every fighter is different in that situation. Some you can't talk to. Not Buster. He was so calm. I looked at him a couple times and said, 'You ready?' He just nodded. And it was a confident nod, not a weak nod. I could see it in his eyes. So I wrapped his hands, put the gloves on him, then warmed him up with the mitts."

When the time came for a representative of the Douglas camp to pay the customary call on Tyson's dressing room, ostensibly to inspect the champion's gloves, Russell personally accepted the invitation.

"Usually I would have sent someone else, but I didn't think anyone else in that room was qualified to do it," Russell said. There was another reason he accepted the job: curiosity. "I wanted to see Tyson myself . . . see what kind of mood he was in . . . how he looked. He knew me, too, but still, when I got there, he looked at me and it was like, *What the fuck are you doing here?* I could sense that."

When Russell noticed that Tyson's gloves apparently had been tied on the insides of the wrists (rather than on the back, in accordance with the rules), and proceeded to voice his displeasure at this indiscretion, the champion's surliness bubbled to the surface.

"If you have a knot [on the inside], and you come up under someone's eye, you can rip their eye open," Russell explained. "So I said, 'You've gotta take [the gloves] off; you have to tie them on the back.' I don't think they were trying to be dirty or anything. Aaron Snowell is a buddy of mine, so I don't want to blast him, but who knows what they were thinking. Anyway, I made them change the gloves, and I swear to God, if looks could kill, I'd have been dead. Tyson was so mad. He looked at me and smoke was coming out of his ears. And they tried to get away with it, too, tried to pull the friendly stuff with me, like, 'John, come on, man . . . What's the big deal?'

The Tyson camp eventually relented and retied Tyson's laces in a manner acceptable to Russell, who decided to get in a parting shot before returning to his own dressing room.

"By that time Tyson was like an animal in there, you know? Walking back and forth, pacing. So as I went out the door—I made sure it was shut first, so that I'd have some space to get out of there—I said, 'We're going to kick your ass, Mike! ' "

Tyson, interestingly, has no specific recollection of anyone from the Douglas camp visiting his dressing room before the fight; although he does not dispute Russell's version of the story, he has a different interpretation.

"Can I tell you something?" Tyson said with a chuckle. "I don't know Mr. Russell that well; I'm not saying that he's a coward or anything, but a lot of people in their minds want to say things in front of my face. At least back then they did. Now? You could do it now. You could probably spit at me now and it wouldn't [make me] do anything. Back then was different. People . . . That was their standard thing, to say: 'I stood up to Mike Tyson.' If [Russell] wants to live that dream, I give him the dream to live. He said it, okay?"

When it was clarified to Tyson that the trainer actually told the story in a self-deprecating manner, with a winking emphasis on the closed-door nature of the exchange, Tyson still seemed to miss the joke. "Listen, that's what I realized in life: Everyone wants to say he stood up to the tough guy: 'I told Mike this or that.' You know what? I'm not a tough guy. I portrayed the image of a tough guy, but I wasn't a tough guy. I don't know, I guess everybody wants to be a man, and maybe that justifies being a man in some small moment in our lives: We stood up to somebody who was supposed to be tough."

As to whether the lacing of the champion's gloves represented an attempt by Tyson's handlers to gain some sort of advantage or simply a bit of benign sloppiness, that, too, is irrelevant. While Tyson appeared, at least temporarily, to have worked himself into an appropriate prefight lather, there was something about his demeanor that concerned his trainers. As Snowell ran through the fight plan—jab, slip, move inside, work the body, cut off the ring, all of the usual Tyson trademarks—the champion exuded neither eagerness nor anxiety, but rather disinterest.

"Like, 'I don't really want to be here, but I'm going to do it anyway,'" Snowell said. Although concerned that his fighter was emotionally (and perhaps physically) unprepared for the challenge that he would face in Douglas, Snowell tried to remain calm.

"I just said, 'Hey, man, focus on the fight,'" Snowell recalled. "That's what trainers do—try to help [fighters] and lift them in spite of themselves. You have to penetrate through hardness and toughness in order to produce a win."

In the dressing room of James Douglas there were no such concerns. By the time he was summoned to the arena Buster's skin was glistening with sweat. His warm-up had been perfectly timed and executed. Physiologically speaking, he was prepared to compete. Words were of little consequence at this point, so there was no prefight speech, no attempt to manipulate the emotions of the challenger.

"You're ready, James," McCauley said to his nephew, just as he had many times in the past. "It's your time."

Russell, meanwhile, continued to emphasize strategy: "Keep your hands up . . . Jab on him . . . Move side to side . . . Don't let him get set."

Douglas took it all in, said nothing, just kept bouncing on his heels, shifting his weight from one foot to the other, sniffing and snorting, throwing soft jabs into the air.

Russell moved closer as they headed toward the door and the long walk to the ring. The trainer's last words to his fighter before leaving the dressing room were: "Let's go kick his ass, James."

There is an oft-repeated story, perhaps apocryphal, but amusing nonetheless, that neatly sums up the overwhelming apathy displayed by the media toward the Mike Tyson–James Douglas fight. The story involves a longtime Associated Press sportswriter named Ed Schuyler, who, when stopped at customs upon arriving in Japan, was asked about the nature of his visit.

"I'm here to cover the Mike Tyson–Buster Douglas heavyweight championship fight," Schuyler reported.

"How long do you expect to work?" the customs agent inquired.

"Oh, about ninety seconds."

A cheap shot, maybe, but seemingly appropriate enough that the story was repeated in the opening minutes of HBO's broadcast of the event, as Douglas and his entourage made their way from the dressing room to the ring. Wearing white trunks, white shoes (with red tassels) and a white robe emblazoned with the red logo of athletic apparel manufacturer Pony, Douglas appeared fit and comfortable as he moved through the cavernous Tokyo Dome, bouncing lightly and tossing off the occasional jab as he climbed into the ring. His entrance was accompanied by gloomy proclamations about the inevitability of the outcome, culminating with Larry Merchant noting that Douglas "now has to go out and fight the most fearsome foe on the planet. He will, however, go away with about a million dollars— and that should cap his professional career quite nicely."

Hindsight puts an interesting spin on that assessment, as Douglas would later earn more than twenty times that amount for a title defense against Evander Holyfield. On this day, however? In the Tokyo Dome?

"It was supposed to be just a walk," Douglas said with a laugh. "Like we were all there just for the workout."

Tyson entered second, befitting his stature as champion and star attraction. As usual, his attire was almost calculatedly spartan: black trunks, black shoes (no socks, or at least none that were visible), and a lazily butchered towel (rather than a robe) draped over his torso. Flanked by cotrainers Snowell and Jay Bright, wearing gray sweatshirts bearing the words "It's a Family Affair: Team Tyson" on the front, and Anaconda-Kaye (a sporting goods retail chain based in Tyson's old stomping ground of upstate New York) on the back, the champion sauntered to the ring with a blank and soulless look on his face. Like the challenger, Tyson appeared to have warmed up adequately; his body reflected the sweat of a rigorous prefight regimen.

As Tyson approached the ring apron Merchant reached clumsily for an image that would set the scene, one that explained to the audience precisely what it was that made Tyson such a pure and unique fighter: "Mike has termed this phase of the fight . . . his favorite phase. He calls it like going out on a date—it's finally going to happen. Of course, his idea of a date is, *Wham-bam, thank you, sir!*"

This pronouncement, while not inaccurate, was a bit on the juvenile (if not downright creepy) side, and thus landed with a thud at ringside, as the rest of the broadcast team, Jim Lampley and Sugar Ray Leonard, responded with utter silence (although after a few seconds one can hear on the videotape what sounds like muffled laughter). At any rate, in light of events that would dog Tyson in years to come, most notably a stint in prison on a rape conviction, the comment seems today almost embarrassingly inappropriate.

As ring announcer Jimmy Lennon Jr. introduced the combatants, Douglas continued to bounce lightly in his corner, the weight shifting silkily from one foot to the other. Tyson, meanwhile, paced about, a look of mild irritation on his face. As the two men were drawn to the center of the ring for final instructions by referee Octavio Meyran Sanchez, they seemed barely to notice one another.

"I don't get into the staring stuff," Douglas said. "I just do my work. My dad always told me to move around the ring, feel the ring, make sure there are no dead spots or anything. So that's what I did. And I was sharp."

That much became apparent within seconds of the opening bell, as Douglas met Tyson in the center of the ring and immediately began dancing and flicking off jabs. Although for the most part harmless, the punches had a startling effect on both the champion and anyone witnessing the fight, for they indicated that Douglas, at least in the short term, would not be casually dismissed. He had come to fight. If there was any doubt about his intentions, they were cast aside roughly ninety seconds into the first round, when Meyran stepped in to separate the fighters and Douglas put together a nasty combination—on the break. Meyran quickly issued a warning to the challenger, who seemed unfazed. The effect of the combination was not so much to hurt Tyson or to flout the rules as to let the champion know that his opponent meant business.

With slightly less than a minute left in the round Douglas easily slipped a big, lazy right hook by Tyson (the first clear indication that the champion's timing and accuracy were off) and then followed with a stinging right-hand lead to Tyson's head, a blow that clearly got the champion's attention. Tyson did not land a solid punch until the final five seconds of the round, and even then it wasn't so much the punch, but rather Douglas's response to it, that hinted at the story about to unfold. Douglas took the punch (a left jab) with little trouble, and then, as the bell sounded, ending the round, he stood stoically for a moment, arms hanging at his side, staring at Tyson just long enough to catch the champion's gaze. If there was no room for such posturing before the fight, during introductions, well . . . maybe this was the right time for it. In a span of three minutes Douglas had proven himself fit and fearless, while Tyson had looked slow and clumsy. Maybe he'd recover, as he always had in the past, even in the sloppiest of his performances.

Maybe not.

Jim Lampley, who has been behind the microphone for dozens of championship fights, said he knew something was different about this particular fight early in the first round.

"Two minutes into the fight you're looking and thinking, My gosh, when [Douglas] throws a jab, he lands it," Lampley said. "And when he throws it, he lands his right hand, too. Mike was already verging toward lunging and slugging, one punch at a time. In those situations when he was great, his defense was his offense, in the sense that it was that radical head movement that got him inside. So extreme that by the instant you try to land a punch, he's already by your glove, and now he's on you, and . . . well . . . good luck. That's what had happened before. But if you have a still head, and you don't have that movement, the jab lands and you're stopped in your tracks. That's what happened against Douglas. Every time Mike wanted to move, Buster just flicked his jab and stuck it right in his face, and then moved away to his left, away from Mike's left hook."

Boxing isn't generally viewed as a statistical sport, but in fact it really is something of a science, and while it's true that a single punch, delivered with menacing effect, can override all that has come before it, there is merit to measuring the effectiveness of a fighter in statistical terms. The simple truth is this: James Douglas landed twenty-two punches in the first round; Mike Tyson landed eight. Between rounds, activity in the corners of the two boxers reflected their respective situations: clarity and confidence in one, concern in the other.

"Use the jab, baby," said Russell as he wiped Douglas's face. "You've gotta use the jab and the short right hand. Shorten your right hand up and then look for two or three shots. Okay, James? Two or three punches, baby." Douglas took a drink of water, swished it around in his mouth, and spat into a bucket. Then he nodded calmly.

At the opposite side of the ring Snowell urged Tyson to "close the gap." He leaned closer and pulled the fighter to him, softly cradling Tyson's head in his arms. This was a pattern that would repeat itself through the evening, Snowell and Bright yelling at Tyson between rounds, when he first hit the chair, and then Snowell changing tactics, hugging and whispering to the fighter just before sending him out for another round.

"A lot of what I told Mike, I told him in his ear, and a lot of what I told him I will not say." Snowell explained. "I spoke to him in his ear so as not to be an embarrassment to him on TV. I'm not there to embarrass Mike; I'm there to get him through the fight. He was getting direction. Mike knows what I told him. He knows and I know, and that's why Mike has never said anything bad about me and I will never say anything bad about him."

Tyson fairly jumped off his chair and ran to the center of the ring at the opening of the second round, but if the gesture was an attempt to intimidate or to provoke timidity on the part of the challenger, it failed miserably. The cloak of invincibility that Tyson seemed to own as a birthright had already begun to fall away. Douglas continued to jab and move, jab and move. Although he would later assess the performance as one fueled primarily by heart, it was clear that Douglas had trained with purpose and awareness and that the game plan sketched by his handlers was now being flawlessly executed. Douglas used a sizable reach advantage to pepper Tyson with jabs and right-hand leads. Equally important was his ability to think on his feet, to remember what Russell had told him: *Move laterally. Don't be a stationary target.* Tyson, conversely, had become an impassive, one-punch fighter. He would take whatever punishment Douglas meted out—two, three, four punches at a time—before flailing wildly with an errant uppercut or hook. In the past these had been weapons that uprooted fighters more capable than Douglas, but without any context, without movement and quickness and defense, they were rendered virtually useless.

Equally impotent, almost from the beginning, were Tyson's thuggish attempts to rattle Douglas. Boxing has forever been a conflicted sport, one that that embraces and lauds both elegance and brutishness, although not always in equal measure or with the same degree of candor. And so the raw violence and baseness of Sonny Liston (and later Tyson) is at once repulsive and compelling; it's easier and somehow more acceptable to admire the sweet sting of an Ali jab than the sickening thud of a Tyson uppercut. And yet, make no mistake, the greatest fighters have in common not only skill and talent and ambition, but a coldness that makes it possible to lean into another man and attempt to drive his brain into the back of his skull. Talk all you want about points and style and grace, professional boxing, distilled to its essence, is a primitive exercise in dominance. At the end of the day, one man emerges victorious; the other, quite often, loses consciousness. On rare occasions, he loses his life.

So if you're looking for gentleness, look elsewhere. Even the prettiest of fighters, with the most delicate features and charismatic personalities—Ali, Sugar Ray Leonard, Oscar De La Hoya—were capable of utter savagery in the ring. They were masterful fighters, gifted and dazzling tacticians. But they were warriors, too; if the fight turned ugly, as it often did, each man was capable of unleashing something deep and primal, and meeting strength with strength.

Whatever was necessary to win.

And so it was with James Douglas, who for one night not only harnessed his considerable athletic ability and crafted a remarkable and strategic display of boxing, but also kicked the shit out of the heretofore baddest man on the planet. That sort of thing doesn't happen by accident, and it doesn't happen without embracing, or at least acknowledging, one's darker side.

In the last half minute of the second round, as Douglas strafed the champion with a withering combination of perhaps a half-dozen punches, Tyson tried to tie him up. Often in heavyweight fights the most critical damage is done in these close encounters: a forehead rises against a chin; an elbow strikes the soft tissue above the eye, opening a gash that can have devastating consequences. While not technically within the legal parameters of boxing, such tactics have always been part of the game (whether an offense rises to the level of a foul and merits the deduction of points is an entirely subjective matter handled by the official in the ring), and one rejects them at his own risk. Tyson was particularly effective at brawling in close quarters, but even here Douglas got the better of him. Near the end of the round, after Tyson missed with a right hand inside, Douglas caught him with an elbow. It was nothing more than a glancing blow, but it had the desired effect.

"Tyson fought the way James made him fight," Russell said. "He was used to going out and destroying people, taking charge. But he never was in charge of this fight. James just focused. He's such an intelligent guy. People don't realize how smart he is. I remember when we were training that we talked about Tyson having a bad habit of fouling. He'd hit you with his elbow—that was part of his arsenal. Throw the punch, miss the punch, then hit you with his elbow. And I told James, 'If he fouls you, he hits you with that elbow, you foul him right back. He hits you low, hit him right back low—right away. Because all they're going to do is warn you. Make sure you do that so he knows you won't let him bully your ass.' Tyson was a bully; we always said that in camp. And when a bully hits you, you have to hit him right back. Don't even give the referees a chance to warn him.

Just pop him. And he hit James in the second round, with an elbow or something dirty, and Buster gave it right back to him, and [Tyson] never did it again in the fight. That, to me, was the turning point."

Although only six minutes old, the fight had already begun to draw gasps of wonderment at ringside; a jaded and cynical press corps, accustomed to stashing perfunctory accounts of Tyson knockouts on their laptops well in advance of the actual fight (all that was necessary was a bit of tweaking on deadline—the inclusion of a name here, a specific time and type of punch there—and a clever scribe could be on his way to the local pub before the fighters had even showered) warmed to the notion that a trip to Tokyo might have been worth the fare after all.

"I think we were going to run something either way, because it was such a long way to go to do nothing," recalled *Sports Illustrated*'s Richard Hoffer, whose magazine, in those free-spending days anyway, routinely blanketed the sports world, assigning coverage of events that ultimately went unreported. (There were, after all, only so many columns of space available.) Hoffer's presence in Tokyo was an insurance policy; in the event that the unthinkable happened, and Tyson was dethroned, the magazine would have a firsthand account by a staff writer. But even Hoffer anticipated that his job would involve nothing more than the cobbling together of a few amusing anecdotes, with placement somewhere in the back of the magazine. Perhaps in the form of a notebook. Rather quickly, his outlook changed.

"It became sort of a joke among the writers," Hoffer said, "because they knew I was unprepared and supposedly had very little to do. But as soon as the action started unfolding, it became a running joke on press row: 'What is it now, Hoffer? One hundred lines? Two hundred lines?'"

Through the first two rounds Douglas beat Tyson in every way imaginable. He was the busier and more aggressive fighter; he also was the more accurate fighter, landing fifty-two punches to just sixteen for Tyson. More importantly, the challenger by this point had already gained a psychological advantage: He had crossed the two-round threshold that Russell had deemed so important; now, anything was possible.

Indeed, Douglas appeared to gain confidence as the fight wore on, while Tyson, in a display of progressive vulnerability that would come to typify the latter stages of his career, became frustrated and ineffective. Rather than revert to the sound defensive principles of boxing that had been a hallmark of Cus D'Amato's tutelage, and thus a fundamental part of Tyson's effectiveness, the champion devolved into a desperate slugger. To the astonishment of those at ringside, including his own cornermen, Tyson stood almost motionless in the center of the ring for long stretches at a time, gazing quizzically at his challenger while absorbing blow after blow, and then periodically interrupting the onslaught by lashing out with a hook. Sometimes these punches found their mark; more often Douglas simply stepped to the side, avoided contact, and countered with a series of left jabs and right-hand leads. Through the first four rounds Douglas connected on roughly 50 percent of his punches, an impressively high percentage, and a figure that reflected just how immobile Tyson had become.

"Cus's style is a very precise style," Jay Bright said. "It's not just standing around, slapping, bulldozing. You're trying to anticipate the punch, slip the punch, counter it with a certain combination. It's a precise style, and you have to be right on the money with it. Otherwise your head becomes a target. That's what I was trying to tell Mike: 'Don't walk straight in. That's what he's waiting for.' But Mike was distracted. His focus wasn't on training and it wasn't on the fight. His mind wasn't on his work."

That much was painfully clear to Kevin Rooney, who watched the fight on television at his girlfriend's house in Rensselaer, New York. It was the first time since Rooney had been dismissed that Tyson had been in any serious trouble in the ring, and Rooney quickly found himself experiencing a maelstrom of conflicting emotions: sympathy for his former friend and fighter; anger at Tyson's current handlers; vindication that his presence in the corner had meant something after all; and frustration over not being able to offer assistance.

"As soon as Mike walked into the ring, I said, 'He's not in shape. He's been out there partying,'" Rooney recalled. "Japan is a party town. You can have a good time there if you want, and that's exactly what Mike did. He didn't do any kind of training. I remember hearing the rumors that two weeks before the fight he weighed 240 pounds, that he was fat and out of shape, then did a crash diet. If I was his trainer and he's doing all this partying, I'd say, 'Look, Mike, you go out there and you let everything go. Try to get out fast.'

"Douglas was always on the cusp," Rooney added. "He had ability, and everything was working in his favor that night. When they came out, and I saw Mike wasn't in shape, and Douglas obviously was in shape, I thought, *Oh, boy, he's gonna have a problem here.* If Mike had called me in a week before the fight and I went out there and asked him, 'What have you been doing?' I'm sure he would have said, 'Well, . . .' And I would have said, 'Yeah, you've been fucking around, huh, Mike? Drinking, partying.' 'Yeah, maybe.' Knowing that, I would have said, 'You've got three rounds in you. Try to get rid of the guy in three rounds, or you're in trouble.' But Mike didn't do anything. He didn't throw any punches. He just kept taking a beating. My girlfriend was even starting to root for Douglas as the fight went on, and Douglas was kicking his ass, and I said to her, 'Come on! I don't want [Mike] to *lose!*' "

Douglas's complete dominance notwithstanding, there was no shortage of onlookers who couldn't shake the notion that Tyson would somehow salvage the fight. There was precedent, after all, for this sort of thing. Frank Bruno, for example, had given Tyson trouble for a few rounds before succumbing, and it wasn't entirely unreasonable to think that eventually Douglas would make a mistake and that Tyson would seize the opportunity. *One punch.* That's all it would take to set the world right.

Douglas would have none of it, though. He continued to strike and move, putting together punishing combinations that proved increasingly effective against the confused and frustrated champion. A big right hand in the opening minute of the fifth round staggered Tyson, prompting the unthinkable: He bowed his head and tried to cover up. This was not a defensive tactic in the manner taught by D'Amato, but rather an instinctive attempt at survival. Clearly, Tyson was hurt. With his corner shouting encouragement, Douglas remained on the offensive, wobbling Tyson with a solid left hand midway through the round; then, as he did throughout the fight, whenever Tyson appeared vulnerable, the challenger instantly bore in, hammer-

ing Tyson with a left jab and an overhand right, and then another series of combinations. For the most part Tyson stood his ground and
endured the punishment. Finally, with about thirty seconds remaining
in the round, he leaped at Douglas and flailed errantly with a right
hook.

Shortly after the bell sounded Douglas took a swipe at, Tyson,
who offered no defense, no protest. Clearly intentional, the late punch
was another measure of the challenger's insistence upon owning the
fight at every level, as was the significant amount of swelling now presenting itself rather dramatically around Tyson's left eye. If evidence
of Douglas's effectiveness and accuracy was needed, here it was. Tyson
had rarely suffered any visible damage in the ring; certainly he had
never experienced anything quite like this.

Cuts and bruises come with the territory in boxing; that's why a
skilled cut man is invaluable. In less than a minute of intense, artful
work, he mitigates swelling, closes wounds and staunches bleeding,
then sends his fighter back into the ring. Good as new. Some cuts,
some injuries, are worse than others, and the degree to which they
inspire unease is not always reflected in the appearance of the boxer.
A cracked rib isn't visible, but it will stop even the toughest of fighters in his tracks; similarly, while a bloody or broken nose might provoke a veritable river of gore, it isn't as dangerous as a cut near the
eye. And a cut *above* the eye (especially along the eyelid) is of particular concern, for this type of wound not only presents a risk of long-
term, permanent damage, but almost always results in blood streaming
into the fighter's field of vision. This is a handicap with potentially
deadly consequences (for a one-eyed fighter is a fighter who can't protect himself), and few ring officials will tolerate it for long.

So it was with a sense of astonishment that one watched the
flurry of activity in Tyson's corner between the fifth and sixth
rounds. As the champion, seemingly exhausted, slumped on his stool,
Snowell crouched in front of him, holding in his hands what appeared at first glance to be a water balloon. The trainer kneaded the
item furiously, then applied it to the area around Tyson's eye in an apparent attempt to reduce the swelling.

If one had no experience with the sport of boxing this might have
seemed a logical approach to the problem. But it wasn't. Swelling is

diminished, or slowed, by applying something cold (and thus reducing the flow of blood) to the affected area. Ice is a natural vasoconstrictor, and while commonly employed in the treatment of athletic trauma, it is messy and impractical in the boxing ring. Preferred during a fight is something that can be embedded in ice (to conduct the cold), then applied directly to the skin. For many years it was common for trainers to use a fifty-cent piece or silver dollar in this way. In the modern era, the coin has been replaced by a device known as an Enswell, a small, smooth-bottomed implement cast of stainless steel or metal (most often rectangular or circular in shape, although it sometimes has the appearance of a tiny, old-school flatiron) with a handle on the back. By the time of the Tyson-Douglas fight, the Enswell (which is sometimes referred to as an "endswell" or "No-Swell") had become as ubiquitous in boxing corners as petroleum jelly, latex gloves, and adrenaline-soaked cotton swabs; even at the club or amateur level it was hard to find a trainer or cut man who would enter the ring on fight night without this simple but indispensable item.

And yet, there was Tyson, sitting impassively on his stool, a bulbous, sweaty mass flopped across his face. To anyone with a modicum of knowledge about the sport, this represented not merely a unique approach to the situation, but a colossal gaffe.

"The corner was woeful," said Jim Lampley. "I mean, the corner was pathetic. And you knew that there would be questions about the corner. But Aaron Snowell, in particular, was supposed to be a boxing person, a professional boxing person. He was trumpeted by King in particular as a guy who knew what he was doing as the trainer. So you never would have thought for an instant . . . You wouldn't have considered, for example, that they would come into the ring without an Enswell. Without any cut material whatsoever. It's impossible. At that level of the sport, it's just not possible. It's like a baseball team coming onto the field without their gloves or something. A corner without an Enswell is like a doctor without his black bag. We were all incredulous. When Ray [Leonard] figured out what it was that they were putting on [Tyson's] face, he was just totally incredulous, and he flatly stated that it's not going to do anything. There was no way that they were going to stop swelling with a little balloon of cold water."

From his home in upstate New York, Matt Baranski, Tyson's former cut man, watched the scene in Tyson's corner with a sense of bemusement.

"Unbelievable. They didn't even have the right equipment to take care of a cut or anything," said Baranski. "I can't imagine going into a fight without an Enswell. I had two of them at all times, laying right there in the ice."

Snowell and Bright absorbed enormous mudslinging for their handling of Tyson's prefight training and, especially, for their conduct in the ring on February 11. Time has offered some vindication on the former. While burning through trainers, Tyson has repeatedly and consistently demonstrated himself to be a fighter with, at best, an inconsistent work ethic and a disinclination to take his sport seriously; whether Kevin Rooney's presence in the Tyson camp during the months and weeks leading up to the fight would have made a difference is debatable. Equally questionable is whether another trainer might have been able to elicit a different response from Tyson as the fight wore on. More problematic, and less open to debate, is the corner's clear mishandling of a crisis. As the fight progressed, and the swelling above Tyson's eye worsened, the absence of an Enswell took on almost comical significance.

Tyson's cut man that night was Taylor Smith, a Detroit-based veteran of the fight game. It is, of course, the cut man's job to come into the ring with the proper equipment, but Snowell would be the first to acknowledge that all responsibility ultimately rests on the shoulders of the trainer.

"The cut man is responsible for having the tools when the person's eye gets cut or swollen," Snowell said. "My teacher, Slim Robinson, told me, 'Always check, don't take nobody's word.' That night I didn't check. I asked him. I said, 'Taylor, do you have all the things that you need for the corner?' This was prior to going to the arena. He told me yes. But never did I check in the bucket to make sure. So when Mike's eye started swelling, I asked Taylor, 'Are you ready? Mike's eye is swelling, you gotta be ready when we go up between rounds.' And he didn't have the stuff. So I had to make a call. I never asked Taylor where and why. I was too upset and there wasn't enough time. As the leader in the corner, I figured something on the eye was better than nothing, so I improvised and made something out of a latex glove."

Not a condom, as has so often been speculated? (Indeed, the item, with no apparent fingers, looked less like a latex glove than a prophylactic.)

"No," Snowell said with a laugh. "It was a glove, and I'm surprised it didn't bust. I just reached down in the bucket and filled it up with water and tied it off. I mean, I had to do something."

While there has been no shortage of people willing to eviscerate Snowell and Bright for their work in the corner that day, Tyson, interestingly enough, has never added his voice to the chorus.

"Hey, it wasn't their fault," Tyson said. "We just didn't think Buster would stand up. Nobody was prepared, man. Nobody thought Buster was going to fight so great that night. We were like, 'Who cares?' We didn't expect the inevitable, you know what I mean?"

So, had Aaron Snowell reached into that bucket and found an Enswell bathed in ice, it wouldn't have made any difference?

Tyson laughed. "Hell, no!"

Contributing to the overall weirdness of the event (and, let's face it, detracting somewhat from the drama) was a distinct lack of enthusiasm on the part of the Japanese audience. Perhaps their reticence had something to do with the fact that the fight was contested at such an unusual hour of the day; or maybe it's just the nature of the Japanese to behave in a more measured and controlled manner than their Western counterparts. Regardless, the crowd in the nearly half-empty Tokyo Dome seemed either unaware of or unmoved by the magnitude of the story unfolding in front of them.

The quiet of the crowd, juxtaposed with the passionate exhortations issued from the fighters' corners ("You got it won! Just stay in control," Russell shouted at Douglas between the sixth and seventh rounds. "This fucking guy is scared to death!") was wildly incongruous. There was no denying the historical impact of a Douglas upset, and yet there was no buzz in the arena, no sense of astonishment or awe. Even in the seventh round, when Tyson was issued a warning by Meyran for hitting Douglas below the belt, and Douglas responded by casually hitching up his shorts and then planting a concussive right hand to Tyson's head, the audience remained oddly disengaged.

"During the first round, if you listen to the tape, you'll start to sense from the announcers that this is different," noted Ross Greenburg. "Part of the reason it's different is that there was an intensity in the ring which was not matched by the spirit of the crowd. What we had were forty-three thousand Japanese fans who didn't know what they were watching. They sat on their hands, never even uttered a cheer."

The backdrop of silence imposed upon the broadcast a restraint not common to major sporting events.

"An incredible thing happened," observed Lampley. "A real good fortune for us and the telecast was that the sepulchral silence of the crowd . . . the absolute stunned silence of the crowd . . . created this sort of hushed, expectant aura, very much like the final three or four holes at the Masters, and our natural kinetic response was to understate rather than to overstate. It would have been almost impossible under the circumstances to blow that telecast up with gushing overstatement because you would have felt like an idiot making that much noise in front of the audience."

If there was moderation behind the microphone, at ringside, there was something less refined in the production room.

"There was a focus by the broadcasters and a focus by the crew because of this eerie silence in the arena," Greenburg said. "But a funny thing was happening: By the time the fight started to roll into the second, third, fourth, fifth round, there was an intense amount of cheering coming from the HBO sports production crew. They knew exactly what they were watching and witnessing, and being a part of, which was one of the greatest upsets in the history of the sport. So what happened was, there were two or three times during the broadcast, early on, in those rounds, when I had to shout at our personnel to calm down, because we had a fight to produce, a broadcast to put on the air: *'Please! Don't scream at the top of your lungs off a vicious Douglas combination when I'm trying to help set up replays of that combination to show our announcers and the American public! Okay?'* We had to calm down our crew, because they were the only ones cheering during the fight."

So subdued was the crowd that one could clearly hear the smack of leather against skin each time a punch landed; audible, too, was the running commentary from Douglas's corner, a mix of cheerleading and coaching, with more than a hint of trash-talking thrown in for good measure.

"You're getting your ass kicked, Mike!" John Russell would scream when Tyson was backed into Douglas's corner. "Where's Cus at? Where's Kevin Rooney? They can't help you now, Mike!"

The memory of those taunts causes Russell to wince, but he figures that if anyone would understand, it's Tyson.

"It wasn't the most ethical thing to do," Russell said. "But at a time like that, the gloves are off and you're trying to win. It's common in boxing, but not too common for me. I try not to be that way. But this was different. This was such a big fight."

By the eighth round, the unthinkable had become, well, thinkable; more than that, actually. By this point, with Tyson obviously tired and hurt, and Douglas feeling a confidence no Tyson opponent had ever known, or at least earned, the outcome seemed almost inevitable.

"We're in the eighth round, folks," Lampley announced soberly at the 1:45 mark. "And a heavyweight champion regarded as completely invincible in these circumstances . . . is in big trouble."

"You got him, Buster!" J. D. McCauley screamed from the corner as the challenger effortlessly flicked off one jab after another. "You got him!"

Lampley: "Can you imagine? Buster Douglas: undisputed heavyweight champion of the world."

Ray Leonard: "It's not over yet, but Douglas has given a good account of himself."

Lampley: "It boggles the mind."

As the round moved inexorably toward its conclusion, the beating worsened. With fifty-four seconds remaining Douglas landed a sharp right hand to Tyson's swollen eye; with twenty-two seconds left and Tyson backed against the ropes, Douglas landed another powerful right hand, followed by a quick combination that obviously hurt Tyson. If not for the fact that he had been leaning against the ropes, the champion might have found the canvas for the first time in his career.

But Tyson was nothing if not stubborn on this day; his reluctance to quit against Douglas was commendable, and even somewhat ironic in light of the fact that history will no doubt regard quitting as a central theme in the later chapters of the boxing life of Mike Tyson. Indeed, with a single moment of brilliance, dredged up from memory and instinct, Tyson nearly salvaged his title, if not his reputation. It happened with seven seconds left in the round, and Douglas again backing Tyson into the ropes. So complete was Douglas's control of the fight that for the first time he let confidence get the better of him. As Meyran pried the fighters out of a clinch, Douglas took a long look at the champion, battered and bruised, before uncoiling a big, lazy left. Not a jab, really—more like a left hook, but delivered with no sense of purpose.

"That was the only time I started to take notice of what I was doing," Douglas remembered. "I was, like, 'Damn! I'm cooking, baby!' I was admiring my work, taking time to reflect, like, 'So, Mike, what do you think? Isn't this incredible?' And then . . . *Wham!*"

As the punch floated past Tyson, Douglas stood flat-footed, one of the few times that he had presented the champion with a stationary target; worse, the act of missing carried Douglas forward ever so slightly, and in less time than it took for him to a draw a breath, Tyson came inside with a right uppercut that landed squarely against Douglas's jaw. The punch, like so many others Tyson had thrown in his tenure as champion, had immediate and profound consequences. Douglas's legs buckled and he dropped to the canvas, landing hard on his backside and then flopping into a prone position.

And that, as they say, was that. With one punch Tyson had voided eight rounds of ineffectiveness; with one punch he had made Buster Douglas a mere footnote.

But then a strange thing happened. As Tyson walked to his corner and Meyran stood over Douglas, counting, the challenger rolled onto his right side and pounded his left fist into the canvas.

"When I saw that," Russell said, "I knew he was all right."

Others weren't so sure.

"Frankly," said *The New York Times*'s James Sterngold, "I didn't know if [Douglas] was saying, 'Fuck! After all this preparation I still got knocked out!' or 'Damn it! I slipped for a moment, but I'm going to be more determined coming back.' My immediate reaction was, This is over. But unquestionably, after a couple seconds, you realized

Douglas was together; he took a serious punch but showed no signs of being glassy-eyed or anything like that."

By the count of six Douglas had propped himself up on his right forearm and turned his attention directly to the official. At eight he was on his knees, waiting patiently. By nine he was nearly upright and ready to resume fighting, although that would prove unnecessary; as Meyran instructed the fighters to engage, the bell rang, signifying an end to the eighth round.

"It was a good shot, but I was coherent," Douglas said of the uppercut that lifted him off his feet. "I was alert and aware of everything. I suppose I could have stayed down and nobody would have given it a thought. They would have said, 'Buster, damn good fight.' But I wouldn't have been able to live with that. *'Hey, you came close, James.'* Fuck coming close! I was pissed!"

From his apartment in New York, Steve Lott watched in amazement as Douglas survived the type of punch that had shorted the circuits of so many other fighters.

"The referee is counting—*seven . . . eight . . . nine*—and Douglas is still on the canvas," Lott said. "And then he gets up. Why? What made him get up? I mean, no one gets up after nine. Nobody! Something in him said, 'Ah, let me get up. What the hell.' "

More aggravated than hurt, Douglas shambled to his corner, a look of disappointment on his face. How many times in training had Russell and McCauley harped about staying active, about never making the mistake of exposing himself to the champion? *Jab and move, jab and move.* For the first time he had failed to heed that advice, and Tyson had punished him. Now there would be hell to pay in the corner.

"God damn it, James!" Russell barked. "I told you never to lean into this guy!"

Douglas said nothing.

"You all right?" Russell asked, the anger draining from his voice.

"Yeah."

"Okay, then get back on your jab. Start doing what you've been doing. Box this guy. Make him run into something."

Predictably, Tyson opened the ninth round energetically, rushing from his stool to the center of the ring and landing a solid left hand to Douglas's head. If this was a test of the challenger's resolve, he passed. As if to let Tyson know he was neither hurt nor dispirited, Douglas fired back with a left-right combination that shook the champion. At ringside, Don King, sitting next to Donald Trump, visibly squirmed. His anxiety was understandable. If Tyson were to lose, King's hold on the heavyweight division would probably be less secure, and certainly less profitable. The promoter had nearly as much riding on the outcome as the fighters themselves.

By the midpoint of the ninth round, Douglas had once more wrested control of the fight. A combination with 1:10 remaining caused Tyson to stumble; again, if not for the support of the ring ropes, he likely would have fallen. Emboldened by the champion's clear distress, Douglas continued to attack. Rather than relying on a knockout punch, Douglas remained faithful to his game plan, busily throwing one punch after another in the final minute—sometimes using his elbows and forearms to straighten Tyson's head and torso, thus presenting a clearer target—in the hope that eventually Tyson would crumble. (Douglas landed thirty-seven punches in the round; more than triple the number landed by Tyson.) Somehow, though, Tyson stayed on his feet. When the bell rang at the conclusion of the ninth round, the champion lurched to his corner, an awkward hitch in his step. His left eye, by this point, was completely closed.

"Mike showed a lot of heart," Douglas said. "Throughout our training camp we talked about how he was liable to quit. He wasn't used to being behind in a fight. But he never quit. And we always thought he might. That was one of the motivating factors going into the fight: If he got down, he might just say, 'Fuck it.' We figured Mike was so used to being dominant that he might not fight back. Wrong."

In actuality, Tyson fought back valiantly, displaying as much courage and conviction as he would ever display in the ring. One could argue that in some ways this was the most memorable performance of Tyson's career.

"I didn't fight well, but I took my beating pretty good," Tyson said. "And that's one of the ingredients to being a great fighter: You have to take it as well as you dish it. Some people like the thrill, but they don't like to take it. When it gets rough, they throw in the towel and say, 'I ain't getting my ass whipped! I'm going to live to fight another day.' "

Tyson threw the first heavy punch of the tenth round, a sweeping right hand that momentarily stunned Douglas. As he had throughout the fight, the challenger showed no lingering effects and quickly fought his way out of trouble. The two men pawed and circled for much of the opening minute, a respite that gave Douglas a chance to catch his breath and perhaps lent Tyson a false sense of security. With 1:59 remaining, after shoving Tyson away, Douglas effortlessly rattled off four consecutive left jabs in a span of three seconds. Each punch found its mark, lashing Tyson in the head and face. Half blind, Tyson marched forward. Douglas flicked off another jab, then followed with a thunderous right uppercut that closed Tyson's eyes and drove his head back at a forty-five-degree angle. It was precisely the type of cataclysmic uppercut that Tyson himself had used to such great effect in his reign, and to see it used against him was startling.

"When James hit him with that uppercut, they were right in our corner," recalled Russell. "And I swear to God, I thought [James] was going to take Tyson's head off."

Any fighter without Tyson's thickly muscled neck (shock absorption for blows to the head) would have gone down immediately; Tyson remained upright but shaken to the point of disorientation. Without hesitation Douglas stepped forward and began punching. This time he would not make the mistake of admiring his own handiwork or presuming that Tyson was so badly injured that he couldn't defend himself. A three-punch combination—*right-left-right*—punished Tyson, who staggered backward, arms falling to his side.

"Finishing was always a struggle for me," Douglas said. "I'd catch 'em, then let 'em go. But you have to finish. You have to punch the guy into the ground."

And so, there was Douglas, right on top of Tyson, stalking the wounded champion, matching him step for step . . . and finally twisting at the waist and throwing all his weight into a left hook, a punch that struck Tyson's head and maintained contact until he was halfway to the canvas. The blow was delivered with such force and conviction that Douglas's momentum nearly carried him down as well, leaving him standing over the vanquished champion, his left foot between Tyson's splayed legs.

"That was poetry," James Sterngold said of the denouement. "It was sort of shocking in its brutality, but it was poetry, too. Because even in that moment, Douglas was an athlete. He was not going to be denied. This was all heart, but it was great, athletic boxing. Douglas knew what he was doing. He wasn't just flailing wildly at his opponent."

The crowd at the Tokyo Dome by now had finally been swept up in the emotion of the event and was filling the arena with noise. As Meyran moved in and began his count, Douglas stepped away, bouncing lightly on the balls of his feet, as if ready to resume fighting that very moment.

Tyson, meanwhile, was engaged in a different sort of struggle. He had ten seconds in which to emerge from the fog. Tyson first rolled onto his side, then propped himself up on his hands and knees—on all fours—as Meyran shouted "Five!" and presented to the champion, within inches of his face, a hand spread wide, fingers extended, in accordance with boxing protocol. Whether Tyson heard or understood the count is debatable.

"When Mike went down, I was probably a foot from his head," said Russell. "He was right there on the ring apron, and I remember screaming at him, 'Stay down, Mike! Stay down!' " Russell paused when relating the story, his voice cracking at the memory. "It's emotional for me, because I like Mike. I wasn't overjoyed at that time. I was happy we won, but I had a little compassion for the guy. I thought if he got up and they let the fight continue, he could have really gotten hurt. So I said, 'Stay down, Mike. Please . . . Stay down.' "

Russell needn't have worried, for Tyson, as it turned out, was not nearly lucid enough to resume fighting. In what would become the defining image of the fight—and, arguably, the defining image of Tyson's career—the champion crawled deeper into the corner and, inexplicably it seemed, began wasting time by scratching blindly at the canvas, like a man in search of a lost contact lens. What Tyson had misplaced, however, was his mouthpiece, which had been dislodged during the preceding onslaught. Now instinct, rather than reason, dictated his response.

"I'll never forget hitting the canvas," Tyson would say many years later. "You don't always remember getting knocked out, but you don't forget hitting that canvas. All I knew was that I got knocked down, and that I was trying to grab my fucking mouthpiece so I could start fighting again. I knew I couldn't fight without my mouthpiece, so I wanted to grab it . . . because I wanted to fight."

"*Six . . . seven.*"

As Meyran continued to count, Tyson scooped up the mouthpiece with his gloved right hand, stuffed it backward into his mouth, and tried to lift himself off the canvas.

"*Eight . . . nine.*"

Stumbling drunkenly, with the white mouthpiece dangling between his lips, Tyson lurched forward and reached out to Meyran with his left hand, as if in desperate need of support. The referee complied, first waving his arms to signal the end of the fight, and then enveloping Tyson in a warm and protective embrace. Officially, the end came at 1:23 of the tenth round.

"It was shocking, that's all I can say," remembered Catskill *Daily Mail* reporter Paul Antonelli. "Here is a guy who is invincible, and he's on the canvas, with his mouthpiece out, crawling around. I know some people don't like him, but at that moment you kind of felt for Mike. That was basically the end of his career. After that fight, he was just never the same."

At ringside, HBO's broadcast team reached for the words to accurately convey the magnitude of the moment. And in that reaching, so pure and heartfelt and genuine, they succeeded in expressing the shock felt by anyone who witnessed the fight.

"It's over!" exclaimed Ray Leonard, stuttering just slightly on the first word. "Unbelievable."

Added Lampley: "Mike Tyson has been knocked out."

And from Larry Merchant, a moment later, as Douglas stood triumphantly in his corner, arms stretched high above his head, handlers and friends and relatives draped all over him: "This makes Cinderella look like a sad story."

In the midst of the postfight chaos, Aaron Snowell climbed through the ropes and walked calmly to his fighter.

"What happened?" Tyson asked.

"You got knocked out," Snowell replied.

Without saying another word, Tyson let his head fall onto Snowell's shoulder. The trainer pulled the fighter close and held him tightly.

"It's okay, man," Snowell whispered. "You're going to be all right."

8

Don King puts up a good image, but he's a monster. He's a gangster—a very bad person who tries to push around all the boxers, managers . . . all the people.

—Octavio Meyran

The scene that played out in the Tokyo Dome for slack-jawed viewers around the world was as touching and heartwarming as any the sport of boxing has ever produced. There was James Douglas, the newly crowned heavyweight champion, bathed in sweat, waving a glove and mugging for the camera, and looking not at all like a journeyman fighter who had just gone ten rounds with Mike Tyson.

Into the celebration stepped Larry Merchant, who sidled up to Douglas and asked the simplest and most pointed of questions: "Why did this happen, James?"

"Because I wanted it," Douglas stated flatly.

No stranger to the madness of a postfight boxing ring, where emotion, rather than erudition, tends to rule the day, Merchant pressed on: "Why did you win this fight that no one thought you could win?"

Douglas paused before answering, and in that moment of dead air someone nearby could be heard yelling, "His mother." With that, the floodgates opened. Douglas nodded, blinked back tears, and echoed the words, "My mother." Then again: "My mother . . . God bless her heart."

He put a glove to his face. From behind, John Russell put an arm around Douglas and asked the champion if he wanted to leave. Douglas shook his head.

"Are you saying the death of your mother focused your mind?" Merchant asked.

"I was already focused," Douglas responded before turning away and crying again.

Merchant continued: "What did you try to do?"

Douglas cocked his head, smiled slightly through the tears. "What I did: whip his ass."

From there the interview settled into a more comfortable rhythm, with Douglas mixing cogent observations about specific elements of the fight (of the eighth-round knockdown he said, "That was a good shot; I was just starting to get real relaxed") with a reasonable and understandable amount of bravado ("I wasn't afraid of him! I fear no man!"), given the magnitude of the accomplishment.

Near the end of the interview Douglas praised his vanquished opponent: "I knew he was going to come on because he's a champion. I knew he'd suck it up and come and get me. And I was ready for it."

As Douglas spoke, the camera pulled back to reveal the champion's entire entourage, including, chest high, his son, Lamar, beaming proudly beneath a cockeyed red baseball cap bearing the team slogan: *Only My Best: James Douglas.*

As Lamar leaned back against his father, Douglas dropped a gloved hand across the boy's shoulder.

"I was aware of everything," Douglas said. Then he hesitated, looked directly into the camera and added, "Dad . . . this is for you. I love you."

What Douglas did not know, could not have known, and certainly would not have had reason to suspect, given the promoter's smiling presence, just a few feet away, was that Don King had already boldly set in motion the machinery of protest that would threaten to take from Douglas the championship he had so obviously earned. But then such was the gleefully duplicitous nature of boxing's greatest show-man. Consider, for example, one of the most infamous entries in the King oeuvre, a frequently told tale of shameless hucksterism and shallow self-interest first reported with great pride and gusto by King himself.

This was back in January 1973, when King traveled to Kingston, Jamaica, for a heavyweight championship fight between Joe Frazier and George Foreman. Frazier was the titleholder at the time, and it was at his invitation that King attended the bout. Technically speaking, King was little more than a fan with a first-class seat in Jamaica; he had only recently begun to build his promotional empire and so had no official duty as promoter or "advisor." What he had were aspirations, and so, perhaps in an effort to broaden his options, he struck up a friendship with Foreman, who was then a scowling, brooding, mountain of a fighter, in other words, the polar opposite of the cuddly, grill-hawking, boxing grandfather he would become. King offered encouragement to the challenger and even provided transportation from the airport when Foreman's relatives arrived in Jamaica.

On fight night, predictably, King's allegiance shifted back where it belonged: to the champion. He shared a limousine with Frazier on the way to the arena, the centerpiece of a motorcade led by police motorcycles with sirens wailing. When the opening bell sounded, there was King, perched in a front-row seat, right behind Smokin' Joe's corner. It wasn't long, however, before Foreman's awesome punching power manifested itself, and soon King felt himself being carried on the winds of change.

"The first round, George hit Frazier with a devastating punch that sent Joe leaping into the air," King recalled. "Every time he'd strike Frazier, I'd move closer to the end of the row, toward George's corner. When the fight was stopped [with Foreman the winner, by technical knockout], I'm into the ring, saying to George, 'I told you.' And George said, 'Come with me.' He took me to his room. Same thing. Motorcycle cops, sirens blasting." When telling this story, King would typically pause here for effect and then let out a knowing little chuckle. "I came with the champion, and left with the champion."

Apocryphal or not, that is a tale that speaks volumes about King and the way he operates; it also helps explain his actions in the wake of the Tyson-Douglas fight. There he was, just a few feet behind the newly minted champion, Buster Douglas, smiling proudly and happily, as befitted a promoter who by his own estimation owned "quite a few" options on future Douglas fights (this was the tariff paid by Douglas in order to secure a meeting with Tyson; it was also an arrangement that King shared with Tyson). Just a few moments earlier, though, after Tyson had been knocked out, King had stumbled through the ropes in a state of intense exasperation.

"I was waiting for him," remembered John Russell. "I said, 'I told you, Don.' And he went nuts, started throwing his arms around, screaming, 'I'm protesting! I'm protesting!' I said, 'Protesting what?' He just yelled, 'Get away from me!' And I did . . . because he's crazy."

Not so crazy, or angry, that he didn't have time to pause in the ring, just close enough to the new champion to make his presence felt, and let it be known that regardless of which fighter wore the crown, a piece if it would always belong to Don King.

Of course, given their respective résumés, coupled with the likelihood that Tyson would remain the most marketable fighter in the game, regardless of his unfortunate and convincing beating at the hands of Douglas, it only made sense that King would throw his considerable weight behind the deposed champion—whatever that meant. There was, after all, a great deal invested in Tyson remaining the champion, most notably an upcoming appointment against Evander Holyfield that promised to provide both men with the fattest purses of their careers. If Douglas were champion, a Tyson-Holyfield fight would lose considerable luster, and in all probability be shoved aside in favor of a Douglas-Holyfield encounter.

And so it was that before the fight even ended, the wheels of conspiracy had begun to turn; soon Douglas would learn that his victory had been challenged and that the man orchestrating that challenge was King.

"My first thought was, *They're going to try to take it from Buster? They're going to put some bad spin on what this kid did?*" John Russell recalled. "It was ridiculous. But boxing is boxing, right? And King is a powerful man, so you have to be concerned."

The thrust of the protest (filed officially with the Japanese Boxing Commission by Tyson's unofficial comanager, John Horne) was this: Douglas had benefited from an error by Octavio Meyran, the ring official, when he was knocked down in the eighth round. In essence, Team Tyson argued, Douglas had been knocked out, and only a long count by the official had allowed him to rise and continue the fight.

"Two knockouts took place," King suggested a few hours after the fight. "But the first knockout obliterates the second. Buster Douglas was knocked out, and the referee did not do his job and panicked. As the promoter of both fighters, I'm only seeking fair play."

Given King's checkered past and disturbingly close relationships with members of at least two of the sport's governing bodies, the WBC and WBA, coupled with accounts of his behavior during and immediately following the fight, it seems at best questionable that fair play was actually high on the promoter's agenda. Interestingly, on the day of the fight, Jose Sulaiman, the WBC president, said that between the eighth and ninth rounds, "someone" in Tyson's corner had voiced displeasure with the alleged long count to both Sulaiman and WBA president Gilberto Mendoza. Sulaiman said, however, that he could not recall which member of Tyson's team had approached him. Two days later, at a news conference in New York, King would slip just slightly by acknowledging that it was he who had protested at that time; the more formal protest was later filed by Horne, allowing King to distance himself somewhat from the proceedings, thus presenting at least a superficial attempt at impartiality.

Eyewitnesses to the fight painted King as openly and blatantly partisan. Consider, for example, this account from a Los Angeles attorney and promoter named Dean Gettleson (who had a ringside seat in Tokyo), as reported in *The New York Times:* "Immediately to my left were Jose Sulaiman and Gilberto Mendoza and directly behind them, in the first row of spectators, were King and Donald Trump. After Douglas got up from the knockdown, King started yelling at

Sulaiman. 'What kind of ref did you bring me from Mexico? You're going to get my man beat.'"

According to Gettleson, "King was yelling at the top of his lungs, and Sulaiman's face was getting redder and redder. And King yelled, 'Stop the fight. The fight's over.'"

As the official walked to the side of the ring to present the judges' scorecards to Sulaiman (an act repeated at the close of each round), King began chastising Meyran: "What were you looking at? You should have known the man was out. You should have counted him out."

Roughly an hour after the fight, according to Gettleson, "We were all going back on the official bus to the hotel. We were where the buses and limos were parked. Well, King called Meyran off the bus and then started yelling at Sulaiman, 'I want a press conference. I want this straightened out.'"

There would be a press conference—two, in fact. The first occurred following a two-hour meeting between King and representatives from the Japanese Boxing Commission, along with officials from the WBC and WBA. At that time King announced that a review of videotape clearly indicated that Douglas had been on the canvas for more than ten seconds. There were more meetings; several hours passed. Then there was a larger, more formal press conference, this one including Octavio Meyran, who sheepishly acknowledged culpability, saying haltingly, in fractured English, "I don't know why I start my count and make my mistake. Yes, [Douglas] was down longer than ten seconds."

Indeed, even a cursory review of the videotape reveals that Douglas spent in excess of ten seconds on the canvas. But to reduce the debate to a simple matter of counting—less than ten or more than ten—is to ignore the subtler aspects of boxing protocol in favor of a rigid (and inaccurate) interpretation of the rules.

When a knockdown occurs, each fighter has an immediate and pressing responsibility. The fighter who has registered the knockdown is required to retreat to the most distant corner; the fighter who has been knocked down is expected to sufficiently gather his faculties in an attempt to discern the actions of the official in the ring. He is required only to focus on the official's count and rise before the count reaches ten; whether the count is accurate or inaccurate, fast or slow, is largely irrelevant—at least in the eyes of the fallen fighter.

The responsibility of the official in the ring is another matter, and one open to some interpretation. Here, for example, is an excerpt from the International Boxing Federation's rules regarding the handling of knockdowns:

Rule 3

When a contestant is knocked down, the referee shall audibly announce the count as he motions with his right arm downward indicating the end of each second of the count. If the contestant taking the count is still down when the referee calls the count of ten (10) the referee will wave both arms indicating the contestant has been knocked out.

Rule 4

When a contestant has been knocked down, the referee will order the standing contestant to the farthest neutral corner and begin the count. If the contestant standing leaves the corner before the count has been completed, the referee shall discontinue the count and order the standing contestant back into the corner. The count will not resume until the standing contestant has returned to the neutral corner.

While the World Boxing Council's rules regarding knockdowns are less specific; the World Boxing Association's rules offer even greater detail:

Rule 3.4

When a contender is knocked down, the referee shall begin the count immediately, in a loud voice, accompanied by a movement of his arm. If the knocked [down] boxer [does] not stand up before the count of ten (10), he will be declared the loser by K.O. (Knockout), and the referee shall make it known by waving both arms.

Rule 3.5

When a contender is considered knocked down, the referee shall order the opponent to retire to the farthest corner of the ring, in relation to the knocked down boxer, pointing at such corner, and he shall immediately count the seconds taking the count from the knockdown judge. If the boxer refuses to go to the farthest corner determined by the referee, or does not stay there, the referee shall stop the count to the knocked down boxer until his opponent retires to the indicated corner, and then the referee shall continue with the count, starting from the point from which it was interrupted.

Strictly speaking, then, on a knockdown, the ring official is expected to pick up the count from the official timekeeper (or "knockdown judge"), who is seated at ringside, rather than starting at "one" when he (the official) stands over the fallen fighter. One can readily see the logic behind this rule: During the intense moments of a knockdown, time can slip away. Precious seconds pass as the ring official ensures that each fighter is safe and adhering to the rules, and then positions himself to begin the count. Such was the case in the Tyson-Douglas fight. A review of the videotape shows that the official timekeeper, wearing white gloves at ringside, began his count at the moment that Douglas's backside hit the canvas near the end of the eighth round. By the time Meyran reached the prone challenger and began his count, the timekeeper was already on "three." The two-second discrepancy remained throughout the count, meaning Douglas (who rose at nine) was actually on the canvas for a count of at least eleven . . . perhaps more. When measured against the official clock, the knockdown of Douglas stretched out over a period of nearly fourteen seconds.

The count, therefore, was long. That much is indisputable. But Douglas bore no accountability for that. He rose before the count of ten, which was all that was required of him. Moreover, considering his response to the count, it seems likely that he would have been capable of rising even in the event that Meyran had picked up the count at three. Douglas, remember, pounded the canvas with his glove, then rolled over onto his forearm and gathered himself as the count progressed. By all indications, he was clearheaded and able to continue fighting well before he actually decided to stand up.

"I was coherent. I was alert," Douglas said. "The protest was bullshit. It just showed they were in denial, crying and whining, trying to take away from what I'd done. It was like, 'Okay, you won the fight, but you're not going to win the war.' It was terrible."

The second press conference, presided over by King, with Tyson (but not Douglas, or anyone in his camp) in attendance, quickly took on the ludicrous atmosphere of a kangaroo court. A videotape of the eighth round was played for an assemblage of reporters, and as Douglas lay on his back, Team Tyson chanted loudly: *"nine . . . ten . . . eleven."* The ex-champ, wearing dark glasses (borrowed from Aaron Snowell) to hide his bruises and swollen eye, seemed less enthusiastic about the entire sordid affair. Tyson nodded his head in agreement as the others counted Douglas out, but he appeared to lack conviction; even as he offered a philosophical assessment of the evening's activities, there was something desultory about his tone and demeanor, as if this were the last place he wanted to be.

"I can handle losing," Tyson said, "if I lose fairly."

The fighter in Tyson bled through at that moment, manifesting itself in the embarrassment that comes with failing to accept defeat gracefully. And one senses that Tyson today, on the cusp of middle age, regrets his participation in King's postfight shenanigans.

"It was a long count, but who gives a damn?" Tyson said. "You know, when you're young, you want to complain. You get sucked into believing that you're immortal. But as you get older, you realize it's just a joke. You have to give people the props they deserve, the respect they deserve.

"People around me were saying, 'Protest!' So I went along with it. But I don't give a fuck. You win the fight, you win the fight. You don't, you lose. You know what I think? You look at this game, and you have to have a little perspective. And if you can't take your lumps, you ain't worth a damn."

If there was a victim in all of this, it was neither Tyson (whose protest had no merit whatsoever) nor Douglas (who not only survived King's shameless challenge, but actually emerged as a man of dignity and character, thanks partly to worldwide condemnation of King's actions); in reality, no one absorbed more punishment than Octavio Meyran, a respected official who regrettably found himself at the center of one of boxing's ugliest controversies.

In any sport, transparency is a referee's greatest virtue. The most effective officials exercise control over the proceedings through a combination of respect, knowledge, and experience. Impartiality is a given, a baseline requirement, since even the pretense or suggestion of favoritism is enough to taint any athletic contest. A subtler but no less important characteristic (or skill) is the subjugation of ego. It is something of a cliché to suggest that no one pays to watch the referee; it's also absolutely true. When an official does his job well, the action flows smoothly and all attention is focused on the participants. The thanklessness of the job can be measured in this way: An official, at his best, becomes merely an afterthought. If he is more than that, then something has probably gone wrong.

Meyran was forty-two years old when he worked the Tyson-Douglas fight, and hardly a neophyte. He had been raised in Mexico City by a father who earned a living as an architect, but whose great passion in life was boxing. Although he never became a serious fighter himself, Meyran spent vast amounts of time around the sport, largely through the influence of his father, who was not merely a former fighter but also a boxing judge and local commissioner. Meyran found his way into the ring as an official and over time rose through the ranks to become one of the more capable adjudicators in the sport. By February 11, 1990, he had been an official for more than two decades, with a résumé that featured twenty-six world championship fights, including the infamous 1980 "No más" encounter between Sugar Ray Leonard and Roberto Duran, which ended ignominiously with Duran (a fighter regarded not only for his skill, but for his almost immeasurable obstinacy) tossing up his arms and quitting in the ring (*"No más!"*). To suggest that Meyran was in any way unsuited or unprepared for working the Tyson-Douglas fight would be grossly inaccurate. He was a good and busy referee who knew his role. As Meyran himself put it, "The show is number one."

Explicit in that observation is an understanding that the official in the ring is not supposed to be an integral part of the show; implicit, however, is the suggestion that sometimes he is sacrificed at the altar of the show. That appears to have been the case with Meyran, who when reached by telephone at his home in Mexico City in January 2006, claimed to have had several conversations with Jose Sulaiman in the weeks prior to the fight, during which the WBC president allegedly told the official, among other things, "Be hard with Douglas, and be nice to Tyson."

When it was suggested to Meyran that this represented a rather startling accusation, Meyran replied, "It's amazing, yes." In thickly accented English, Meyran added, "But I'm a professional, and I said I'm not going to do anything . . . not legal. Those were my words."

Sulaiman's reply, according to Meyran, was, "That's okay, don't worry. Just do your job."

And so he did, without incident—until the eighth round. When Tyson's uppercut sent Douglas to the canvas, Meyran responded with the measured assuredness that comes with experience. He first ushered Tyson away, quickly and efficiently (and correctly), and then began his count, thrusting his fingers directly in front of the fallen fighter, and announcing each number loudly and clearly. It was suggested afterward in some circles that a lack of communication between the timekeeper (who was Japanese) and the ring official (Meyran, whose primary language is Spanish) contributed to the discrepancy in their respective counts, that somehow Meyran failed to understand the timekeeper's count simply because he (Meyran) did not speak Japanese.

In reality, the language barrier played no role whatsoever, since Meyran, by his own acknowledgment, did not look to the timekeeper for advice on when to begin the count. This is not a condemnation of the official, as it was routinely and widely interpreted in the days immediately following the fight, but rather an explanation for his handling of the knockdown. While it is true that Meyran failed to pick up the official timekeeper's count, in strict accordance with the rules, it is also true that the referee in the ring is allowed some discretion in these matters (he is permitted, for example, some leeway in ordering the standing fighter to a neutral corner before beginning his count), and that Meyran's handling of the knockdown, far from representing incompetence, was entirely in keeping with the protocol of the sport, and in fact was quite ordinary.

Consider that a similarly meticulous evaluation of a videotape of the fight reveals that Meyran handled the tenth-round knockdown of Tyson in precisely the same manner that he had handled the eighth-round knockdown of Douglas; indeed, Tyson, too, was on the canvas for nearly fourteen seconds (measured against the official clock) before he was officially declared a loser by knockout.

It is worth noting here that neither the official timekeeper nor the ring official is guided by the clock when administering his count. It is an entirely human process, one subject to interpretation and nuance. The videotape, for example, reveals that when Douglas was knocked down, the official timekeeper raised his index finger (indicating the count of "one") the moment Douglas hit the canvas; this was an error, technically speaking, since the timekeeper is supposed to wait until a full second has passed before indicating the count of "one."

"The letter of the rule presents a paradox between the count of the referee and some imaginary timepiece that neither he nor the timekeeper uses in the heat of battle," Larry Merchant suggested a few days later, following HBO's rebroadcast of the fight. "The fourteen-second knockout is commonplace."

The most important thing is consistency, and in that regard Meyran's performance was flawless.

"Both boxers, I made the same count," Meyran explained. "I never take the timekeeper's time. I make my own count. In twenty-seven years of officiating, I did it in the same form . . . the same manner."

When asked if this was because turning one's attention away from the action and toward the timekeeper represented a risk of negligence to one's own job, Meyran responded, "Yes, correct. Because the health of the boxer is most important for me."

In the aftermath of the Tyson-Douglas fight, Meyran was alternately lionized (for standing his ground against King, when the promoter, he said, pressured him to acknowledge his mistake and even reverse his decision) and criticized (for mishandling the count). The hours following the fight, he said, were among the most difficult of his life, for he was held up to ridicule and pressured to compromise his integrity. In the beginning, at least, Meyran did not waver. To

Western journalists he repeatedly proclaimed his innocence, arguing that while the eighth-round knockdown resulted in a long count, it was neither inaccurate nor favorable to Douglas. Over and over, he said, there was no mistake, no error, no faulty judgment.

"For me, all the time, in all my career, I try to protect the boxers," Meyran would say many years later. "The boxers are the main persons in the sport. Then, when some people tried to push me to change my mind, and the show became more important than the boxers . . . it's not good for me. At that moment Tyson was the iron man, the best boxer in the history of the heavyweight division. In reality, that's not correct. We know in that moment who is Don King and who is Tyson. He's just a good boxer. . . . I prefer to try to protect boxers, no matter what's the name. Tyson, Douglas—any name. To me, it's only boxers."

If Meyran has any regret about his conduct in the entire Tyson-Douglas affair, it is only this: that in the glare of the spotlight, in front of the media, he supported the company line by acknowledging that an error had been made.

"I don't know why I start my count and make my mistake. Yes, [Douglas] was down longer than ten seconds."

There it was: an admission of guilt and a tacit declaration that the previously unbeaten champion had been somehow dealt an unfair hand. It is a quote that dogged Meyran for years, casting a shadow over all that he accomplished in the ring and forever tainting him as either a poor official or a man who lost his nerve. Either assessment seems unduly harsh in light of the circumstances.

"In the press conference after the fight," Meyran explained, "at my left hand was sitting Jose Sulaiman; to my right hand in first place was Don King, and in second place was Tyson. Then Sulaiman start to tell me in a low voice, 'You make a mistake, tell them that.' And I will, because in that moment I was very confused and I feel under pressure from them, especially from Sulaiman."

Meyran offered nothing else in the way of support for King or Sulaiman, and certainly never suggested that the decision should be overturned. And yet, for a few days at least, the official outcome of the fight was uncertain. Both the WBC and WBA announced that they would temporarily withhold recognition of Douglas's victory, pending an official review that could take as long as two weeks to complete (Sulaiman announced that WBC officials would meet February 21 in Mexico City; Mendoza suggested that the WBA would convene somewhat sooner, probably within ten days).

"Personally, I feel there were two knockouts in the same fight," Sulaiman said at the time. "Douglas was down for twelve and a half seconds in the eighth round. Tyson was knocked out in the tenth round." Whether Douglas benefited from the long count, Sulaiman added, "becomes a matter for review."

That comment, combined with Sulaiman's stated opinion that a rematch between Tyson and Douglas would best serve the interests of boxing, made many boxing insiders cringe, including some in Sulaiman's own organization.

Said WBC ratings chairman Dick Cole, "It was another one of those things Jose says that makes it look as if there's impropriety in boxing and that Don King runs the WBC."

In a curious bit of irony, boxing's third sanctioning body, the IBF, immediately declared Douglas to be its new heavyweight champion; this despite the fact that the IBF, which was not recognized as a legitimate governing organization by the Japanese Boxing Commission, did not even have a representative in Tokyo. Regardless, Douglas would hold at least one of the sport's alphabet titles. Whether he would add the word "undisputed" to that title remained to be seen.

Virtually all of what transpired in the hours after the fight went unwitnessed by Douglas, who had retreated to the comfort and quiet of his hotel room, where he relaxed in relative tranquility with his son and trainer. As word of a Tyson protest leaked out, Douglas grew anxious. Russell attempted to reassure his fighter that there was nothing to worry about, that in the court of public opinion, at least, James Douglas would emerge victorious, and King would be perceived as nothing more than an unscrupulous opportunist.

And, indeed, that is precisely what happened.

"The press jumped on it and nailed [King's] butt to the wall," Russell said. "They got him so bad that he had to back off. I take my hat off to the media on that one. He backed up completely."

Although the protest was formally lodged by Team Tyson, of which the former champion was the titular figure, Tyson himself largely eluded public excoriation, the bulk of which was reserved for King. Reportorial accounts of the proceedings in Tokyo tended to focus on two things: (1) Douglas's courageous performance, and (2) King's arrogance, which, to many eyes, extended to Sulaiman.

"Sulaiman was essentially a King henchman," offered *Sports Illustrated*'s Richard Hoffer. "I remember him sweeping through the room afterward, and he sort of nodded to me—I had casually known him when I worked at the *L.A. Times*—nodded and winked . . . I don't remember exactly what he said, but the impression was, *Don't worry, we're going to take care of this.* They were so mistaken. They assumed that everybody wanted this decision reversed and Tyson restored to his glory, as if that could happen just by virtue of being so far away. They felt they could do it, and they thought they were acting in accordance with the world's wishes, I guess. Not until they got back [to the United States] did they realize they were wrong."

Surely neither King nor Sulaiman—nor anyone in Tyson's camp—anticipated the blisteringly negative response to the news that the WBC and WBA had temporarily withheld recognition of the outcome. And yet, they should have known better. To the average sports fan Buster Douglas was *Rocky* made real. His was the everyman story, the heartwarming tale of an underdog who triumphs over monumental adversity and wins the heavyweight championship. One does not tread on such iconic characters casually; indeed, it was an act of immense hubris to even suggest that Douglas was somehow undeserving.

"It was a career performance [for Douglas]," observed Bert Sugar. "No matter what anyone might think—and I know some people will talk about Cinderella Man [James Braddock, the Depression-era boxer who upset Max Baer, like Tyson an imposing brute of a fighter, to win the heavyweight title]—this was boxing's biggest upset. Braddock resonated more because he was a hero for the Depression. People couldn't feed their bellies, so he fed their hopes. Douglas didn't do anything like that for a couple reasons. First, it happened so far away and so late at night. And what Don King tried to do afterward certainly didn't help."

Then again, one could argue that King's antics backfired spectacularly, serving not only to amplify Douglas's accomplishment, but to endear him to millions of people who might otherwise barely have noticed. Thanks in no small part to King's *trickeration,* Douglas's story quickly transcended the world of sport.

"Buster Douglas was a guy who pulled off the unthinkable, who for one night in his life, for whatever reason, galvanized all his forces to be the best he could possibly be," said Larry Merchant. "To realize his fullest potential, he had to endure the death of his mother; he was separated from his wife. And yet he seized an opportunity instead of being intimidated by it and taken down by it. That's a great story in itself—that a guy had that in him. We all want to believe we have that—whether it's a B-level writer who writes the masterpiece, or the painter who paints the masterpiece. For one moment in time, his talent and the opportunity and the inspiration . . . there's a confluence between all of those things that makes for a mighty moment."

No one outside of King's sphere of influence wanted that moment spoiled. As Tom Callahan wrote of King in *Newsweek* after the fight, "He is a self-promoter, a silent manager and a collector of human beings. When his multimillion-dollar meal ticket was beaten bubble-eyed by the 42-to-1 long shot in Tokyo—and then knocked cold as Carbo in the tenth round—King circled frantically with his World Boxing Council and World Boxing Association buddies. Using a long-count controversy, they managed to delay Douglas's recognition for two days until the public shouted them down."

Assisting in the backlash were boxing insiders like promoter Bob Arum, a King rival so appalled by the controversy that he implored the Nevada Boxing Commission to ban the WBC and WBA from conducting business in the state of Nevada—the equivalent of a death sentence, considering Las Vegas was the professional boxing capital of the world.

"It has made boxing ludicrous," Arum said of the delay in recognizing Douglas's victory. "It's absolutely mind-boggling. These organizations are immoral. They will do anything to be expedient for their own interests. They have no kind of standards of right or wrong."

So relentless and one-sided was the beating absorbed in the media by King, Tyson, the WBA, and WBC that within forty-eight hours all previously skeptical parties had reversed their positions. On the morning of February 13, both the WBC and WBA announced that they would recognize James Douglas as the heavyweight champion of their respective organizations. There would be no further review, no mandatory rematch against Tyson.

Jim Binns, the WBA's legal counsel, stated that his organization now considered Douglas to be "an unfettered, unencumbered champion."

Sulaiman concurred, proclaiming not only that Douglas was the new WBC champion, but also offering an apology for any discomfort the delay may have caused: "I am sorry and embarrassed for my timing."

A news conference conducted that afternoon at the Grand Hyatt Hotel in Manhattan featured a humbler Mike Tyson ("I'm not going to make excuses. The new champion won the title.") and an impressively elastic Don King, who in one breath praised Douglas ("The man was magnificent!") and in the next breath reminded him that while a rematch with Tyson was not mandatory, it was, shall we say, practical.

"The name of the game is money," King pronounced. "Buster Douglas is not going to fight anybody else in the world and make as much money as he will fighting Mike Tyson."

That remained to be seen, and for the moment, at least, it was not a matter of paramount importance to Douglas, who returned to a hero's welcome in Columbus and an avalanche of publicity and marketing opportunities that would dominate his life for months to come.

For the embattled referee Octavio Meyran, things did not turn out so well. He said he received the equivalent of $2,800 from the Japanese promoter of the fight—less than half the standard fee of $6,000 typically paid to officials of heavyweight championship events at that time. Meyran returned to Mexico City and his job as a manager in a factory that manufactures blue jeans. Although he continued to officiate smaller, local fights for the next few years, Meyran served as a ring official in only one subsequent championship event: a WBO flyweight bout on November 3, 1990, in Acapulco. He never worked another world championship fight sanctioned by any of boxing's other governing bodies, a result of what transpired in Tokyo and, he believes, a subsequent blacklisting by King and Sulaiman. In 1994, Meyran retired from officiating.

"I lost . . . how you say . . . the gusto," Meyran said. "I prefer to stay out of the sport of boxing."

Although willing to share his side of the story, Meyran was reluctant to be portrayed as a tragic or even sympathetic figure. He had moved on with his life, he said. His time and energies were now devoted largely to his job and his family, which included a wife and a six-year-old daughter (Meyran also has two older daughters from a previous marriage). His father had died in 2002, severing Meyran's last link to the sport of boxing. He no longer had any interest in watching boxing on television; as for the last time he had attended a match in person . . . well, he couldn't recall. It had been many years.

There was, in Meyran's voice, a resignation—if not necessarily a sense of peace—that comes with age. When asked if he harbored any resentment toward King or Sulaiman, he said, "Not anymore. I'm not angry."

In the background, as Meyran talked on the telephone, his wife, Blanca Eugenia, listened to the conversation. It was she who had facilitated this interview, who had helped make Meyran available after years of comfortable obscurity. As her husband talked, she said something aloud.

Meyran paused.

"What was that?" the interviewer asked.

"My wife says that I am sad."

"Is that true?"

He paused again. "Yes . . . I'm sad."

When it was suggested to Meyran that he might still be able to resurrect his officiating career, he demurred. "I'm too old for beginning again."

Too often lost in the controversy over the long count and the officiating of Octavio Meyran is the implausible scoring of the Tyson-Douglas fight by the three ringside judges. Through nine rounds Judge Larry Rozadilla of Los Angeles had Douglas winning the fight by a large margin, 88–82. The two Japanese judges saw the fight differently. Judge Ken Morita had Tyson leading by a score of 87–86, and Masakazu Uchida scored the fight even, 86–86.

What this means, of course, is that if the bout had ended in a judges' decision, it might well have been ruled a draw, and Tyson, despite clearly losing the fight in every sense of the word, would have retained his title.

As Meyran observed of the scoring in an e-mail message a few days after he was interviewed, "Is not a very strange thing?"

We were like a close-knit family going into the Tyson fight. After-ward . . . it was like everyone wanted the limelight. It fell apart so quickly.

—James Douglas

When James Douglas left Columbus for Tokyo in late January, he did so under a cloak of anonymity. He returned a conquering hero—*undisputed heavyweight champion of the world*—and with that designation came the unmistakable realization that everything had changed. There are no guidelines for this sort of transformation, no handbook for adapting to sudden celebrity. One simply climbs aboard the roller coaster and hangs on for dear life. Douglas, a laid-back fellow who was almost devoid of pretense, seemed at least on the surface better suited than most to avoid the trappings and pitfalls of wealth and fame. He'd led a simple life in the past and wasn't averse to living simply in the future. A more comfortable life would be fine, but he saw no pressing need for a fleet of new cars or a private jet or, for that matter, any of the gaudy accoutrements traditionally bestowed upon the heavyweight champ.

It is a dizzying ride, however, and almost anyone can be thrown off balance, as Douglas discovered shortly after his plane touched down on U.S. soil. On his first morning back in Columbus, Douglas rose early and visited the modest brick bungalow in suburban Westerville owned by John Johnson and his wife, Susan. Jet-lagged and groggy, Douglas took a seat in a living room jammed with television equipment and technicians and began conducting interviews: *Good Morning America* at 7:10; the *Today* show at 7:30. Then came the local network affiliates and a slew of requests from print media. Everyone wanted a piece of Buster, including Don King, who called that very morning, only to be rebuffed, at least temporarily, by Johnson, who wasn't above exercising a little managerial muscle in the wake of his boxer's triumph. King, after all, had made them squirm for the better part of a year, first compelling Douglas to sign an onerous promotional contract; then there was the stunt in Tokyo, the protest that King would later casually dismiss as an innocuous publicity gimmick intended to drum up interest in a Tyson-Douglas rematch.

Johnson understood, and on some level probably even appreciated, King's role as the ringmaster of professional boxing; at the same time, he wanted to make sure that King realized there had been a seismic shift in the heavyweight division and that if King wanted to play a significant role in the new world order, he would have to cooperate with Douglas and his manager. There would be no more bullying. Granted, King had a promotional contract with Douglas, but as the following weeks and months would demonstrate, contracts in boxing are not exactly viewed as unbreakable.

On February 14 (Woody Hayes's birthday, as Johnson pointed out), the manager and his fighter traveled to New York at the behest of HBO, which had invited both fighters to its studio to tape interviews that would supplement the network's rebroadcast of the championship fight. The original broadcast had been viewed in approximately 6.6 million homes and earned a rating of 31.1 (meaning that percentage of HBO subscribers had witnessed at least a portion of the broadcast), making it the third-highest-rated fight in HBO history, a distinction it holds to this day. Numbers one and two were also Tyson fights: against Frank Bruno and Larry Holmes. There was, however, a perception (and this extended into the corporate offices of HBO) that a large percentage of the potential audience for Tyson-Douglas had either missed the fight entirely or, at the very least, tuned in late.

"Every Tyson fight was registering those kinds of numbers," explained Ross Greenburg. "But I think what happened in this case was—and I started hearing stories when I got back to New York—that people who were watching the fight were actually calling friends frantically after the first round and saying, 'Are you watching this?' And then there were more calls after each round. Now, of course, we measure those quarterly breaks. Every fifteen minutes you can see whether there is an increase in the ratings. We didn't have that back then. But I'm sure the rating increased every quarter hour of that fight; there is no doubt in my mind."

With the goal of securing new subscribers and setting records for cable programming, HBO aggressively promoted its rebroadcast, which would include observations by Tyson and Douglas and detailed analysis of the more controversial aspects of the fight. The package, network executives hoped, would lure viewers to HBO in even greater numbers than those that had been achieved by the initial telecast. (In actuality, it fell far short of that goal.)

First, however, there was business to conduct. On the night he arrived in New York, Johnson met with Top Rank promoter Bob Arum, whose sales pitch included a $30 million offer for a fight against Evander Holyfield, and $50 million for a rematch with Tyson. Then came a ninety-minute meeting with King at Johnson's suite at the Parker Meridien Hotel. Considering their recent history, and Johnson's open contempt for the promoter, the meeting went reasonably well, although King's offer of $10 million to $11 million for a Tyson–Douglas rematch sounded, to Johnson's ears, almost comically cheap. Business is business, though, and Johnson, good-ol'-boy rhetoric notwithstanding, knew how to play the game. Personal animosity aside, if King could put together a strong package for Douglas's first title defense, then Johnson was obligated to consider the offer, not only to serve the interests of his fighter, but to avoid the painful (and expensive) litigation that would almost certainly accompany any attempt to jettison King.

Whatever goodwill King might have engendered during his meeting with Johnson evaporated the following day when members of the Tyson and Douglas camps converged upon the HBO offices in Manhattan. Douglas arrived at the appointed time; King and Tyson showed up an hour late, a regrettable but probably benign offense (the pair had first gone to the wrong HBO building and then were delayed by fans who had gathered for the boxers' appearance). Douglas and

Johnson nevertheless interpreted it as an example of Tyson's inherent lack of respect for the new champion.

The taping itself did not help matters any. Douglas wore a suit and showed no obvious signs of physical distress from the fight. Tyson wore jeans and a long-sleeved T-shirt; dark glasses hid the bruises and swelling that still marked his face. The two boxers did not even acknowledge each other until Larry Merchant, acting as moderator and studio host, urged them to shake hands, which they did, rather perfunctorily. Anyone who knows Douglas can attest to his dry wit and deadpan sense of humor, qualities that can make him an enormously interesting interview. But on this occasion it quickly became apparent that Tyson would be the focus of attention; not that this represented much of a surprise. Fans of boxing might have been curious about Buster Douglas, but it was not unreasonable to assume that they were even more puzzled by the unraveling of Tyson, and so that was the interrogatory path chosen by Merchant. The first three questions were directed at the ex-champ, prompting Ross Greenburg to interrupt and urge Merchant to "mix it up." Douglas later complained that he felt almost as though "I might as well not have been there."

What most irked Johnson was King's apparent disdain for the new champion. When Johnson got word that the promoter was watching the taping from within the HBO control room, and mocking Douglas's performance, Johnson went ballistic, storming into the room and shouting at King, "Are you laughing at James Douglas? If you are, you're finished."

King is not a man easily threatened, and this challenge, like most, rolled off his back. The promoter's arrogance was hardly shocking: As Tyson's promoter and "advisor" he still owned a huge chunk of professional boxing's most marketable commodity; he also had a promotional contract with the new champion. How could he go wrong?

Johnson wasn't about to be pushed around, though, and just as King would brazenly continue to operate under the assumption that he would be included in any fight involving either Douglas or Tyson, Johnson would proceed as though Douglas's agreement with King was not worth the paper it was printed on.

To a degree, both men were right. And wrong.

"We never really got a chance to enjoy beating Mike Tyson," Johnson said. "As soon as it was over, we were basically involved in a lawsuit with King."

Had Johnson and King been able to reach an agreement that satisfied both camps (in other words, if King had been the highest bidder), things might have turned out differently. But King had a contact and thus felt no obligation to push the numbers upward. So Johnson continued to entertain other suitors.

On Friday, February 16, Douglas returned to Columbus. The following morning, despite bitter cold and nasty, wind-driven snow squalls, some 25,000 people turned out for a parade and celebration in honor of the new champ, who also took the time to attend a less formal, but no less adulatory, function, at the Windsor Terrace Recreation Center in his old North Side neighborhood. In an area beset by crime and poverty Douglas emerged from a stretch limo and began shaking as many hands as he could, smiling widely at a crowd of 1,500 people, many of them waving bouquets of roses and carnations. The boxer whose presence had barely caused a ripple of excitement when he walked through Columbus Airport on his way out of town listened as Mayor Dana Rinehart said to the assemblage, "The other day CBS asked me what Buster Douglas meant to Columbus. I said, 'That's easy. He's our hero. He loves Columbus and we're proud of him.'"

The world, it seemed to Douglas, had been turned upside down. Why, the last time he'd attended a homecoming parade in Columbus, in the summer of 1984, the honoree had been native son Jerry Page, who recently had won a gold medal in boxing at the Summer Olympics in Los Angeles. Acting less out of community service than self-interest, Douglas had stood on the corner of Broad and High Streets that day, distributing fliers promoting his upcoming fight against Dave Jaco at the Sheraton Center Ballroom. Tickets were a bargain—just ten dollars. Apparently, though, even that was too steep a figure for a James Douglas headliner. The card was eventually canceled and the fight later moved to Las Vegas, where Douglas won by a unanimous decision.

How strange and wonderful it was that some of the same people who once balked at paying ten bucks for a Douglas fight were now standing outside, clutching flowers on a frigid Midwestern winter morning, hoping for just a glimpse of the heavyweight champ.

"No one could have expected it," Douglas would say many years later, when reflecting on that day in Columbus. "But they put something together so quickly."

In some ways the parade in Columbus was merely the beginning of an extended victory lap by Douglas, one that took him all over the country, to an assortment of functions that would test not only his endurance but also his commitment to boxing. Over the next two weeks Douglas would spend time in the following cities, among others: Los Angeles, for a chat with Johnny Carson on *The Tonight Show* and a series of meetings with film producers (including Clint Eastwood) interested in optioning his life story; Detroit, where he served as a celebrity referee in a professional wrestling match between two of the business's biggest stars, Hulk Hogan and Randy "Macho Man" Savage; Kansas City, Missouri, home of promoter Payton Sher, a friend of Johnson's who had supported Douglas early in his career (the mayors of both KCs—Missouri and Kansas—showed up that day); Los Angeles (again), for an appearance at the Easter Seals Telethon; and, of course, Las Vegas, the likely host of his initial title defense.

Douglas and Johnson first visited Vegas on February 18, flying from Columbus on a private jet owned by Steve Wynn, owner of the Mirage Hotel and Casino, following an earlier meeting in Columbus with Bob Halloran, who arranged fights for the Mirage. They returned on March 2 for another round of meetings. In this same time frame Douglas met with Bill Cosby about potential business opportunities; filmed a commercial for his new 900 phone number (where, for two dollars a pop, fans could listen to the new champ discuss his victory over Tyson); and, at the opposite end of the PR spectrum, visited tiny Duluth, Minnesota, a city that had shown Douglas uncommon kindness and courtesy when he last visited, in 1988, as a struggling heavyweight who earned a paltry $2,500 for a fight against Percell Davis.

Although the pace would naturally slow as the months wore on, a pattern of self-promotion (with its implied determination to cash in as quickly and heavily as possible) had been established, a fact that concerned John Russell, even as he watched from his home in Akron.

"After the Tyson fight Johnson took Buster all over the country, almost like taking a show horse barnstorming," Russell said. "He's taking him to Carson; he's taking him here, there, everywhere. Why? Because Johnson wanted to do it more than James.

"Steve Wynn was sending his private jet to Columbus every three weeks and flying them all out to Vegas, partying at the hotel. And here's a guy who needed to be in the gym. I told Johnson, 'He don't need to be going to Vegas, he needs to be training.' Johnson said, 'Ah, he'll be fine. We've got plenty of time.' He wanted to party more than James did. I remember one time when I went with them [to Vegas]—and I only went once—we were at the Mirage, and I remember going down to Buster's room. Him and his buddies were in there, and I was going down the hallway and I heard Buster screaming. I listened at the door, and he was screaming, 'These guys are hauling me all over the country. I want to be home. I want to be with my family.' So I went into the room and said, 'Shit, James, then let's go home.' He said, 'Fucking Johnson, man.' . . . I tried to tell him he was the boss. If he wants to go home, then go home. But you see . . . that's Buster. He doesn't like to cause trouble. You can only put the blame where he lies, but that's the way he is."

Even as Douglas found an important measure of peace in his personal life, in the form of a reconciliation with Bertha (the couple's first child would be born the following winter), his professional life became increasingly tumultuous. Whereas Team Douglas once had been the boxing equivalent of a mom-and-pop store operating on a shoestring budget, it now bore the privilege and responsibility of a major corporation. Money indeed changes everything, and suddenly Douglas found himself at the center of a battle over control of his own future, both in and out of the ring. Factions were formed in this struggle. In one camp were Johnson and McCauley. In another camp were Rodney Rogers and Larry Nallie, a pair of Douglas's old high school buddies who had begun to take an active role in his business and managerial activities (Nallie's title was "financial advisor"; Rogers's was "camp coordinator"). In a third and more neutral camp was the trainer, John Russell. Interestingly enough, Russell would be the only person from any of the groups to build a friendship with Douglas that endures to this day.

"John Russell is a good person," said Bertha Douglas by way of explanation. "He and James are buddies. John cares about what happens to James. Those are the people you want to keep around you, because once you get to a certain level, you've got a lot of sick people around you, people who don't care about you, and who suck the life out of you."

James Douglas would later refer to Nallie as a "joke," but as the conflict over control of James Buster Douglas, Inc., escalated in the spring and summer of 1990, it was Johnson who emerged the loser.

"James basically said to me, 'Hey, man, you did a great job, but from now on I'm going to make my own decisions,'" Johnson said. "As it turned out, he leaned much more toward listening to Larry Nallie than he did to me. And a major conflict took place because some of the decisions that were made, I disagreed with tremendously."

Among these was the dismissal of Johnson's son, John Johnson Jr., from his position as the team's public relations coordinator. The stated reason for the firing: insubordination. Johnson Jr., a former sportswriter who had left his job to work for Douglas, and who would later obtain a law degree from Ohio State University, seemed to bear no ill will toward Douglas when he discussed the situation with the *Philadelphia Daily News* in 1993. Indeed, the son sounded impressively diplomatic.

"He's my father and I want to protect him," Johnson Jr. said of John Johnson Sr. "But there were places where he made errors in judgment. He definitely tried to achieve his own little agenda: 'I've got the heavyweight champion, so now people will listen to me. I have a platform to speak to people and I can take Buster here and say this and do that.' Buster didn't like that, and I don't blame him."

Eventually the discord led to Douglas taking greater control of his own affairs—acting as chief executive officer of James Buster Douglas, Inc., in a manner of speaking—and Johnson accepting a reduced and quieter role.

"Tyson opened the door to the megamillions," Bertha Douglas

said. "And when that happens, the fools really go crazy. Here you have a manager who is so fixated on that bone they're dangling that he'll accept and do anything. . . . That's not the kind of person you want representing you."

She paused momentarily, then offered a less rancorous assessment of the former manager. "John Johnson did his job. He took James as far as he could take him. But there comes a point in life where you come to a crossroads, and you either carry the baggage you have, or you let it go. James decided to let it go."

Johnson continued to serve as Douglas's manager (contractually, he was entitled to 23 percent of the fighter's share of the gross purse), but by the summer of 1990 he had clearly become a less prominent and influential member of the boxer's team, something that causes Johnson both comfort and sadness when one mentions the rather sudden downfall of Buster Douglas. Comfort in the sense that by the time Douglas walked into the ring to defend his title for the first (and last) time, Johnson had been exiled, and thus could bear little or no responsibility for what would befall the champion. But that was not, he would say, the overriding emotion.

"I was there, but I had no say in anything," Johnson claimed. "I was heartbroken. It was one of the most depressing times of my life. When I think about it even now, it hurts. I mean, at one time, James and I were unbelievably close. John [Russell] and I were pretty close for a while, too, for a few months after the [Tyson] fight. Then all of a sudden the power shifted, and I was . . . well, I don't know what you'd say I was. An asshole or something, I guess."

That is, in fact, one of the words boxing insiders employed in their descriptions of Johnson during the time that he managed Douglas. As Johnson battled with Don King, rival promoter Dan Duva, concerned that his heavyweight, Evander Holyfield, would miss out on a title shot, criticized Johnson for mishandling the dispute. Bob Arum labeled Johnson a "hick." John Russell said Johnson's fiery temper (manifested in sometimes profane exchanges with the press and confrontations with members of the boxing establishment), combined with a propensity for partying, proved ultimately to be an embarrassment.

"There were times I thought, *We've got the heavyweight champion of the world and we've got this hillbilly running around with us?"* Russell said. "I mean, it was a joke."

Douglas is less bilious in his assessment of Johnson, although his recollection is essentially the same.

"John did what he did," Douglas said. "But to me, he was just out there, caught up in the moment, I guess. And it was an unbelievable thing. People would tell me later—influential people in the boxing world—they would tell me, shaking their heads, 'My God, John Johnson has the heavyweight champion.'"

Time has at once intensified and blurred the differences between the warring factions, to the point where it's difficult now to ascertain whether the split was attributable primarily to personal or professional differences, or some combination of the two. This much is certain: The bickering and posturing disturbed Douglas to the point of distraction, at a time when distraction was the last thing he needed.

In early June of 1990, Douglas agreed in principle to defend his title against Holyfield, a former cruiserweight champion who had trained madly in an attempt to metamorphose into a heavyweight, thereby gaining access to boxing's most lucrative and glamorous division. The fight would be held at the Mirage, which had earned the right to stage the event with a purse bid of $32 million. Of that figure, $24 million would go to Douglas (at the time, this represented the single biggest payday in the history of boxing; it also ensured that, for one year, anyway, Douglas would be the highest-paid athlete in the world); Holyfield, the challenger, would receive $8 million.

Later that month Douglas opened training camp for defense of his title, only to shut it down a few days later under the pressure of a series of escalating legal battles. Douglas had thrown the first punch in this fight back in February, when he signed a conditional two-fight contract with the Mirage. In March came round two, when Douglas (along with coplaintiffs Johnson and the Mirage) sued to break King's promotional hold on Douglas. The plaintiffs' claim: that the contract was illegal in the state of Nevada, and that, regardless, King had breached the contract through his actions in Tokyo and afterward. Not surprisingly, King countersued in New York for breach of contract. A third lawsuit was filed by Donald Trump, charging Douglas, Johnson, and the Mirage with interfering with a contract between Trump and King to stage a Douglas-Tyson fight in Atlantic City in June.

Negotiations between King and the Douglas camp had ended rancorously following a late February meeting in Las Vegas, during which the outraged promoter had referred to John Johnson as a "stupid motherfucker" and vowed to "kick [your] ass." King later fell back on the divide-and-conquer tactics that had proved so beneficial throughout his career: He moved into a Columbus hotel and shamelessly played the race card to promote chaos in the Douglas camp, enlisting the help of NAACP director Benjamin Hooks and befriending Douglas's father, Bill Douglas (who needed no great encouragement to express disdain for Johnson), in an effort to engender support for his argument, namely, that Douglas had made a grave mistake in putting his trust in a white manager.

"That wasn't a good time at all," Douglas recalled. "It was like dealing with a bunch of sissies. First they bully you, then they become whiners, criers, complainers. King and the whole gang. They refused to let it go. They harassed me and continued to harass me. I was harassed every day I was heavyweight champion of the world. By the time the Holyfield fight came around, it was total chaos in our camp."

From late February through the middle of July, Douglas spent more time in courtrooms and law offices than he did in the gym.

"I was constantly flying to New York, flying to Los Angeles, giving depositions all the time," Douglas said. "I remember going on a talk show, and here I am, walking to the studio, and somebody comes up to me and says, 'Hey, how are you doing?' and he hands me a piece of paper. I'm thinking he wants my autograph or something, until I look down . . . and it's a damn subpoena! I was getting hit with stuff like that every day."

At the time, the Douglas camp, Johnson in particular, presented an image of sturdy resolve in regard to the litigation. ("We're fighters . . . James didn't back down from Mike Tyson and he won't back down from Don King and Donald Trump.") Johnson also believed, or said he believed, that "all this legal stuff may be helping the world rally behind us. I know there are a lot of people who are going to want to see this next fight."

There may have been some truth in that observation, but unstated was the effect the turmoil was having on the person who mattered most: Douglas. In early July, with the parties unable to reach a settlement, King's multimillion-dollar lawsuit against Douglas went to trial in United States District Court in Manhattan, with Judge Robert Sweet presiding. Over the course of two weeks jurors, along with the public, were treated to testimony that was alternately enlightening and farcical. Among the unlikely witnesses scheduled to testify on behalf of the plaintiff were Douglas's father, Bill Douglas, and Bob Arum, who had long been one of King's most vocal critics.

A Harvard Law School graduate and former federal prosecutor, Arum was, superficially at least, the polar opposite of King. Each, however, was a shrewd and ferocious businessman who had thrived in the cutthroat world of professional boxing. That Arum was now aligned with King was less the result of some revelatory truce between the warring promoters than a cold and simple act of retribution on the part of Arum, who felt betrayed by Steve Wynn. In his biography of King, *Only in America,* Jack Newfield explains that Arum had helped Wynn devise a strategy for wresting promotional rights to Douglas from King by filing a lawsuit in the state of Nevada (where both Wynn and Arum held considerable sway). Arum wanted to be included in the proceedings and was hugely offended to discover that Wynn had neglected to name him as a coplaintiff.

"Steve Wynn stabbed me in the back and now I am about to get even," Arum told Newfield before offering testimony in the trial. "He double-crossed me and made his own deal with Douglas. He froze me out. Everything I ever said to you about King is still true, but I'm going to go in there, swear to tell the truth, and kick the shit out of Wynn and help Don win this case. Wynn is a greedy, stupid fuck. He and I could have shared control of Douglas, and of the heavyweight championship, and King would have been out in the cold. But Wynn got greedy. He wanted to hog it all for himself. He filed the Vegas suit too late, and without my name on it. That's why King's case went first in New York. I was forum-shopping, handing Wynn the home-court advantage before a state judge in Las Vegas. He blew it because he is a dumb schmuck. And that's why I am here today, as King's witness."

Arum's testimony was offered in support of the notion that King's actions in the wake of the Tyson-Douglas fight represented little more than an attempt to fuel interest in a rematch.

"That's how we fight our battles in boxing—through hyperbole," Arum said. "Hyperbole is not lying. Hyperbole is exaggerating. In the heat of battle we all say crazy things that we are not accountable for."

As King has demonstrated countless times through the years, battles in boxing are also fought in the courtroom, and few men have survived as many attacks. On July 17, as the trial seemed destined for a third full week of testimony and subsequent jury deliberations, an agreement was reached, sparing Douglas the pain of watching his father testify on behalf of King and freeing the champion to defend his title against Holyfield on October 25 in Las Vegas. But the victory, such as it was, came at a significant cost: King would receive $4.5 million from Wynn and the Mirage. (Donald Trump settled for $2.5 million in exchange for turning over his promotional rights.) In other words, King would be paid $4.5 million to do *absolutely nothing!* All he had to do was walk away. Not only that, King would retain promotional rights to a Tyson-Douglas rematch (presuming Douglas successfully defended his title against Holyfield).

Small wonder that afterward, outside the courtroom, King told reporters, "Due process is a wonderful thing. I'm glad to be an American."

In reflecting on the settlement, fifteen years down the road, Douglas could only offer King grudging respect. "He's a hell of a businessman, I guess."

The conventional wisdom was this: Evander Holyfield, not unlike Michael Spinks, was a natural light heavyweight or cruiserweight who had gone to enormous lengths to thicken his comparatively slender frame in what would ultimately prove to be a misguided attempt to compete at the heavyweight level. Skeptics and boxing purists viewed Holyfield as an experiment in physiological tinkering and pointed to his spindly legs as evidence that he was merely masquerading as a heavyweight.

Holyfield's supporters, and they were not small in number, countered with an impressive list of reasons for believing that Holyfield would live up to his nickname: "the Real Deal."

In winning all twenty-four of his professional fights (including twenty by knockout), the reasoning went, Holyfield had repeatedly demonstrated the skills of a boxer and the punching power of a heavyweight. Far from being a bloated cruiserweight (and, thus, a "soft" heavyweight), Holyfield had achieved legitimate heavyweight status through a revolutionary (at the time, anyway) regimen of diet and fitness, as evidenced by his chiseled physique. In addition to employing three old-school boxing traditionalists in his corner, trainers George Benton, Ronnie Shields, and Lou Duva, Holyfield had transformed himself with the aid and expertise of a diverse group of trainers that included Houston-based fitness specialist Tim Hallmark, ballet instructor Marya Kennett, and bodybuilder Lee Haney, a former Mr. Olympia. Together they had sculpted Holyfield's body and provided him with a combination of strength, flexibility, and cardiovascular conditioning unprecedented among heavyweight boxers.

As for the skinny legs? Well, thoroughbred racehorses accomplished miracles while running on veritable twigs. So it would be with Holyfield, a thoughtful man who possessed the heart and desire of a champion and, now, the machinery to fulfill his dreams.

The plan was for Holyfield to use his fitness as a weapon. Just as Douglas would rely on his jab, Holyfield would utilize superior conditioning to offset the champion's advantage in size and reach. At 6 feet 2½ inches tall and weighing 208 pounds, Holyfield was significantly smaller than Douglas. In studying video footage of Douglas, though, Holyfield's handlers had determined that the champion was most effective when facing a docile or confused opponent, as Tyson had been back in February. Holyfield would be neither; instead, from the opening bell, he would try to overwhelm Douglas with a flurry of carefully choreographed activity. "Busy" was his buzzword.

"I want that left hand of yours growing out of [Douglas's] face," Benton told Holyfield.

Twelve days before the fight, while training in Reno, Nevada, Holyfield endured a particularly demanding session involving twelve rounds of sparring against three different opponents. Astonishingly, Holyfield seemed to get stronger as the session went on. He averaged sixty punches per round for the first eleven rounds, then threw seventy punches in the twelfth, culminating with a heavy left hook that knocked out his sparring partner, Phil Brown.

It was a performance that left Holyfield's camp breathless with anticipation. Lou Duva had said that the game plan for beating Douglas involved a combination of power and stamina. On paper, they divided the fight into three segments: four rounds of jabbing followed by four rounds of brawling.

"And Part Three?" Duva was asked by a reporter.

The trainer scoffed. "There ain't gonna be no need for Part Three."

A prescient observation, although a bit of an understatement. As it turned out, there would be no need for part two, either.

While Holyfield pursued the heavyweight title with an almost religious fervor (much as Douglas had done in the months prior to meeting Tyson), the champion aggressively pursued an agenda of inactivity. Either unable or unwilling to set aside the legal and personal conflicts that devoured so much of his time and energy, Douglas gained weight and lost confidence in roughly equivalent measures. By the time he officially opened training camp in Las Vegas, in late August, Douglas was in dreadful shape. He had no interest in fighting; nor did he have the physical capacity to fight. And yet, there was so much money at stake, so much riding on this one performance. If only he could get through it, hang on for one more night. Published reports at the time speculated that Douglas allowed his weight to reach 260 pounds in the months after the Tyson fight. Maybe 270. According to Douglas, those were conservative estimates.

"When I got on the scale at the start of camp, I weighed 300 pounds," he recalled. Douglas shook his head, clearly uncomfortable with the memory. "John [Russell] was, like, 'Oh, shit!' "

Douglas's fitness became a primary concern for the duration of camp. There were stories of aborted sparring sessions, of training runs skipped or cut short or completed on the back of a golf cart. One of the enduring tales associated with Douglas's fall from grace involves Steve Wynn, who tried to protect his investment by offering

Douglas a penthouse suite and private use of a hotel sauna. Imagine Wynn's distress when he learned that Douglas had placed a $98 room-service order—from the sauna.

With Johnson nudged to the sideline, Bill Douglas returned to his son's corner to assist with training, a change that, while offering some reassurance and emotional support for James, also led to an escalation of tensions in the Douglas camp. It was almost as if the Tyson fight had never occurred. Suddenly it was 1987 all over again, with all that bad blood in the air, his father jousting with McCauley and Johnson, poisoning the gym with bitterness and rancor.

"Buster wasn't able to focus," recalled Russell. "Johnson and J. D. would stay on one side of the gym, and then it would be me and Billy and James on the other. There was a lot of animosity there. I tried to stay neutral and do my job, but there was a lot of turmoil, and James hates turmoil. I could see in training that he had basically given up."

As fight night drew near and Douglas continued to slog halfheart-edly through workouts, it became apparent to Russell that a disaster was imminent and unavoidable. Two weeks before the bout he ap-proached Douglas and proposed the unthinkable.

"Let's cancel the fight."

Douglas thanked the trainer for his concern, but said such drastic measures would not be necessary. He'd be fine. And anyway, there was just too much money on the table, too many people counting on him. He couldn't back out. Not now.

"I was very concerned because our training wasn't going the way I knew it needed to go," Russell explained. "For my own conscience, I had to say how I felt. So I got it off my chest and then we went forward."

Looking back on it now, Douglas realizes he made a mistake. He should have listened to the trainer.

"I wish somebody would have [postponed the fight]," he said wistfully. "We were done."

Not that anyone in the Douglas camp publicly expressed their anxiety. It is an unwritten rule in sports (dangerous sports, in partic-ular) that one display only confidence and self-assuredness in advance of the contest. So it was that the acrimony within the champion's business and managerial team was rationalized as a natural part of the growing process. Rumors of Douglas's indifferent attitude toward training were dismissed as . . . well . . . just that: rumors, devoid of merit or even serious consideration. At a press conference in early August Douglas had uncharacteristically insulted his opponent, asserting that Holyfield's résumé had been padded with "cupcakes" and promising that when they met in the ring, the challenger "will go down." That sort of rhetoric continued throughout training camp, a drumbeat of insistence in the face of accumulating evidence that the champion was in serious trouble.

Every championship fight needs a good moniker, a catchy marketing phrase that neatly and succinctly captures the mood of the event. Holyfield–Douglas was billed, rather prosaically, as "The Moment of Truth." In reality, that moment occurred not on October 25, but one day earlier, at a ballroom in the Mirage Hotel and Casino, when the two fighters were officially weighed in. The weigh-in is a grand boxing tradition that serves a dual purpose: to ensure that each fighter's weight falls within the stated parameters of the contract, and to hype the fight by giving the media and the public a glimpse of the combatants in the semibuff.

Appearances can be deceiving, especially in the heavyweight division, where it isn't uncommon for fleshy fighters (consider Larry Holmes and the reincarnated version of George Foreman) to throttle opponents who possess superficially impressive physical attributes but little in the way of heart or skill. A weak chin is a weak chin, and no amount of vasculature is going to change that.

And yet . . .

How could one not be impressed by the appearance of Holyfield as he stood on the scale, tightening his biceps and smiling proudly as his weight—208 pounds—was announced? Whatever else you might have said about him, Holyfield was clearly a man who had trained seriously and diligently for this fight.

The same could not be said of the champion. When Douglas slipped off his shorts and stepped onto the scale, wearing only gray briefs, a murmur filled the room. Although it would be unfair to suggest that Douglas appeared grossly overweight, it was obvious that he had trained with something less than the dedication that had fueled his preparation for Tyson. His midsection was round, his chest and upper arms soft. In fairness, it should be pointed out that Douglas had never been mistaken for a bodybuilder, but there was something in his appearance—a complete lack of definition—that belied the confidence voiced by his camp. When Douglas's weight was announced, audible gasps went up from the crowd.

"Two hundred forty-six pounds."

That was the instant that many boxing observers were compelled to reevaluate their analysis of the impending title fight.

"You know, fighters are all crazy," said Jim Lampley. "Otherwise, they wouldn't be fighters. And there are many fighters who can achieve a moment of success and then cannot handle it afterward, or resist being able to handle it afterward. Watching Buster destroy Tyson, looking at who Holyfield was, I foolishly told all my friends and coworkers, 'This is an easy fight for Douglas. This is an easier fight than the Tyson fight. Evander is smaller, he's a total trader—he's willing to engage. He's going to go in and stand toe-to-toe with a guy who is bigger, has a better jab, and a far bigger right hand.' That's an easy fight to call if Buster Douglas shows up—or so it seemed to me. Then the Buster Douglas who shows up is an entirely different person than the guy who had his moment in Tokyo."

Two hundred forty-six.

So startling was the number that members of the Douglas camp initially asked that their fighter be reweighed. Then they reconsidered, perhaps realizing that confirmation would only have served to magnify their plight. Better to take the high road, whereby one expresses not shock or dismay, but cool confidence. Accentuate the positive—a whopping thirty-eight-pound advantage over Holyfield; eliminate the negative—a fourteen-and-a-half-pound increase from the Tyson fight, during which Douglas had been fitter and quicker than at any point in his career.

"It don't make no difference," John Johnson calmly stated. "We know he's been working hard and is in shape."

Added J. D. McCauley, "I've been with him every morning when he does his five-mile run and rides the Lifecycle. I guarantee you, Buster Douglas is ready to fight."

To this day McCauley insists he wasn't merely spinning the story in his favor. The trainer noted that Douglas was hardly a naturally svelte man, and had routinely entered the ring weighing in excess of 240 pounds. (This is true. On six occasions prior to 1990, Douglas weighed *more* than he weighed for the Holyfield fight.) The Tyson fight, McCauley said, was an aberration. Of course, one could reasonably argue that it was precisely because of this aberration that Douglas pulled off the upset of the century. Regardless, McCauley believes that, despite his appearance, Douglas should have retained the title.

"He fought at that weight his whole life," said McCauley. "If Buster did what he was supposed to do, what he could have done, Holyfield couldn't touch my nephew. But Buster didn't fight him. That's my opinion. Buster didn't fight. It wasn't the same person [who beat Tyson]. Not even close."

The challenger's camp could barely contain its glee at the weigh-in. Gone was the earnest modesty that had long been a hallmark of Holyfield's, replaced by outright braggadocio on the part of his handlers.

"We're home free," said Lou Duva, adding, of Douglas, "Roll him in and carry him out. How can any heavyweight champion fight at two hundred forty-six?"

The next night, as he walked to the ring in front of a crowd of 16,000 people, with Douglas right behind him, the fighter's gloves resting on the trainer's shoulders, John Russell felt a crushing sense of helplessness. Less than an hour before the fight, in a display of almost incalculable ambivalence, Buster had fallen sound asleep on a table in his dressing room. There is only so much you can fake, Russell thought. Preparation breeds confidence, and the trainer knew that Douglas was thoroughly unprepared—emotionally and physically—as he climbed through the ropes to meet the challenger.

"I don't know how in the hell James went up the steps that night, to be honest with you," Russell said. "And Holyfield looked great. He was hungry, fit. They played us like a fiddle."

By the time the fight went off, Douglas's detractors outnumbered his supporters by a sizable percentage. Even the betting public had lost faith, installing Holyfield, in his first heavyweight championship fight, as an 8 to 5 favorite. The designation, as it turned out, was deserved. Holyfield owned the fight from the start, following his game plan to perfection and swarming all over the bewildered and plodding champion. In the first two rounds Holyfield was every bit as busy as Douglas had been against Tyson, and even more accurate, landing an astonishing 66 of 100 punches. Douglas, conversely, spent the first six minutes on his heels, gasping for breath, alternately backpedaling and covering up. He threw 69 punches, a respectable figure, although only 20 found their mark, and not one inflicted the slightest bit of damage.

On several occasions Douglas tried to use a right uppercut—the punch that had nearly dislodged Tyson's head in Tokyo—in an attempt to slow Holyfield's attack. Each time the challenger either slipped the punch or easily absorbed the blow. Holyfield had been trained to look for Douglas's uppercut, and to use it to his advantage. There were times, Holyfield knew, when the champion relied too heavily on his favorite punch, to the extent that he would throw an uppercut even when out of position. When Douglas mistakenly tried to throw another uppercut less than one minute into the third round—despite the fact that too much space separated him from his target—Holyfield responded artfully. The challenger stepped to the side and watched as Douglas's right hand whistled past his head. The momentum carried Douglas forward, face-first, and into a brutal right cross by Holyfield.

What happened next would haunt Douglas for years to come. On the way to the canvas he reached out with his left hand and pawed at Holyfield, as if looking for support. The two fighters cracked heads as Douglas fell; the champion landed first on his left side and then, after wiping his right glove across his brow and briefly examining it, rolled onto his back. As referee Mills Lane shooed Holyfield to a neutral corner and began his count, Douglas lay motionless, save for the rhythmic heaving of his chest. Then the oddest thing happened. Douglas drew his left glove across his face and glanced at it, as if searching, maybe even hoping, for signs of damage—a trickle of blood from the nose, perhaps—or maybe he was wiping sweat from his eyes. Then he did it again. Three times Douglas brushed his face. Not once did he make an attempt to stand. The man who had so impressively—*so courageously*—risen from the canvas after getting knocked down by the most fearsome heavyweight in history could summon neither the energy nor the will to fight.

And so, it was suggested afterward, Buster quit.

"That's a question only he can answer," said John Russell. "In my heart, I don't think James would lay down for anybody. I think he got cracked and he knew he was in trouble, and . . . I don't know if he could have gotten up or not. I do know he got hit."

No one disputes that Douglas took a shot. Open to debate, and ultimately answerable only by one person, is whether he could have gotten up off the canvas before the count of ten and continued fighting.

"I don't know if he could have got up, but he sure never tried," said referee Lane. "I looked into his eyes, and his eyes looked good to me."

Well after Lane had completed his count, even as Holyfield's corner erupted in wild celebration, Douglas remained supine, blinking at the lights above, listening to the roar of the crowd—a deafening storm of applause and howls and catcalls. For more than two minutes the fallen champion remained on his back with the ringside physician hovering nearby, time enough to clear his head, and to think about where he had been, and where he would go from here. And yet, the only thought he could muster, the one that kept coming back to him, over and over, was this: *I'm so tired*.

On March 25 boxing will be lifted from the pages of Ring *maga-zine and into those of* Newsweek *and* People—*and the* National Enquirer. *It will be removed from the sports anthology shows to* Dateline *and* 20/20—*and* Inside Edition. *It will emerge from the casinos of Atlantic City and Las Vegas, where for three years it has merely survived, and assume a prominent place at bar stools, on street corners, maybe even in sewing circles. The awakening will happen around the world. Boxing comes back on March 25. . . . Because the day [Mike] Tyson walks into his freedom, boxing once more be-comes the kind of personality-driven riot that galvanizes globally. With his return it is newly dangerous and unpredictable, freshly sen-sationalized with theatrical themes. There will be, finally, something for everyone—from boxing fan to tabloid consumer—in a sport that has hardly had anything for anybody.*
　　　　　　　　　　　　　—Richard Hoffer,
　　　　　　　　　　　　　Sports Illustrated, March 27, 1995

Since Tyson lost to Douglas, nobody has cared about boxing, other than the hard-core boxing fan. That was the beginning of the end.
　　　　　　　　　　　　　—Kevin Rooney, April 2005

Nearly every day, for months on end, Steve Lott would sit down and compose a brief letter, in longhand, to his old friend. The content of the letters varied—small talk about the sport of boxing, up-dates on mutual acquaintances—but always they ended the same way: with Lott, a cornerman for Mike Tyson in the glorious early days, ex-pressing his desire to visit the fighter. This was no small undertaking, seeing as how Tyson, at the time, was an intensely famous and reluctant guest of the Indiana State Department of Corrections. One could not simply show up, unannounced, knock at the front gate, and expect to be granted an audience with an inmate of one's choosing. There were rules to be followed, protocol to guide one through the process. (Kevin Rooney, Tyson's former trainer—and a man who had worked as a prison boxing instructor and thus knew a little something about the regulations regarding such matters—discovered this when he drove to the Indiana Youth Center on a whim, only to find that his name had not been included on a list of approved visitors; Rooney was turned away and never did get a chance to see Tyson behind bars.)

Inmates have rights, too, and if Inmate Number 922335, Michael Gerard Tyson, did not feel like sitting down in an interview room and chatting amiably with ghosts from a previous life, that was his prerogative. Anyway, Don King had made certain that Tyson would have no shortage of visitors. Rory Holloway and John Horne were still on the payroll (at salaries of $20,000 per month), and part of their job description included the nurturing of a friendship with Tyson, which they dutifully fulfilled. (Indeed, so convincing and reliable were Holloway and Horne that on August 16, 1994, while still in prison, Tyson would sign a contract making the pair his official comanagers.) There were other visitors as well, many of them famous—actors, fighters, politicians, musicians, writers (especially writers—who doesn't like a good morality tale?)—so it wasn't like Tyson was so lonely or starved for conversation that he needed to reach into the past and dredge up the anger and regret that would likely accompany a visit from a charter member of Team Tyson.

But Lott persisted. He kept writing, asking for permission. He heard nothing in response. Finally Lott turned to a friend for advice. The friend had some, shall we say, *familiarity* with the penal system (he was an ex-con), so he advised Lott to try a different approach: Write a letter to the warden requesting a special visitor's permit. The request ultimately would have to be approved by Tyson, of course, but at least this way it would be communicated through formal channels, and therefore somewhat more difficult to ignore. Sure enough,

Lott's request was approved, and before long he found himself sitting in a sterile room at the Indiana Youth Center, a "high-medium security" facility near the Indianapolis International Airport, waiting for Tyson to walk through the door. Several years had passed since they'd spoken, so Lott wasn't sure what to expect, but the reunion proved less awkward than he'd anticipated. Tyson entered the room with a smile on his face and the two men immediately fell into a warm embrace. They talked for nearly three hours about anything and everything, Lott occasionally lapsing from "friend" mode into "big brother" mode, scolding Tyson for things he had said in the press about Jimmy Jacobs and Bill Cayton, or advising the fighter to get his own lawyers and stop relying on King to fight his battles . . . *and to stop trusting King, for Christ's sake!* Generally, though, the mood was light, and it remained that way on Lott's two subsequent visits.

Not until after they had hugged and parted and Lott was safely behind the wheel of his car, with the prison walls and razor wire in his rearview mirror, did he allow the tears to fall.

"For me, each time, it was sad," Lott recalled. "Mike isn't that emotional, but I am. Even now, when I watch videos of Mike, I have to walk away from the room sometimes. But I knew I had to compose myself. I knew I had to show him strength because, I mean . . . he's in prison. I could leave any time. So just for today, I thought, *Suck it up. And when you leave you can cry or do whatever you want. Just don't make him feel worse than he already does.*"

Whether Tyson deserved sympathy or scorn was mostly a matter of personal preference, and it's not unreasonable to point out that any sorrow expressed by the fighter typically stemmed not from remorse over misdeeds (in particular those that led to his incarceration), but rather from a vague sense of embarrassment or self-loathing. Tyson would acknowledge over the years errors in judgment, mistakes in assessing friendships and business relationships, and, repeatedly and most vocally, his own inability to control his baser impulses. ("Testosterone—that's what it is. Testosterone really takes it out of you. I don't care what anybody says.")

Indeed, so infamous was Tyson's reputation for prodigious and virtually uncontrollable and unrepentant carousing that when he stood trial on charges of rape in the winter of 1992, defense attorney Vincent Fuller actually put forth as a legitimate explanation the notion that the fighter was, at his core, an incorrigible street thug whose libido dictated his every action; therefore the victim should have been aware of the risks associated with anything beyond the most casual encounter with Tyson. So far had the champion fallen that he tacitly endorsed, or at least permitted, a desperate defense strategy that hinged on the perception that he was little more than an animal acting on instinct; and so implausible and condescending was this approach that Tyson could not possibly have engendered less support and respect had he stood up in the courtroom and cried, "The devil made me do it!"

"I feel sympathy for the fact that Mike never had a childhood," offered Jim Lampley, one of many boxing observers drawn inexorably to the parlor game that is the psychological deconstruction of Mike Tyson. "For the fact that Mike was trashed by the unfortunate culture in which he lived his first eleven years, and then went to a situation where he became a commodity and was given all the privileges and excuses and avenues around growing up that a commodity gets. And so any chance for him to be a legitimate, integrated human being was short-circuited a long time ago; he's intelligent enough to know that, and deep in his heart he's angry about it. And all of his self-destruction comes from that. He needs to keep proving the point that he's been trashed. So he destroys himself on a daily basis to make us observe it.

"I do feel sympathy about all that. On the other hand, nobody has ever been clearer about Mike than [former heavyweight champion] Lennox Lewis was, the day Lennox at a news conference said, 'Hey, I had it tough, too.' At some point you're responsible for yourself. That's the bottom line on Mike Tyson."

It is less a comment on his athleticism and boxing acumen than a testament to the perverse power of celebrity that Tyson remained the dominant figure in professional boxing for a good ten years (some would say longer) after being first stripped of his titles (as well as his veneer of invincibility) by Buster Douglas. The natural eroding of physical skill that comes with the passing of time was, in Tyson's case, exacerbated and accelerated by a variety of factors, not least of which was a declining interest in the sport that had made him rich and famous. As time went on and the personal problems and debts mounted, as he burned through friends and advisors and sycophants and trainers, boxing became something else entirely.

"Mike has said his heart isn't in it," observed his friend and former trainer, Jay Bright, in the fall of 2005. "[He fights] because he has a bill; he has to make money. That's basically it. He doesn't have the dedication he once had because it's all about money. Before, it was about titles and beating people and being the best fighter he could be—beating everybody. At this point it's just to get people off his back."

Although no rational observer could dispute the obvious—that Tyson had demonstrated in Tokyo that he was no longer the spectacularly kinetic fighter he'd once been—neither could one make the claim that he was suddenly suited for retirement. Having lost his taste for serious training and having abandoned the defensive-oriented posture espoused by Cus D'Amato, Tyson hardly resembled the boxer who had dominated the heavyweight division in the mid-to-late 1980s. But punching power is the last vestige of a fading fighter, and more than one heavyweight has salvaged a career on the concussive potential of a single blow. (Just ask George Foreman, whose second rise to the top of the heavyweight ranks would coincide roughly with Tyson's descent.) Even as Tyson's quickness evaporated—even as he became a trader of punches—he remained one of the sport's most dangerous and successful practitioners.

Just four months after losing his title, while Douglas was embroiled in legal disputes, Tyson and his revamped corner (which now included veteran trainer Richie Giachetti) returned to the ring. If the opponent (Henry Tillman) was unimpressive, the result (a first-round knockout) nonetheless signaled a reincarnation of Tyson. This version would be slower, less frenetic—less fearsome—but still quite capable of laying sideways just about anyone foolish enough to lead with his chin. On December 8, 1990, in Atlantic City, Tyson dispatched Alex Stewart in the first round. Then, on

March 18, 1991, came a seventh-round technical knockout over Donovan "Razor" Ruddock in Las Vegas, in a fight steeped in controversy thanks to referee Richard Steele's decision to end the proceedings with Ruddock on his feet and seemingly capable of defending himself.

Tyson and Ruddock met again a little more than three months later in Las Vegas in a fight remembered less for its outcome (Tyson emerged with a lackluster twelve-round decision) than for the bilious prefight ranting of the former champion, who, in what would come to be standard behavior, referred to Ruddock as a "transvestite," and vowed, in time-honored jailhouse rhetoric, to make the Canadian fighter the latest in a long line of Tyson's sexual conquests. The harangue raised eyebrows at the time, although in the latter stages of Tyson's career, prefight posturing and vulgar tirades—directed at opponents, the media, anyone within earshot—would become an accepted part of the show.

"Mike is an extremely complex individual," observed Paul Antonelli. "He can be the sweet son, the way he treated Camille, the way he calls people Mr. or Mrs. On the other hand he can be a totally different person, a very harsh person. I think that's why he captivated audiences: because of his bizarre and unpredictable behavior. And I think it started with the Douglas fight. Mike had always respected his opponents. If he knocked someone out, he'd go over and make sure they were okay. For some reason that all changed. He was not respectful of his opponent anymore. I mean, he had always talked trash before a fight, but once the fight was over, he realized, 'Hey, that guy is just like me,' and he'd want to make sure [the other fighter] was okay. For some reason, that part of him seemed to go away after the Douglas fight."

With each successive outburst or transgression, Tyson's weirdness quotient increased, drawing ever more curiosity seekers, like moths to a flame. Boxing purists, though, were repulsed as much as they were fascinated.

"On a human level, he's a tragic figure of what I call the sky above and the mud below," said Larry Merchant. "Tyson had the talent and the ambition to escape his background, and to reach very high, but he couldn't deal with it. He fell to the earth. In that sense, as a human, he's a tragic figure. But my feeling for him as a fighter was that he abused too many people around him—people who helped him get where he got—and over time that he was a sociopath if not a psychopath, and overall I thought he was a cancer on boxing."

When it was suggested that this seemed a coarse and ironic assessment, given that Tyson almost single-handedly aroused a sport that, in the eyes of the general public, had been dormant for years, Merchant disagreed.

"Well, I think what he did, he did for himself. He got a lot of people interested in Mike Tyson; I don't know if he got a lot of people interested in the sport. It's fair to say he became this tabloid figure that everybody followed and was curious to see what his next breakdown would be, his next train wreck."

Intentionally or not, Tyson fed the gaping maw of celebrity journalism throughout the 1990s, reaching a zenith of sorts (although one might argue persuasively that it was more of a nadir) in the winter of 1992, when he stood trial on charges of raping a contestant in the Miss Black America pageant. The incident had occurred three weeks after Tyson's rematch with Ruddock, in the early morning hours of July 19, 1991, in Room 606 of the Canterbury Hotel in Indianapolis. It was there, a jury would later determine, that Tyson had sexually assaulted eighteen-year-old Desiree Washington. More than six months would pass between the time Washington filed a formal complaint with police (on July 22, 1991) and the case went to trial at a Marion County Courthouse, providing ample opportunity for media saturation and political exploitation.

As Richard Corliss wrote in *Time*, "They met by a fluke of fate, like a tank and a tricycle at an intersection. He was the most dangerous man in sports, the once and (we supposed) future heavyweight champion of the world, whose conquests included forty professional boxers and countless women. She was (we now suppose) the last innocent child in America, an eighteen-year-old Sunday school teacher fresh from high school graduation in a tiny Rhode Island town. When Desiree Washington met Mike Tyson at a beauty pageant last July, she saw not the pug and thug of tabloid legend but a young man wearing a *Together with Christ* button who was praying with Jesse Jackson. Tyson, it appears, saw a late-night snack."

That about sums up the polarizing effect of the trial, which not only pit the defendant, with his $5,000-a-day defense attorney (Fuller was a prominent Washington, D.C.—based lawyer who, a decade earlier, had successfully argued an insanity defense for would-be presidential assassin John Hinckley; not coincidentally, he had also earned an acquittal for Don King on charges of tax evasion in 1985), against the victim, but served as a combustible agent for broader disagreements as well. Oddly (given the fact that both the accused and the victim were African American), although perhaps inevitably, the Tyson rape trial became a divisive event on a racial front, with Tyson's black supporters conducting prayer vigils in support of the former champion and railing against supposed racial injustices committed by the prosecution (which, the argument went, catered shamelessly to the fears of white America by perpetuating antediluvian stereotypes of the black male as an unrestrained and unrepentant sexual predator).

In reality, it was Fuller who served up the more unsettling and racially charged argument, teetering as it did on the fault line between vigorous defense and outrageously chuckleheaded counterintuitiveness. The "stud defense," as it was termed, presented to the public, and to the jury (comprised of ten whites and two blacks), a defendant so obviously and famously driven by his primal instincts that no sane person (especially a woman) could accept an invitation to his hotel room or limousine without understanding that a verbal contract had been executed. It was, as Sonja Steptoe, an African-American journalist, opined in *Sports Illustrated,* "a Faustian bargain if ever there was one. In Fuller's attempt to win his client an acquittal, the defendant was affixed with a label: *Beware—Dangerous Sexual Animal.*"

And so it went, day after queasy day, the defense awkwardly portraying Washington as a willing participant in a late-night dalliance with the former heavyweight champion, a young, but hardly inexperienced woman who flirted with danger and got precisely what she deserved . . . probably even what she wanted. Conversely, prosecutor

Greg Garrison took the high road. Rather than relying on shrill personal attacks, he skillfully and coolly presented the facts of the case, culminating with an impressive cross-examination of the defendant, whose decision to take the stand proved to be a serious error. Simply put, Tyson came across badly, and his description of the evening—from conflicting time lines to recollections of breathless dialogue, like outtakes from a porno flick—ultimately rang false. In contrast, Washington seemed believable and determined, characteristics bolstered by the surfacing of reports that her father allegedly had been offered one million dollars by the Rev. T. J. Jemison, head of the National Baptist Convention and an acquaintance of Don King's, to entice the young woman to withdraw her complaint against Tyson. The alleged offer was rejected and the matter referred to authorities. (Jemison was later indicted on federal perjury charges for statements made while serving as a character witness in an unrelated trial, during which he denied having offered hush money to the Washington family. A federal judge ultimately threw out the perjury charges.)

In the end (which came on February 10, 1992, nearly two years to the day after Tyson's upset at the hands of Buster Douglas), the jury sided with the victim, returning at 10:52 in the evening, after nine hours of deliberation, to Courtroom 4 of Marion County Superior Court, and pronouncing Tyson guilty on one count of rape and two counts of deviate sexual conduct, crimes punishable by up to sixty years in prison. Save for a slight and sudden tilting of the head, the fighter betrayed no emotion as Judge Patricia Gifford read the jury's verdict. Similarly transfixed was Don King, who sat quietly in the front row, clutching a Bible. Defense attorney Fuller immediately requested that his client remain free on bail pending an appeal, claiming, somewhat disingenuously, that Tyson was "a celebrity with no place to go." Gifford granted the request, set bond at $30,000, and demanded that the fighter (who was now a convicted rapist, and not merely "the accused") surrender his passport.

"Here it is," said King, reaching into a leather shoulder bag.

On March 26, 1992, Tyson stood again in front of Gifford, awaiting sentencing. Previously, at a three-hour hearing, Tyson had testified on his own behalf. In a rambling, ten-minute statement, he proclaimed his innocence (a stance he maintains to this day), saying, among other things, "I didn't hurt anybody. Nobody has a black eye or broken ribs. When I'm in the ring, I break their ribs, I break their jaws. To me, that's hurting someone . . . I have not raped anyone, attempted to rape anyone or harmed anyone in any means. I'm sorry that Ms. Washington took it personally and I agree that I've done something, but I by no means meant to hurt her or do anything to her, and I'm sure she knows that well."

Tyson did acknowledge that his behavior was "kind of crass"; not surprisingly, this was an admission that did little to sway Judge Gifford, who sentenced Tyson to ten years on each count, then suspended four years. The six-year sentences would run concurrently. He was also fined $30,000, the maximum allowed by law. Since Indianapolis law permitted an inmate to shave one day off his sentence for each day served without incident, Tyson could earn his release in as little as three years.

A motion for bail was denied, and the newest member of Tyson's legal team, renowned Harvard law professor and celebrity defense attorney Alan Dershowitz, filed an appeal of that denial. In the short term, at least, this meant that Tyson was going to jail. There was no way around that now. The fighter calmly removed his watch and tie pin, handed both to Vincent Fuller, then turned to embrace Camille Ewald, who had made the trip from Catskill to show her support. Moments later Tyson was led out of the courtroom in handcuffs. The woman he called his mother waited until he was out of sight. Then she began to cry.

Whether Mike Tyson emerged from the Indiana Youth Center a rehabilitated man is a question too broad and complex, and littered with psychological and sociopolitical land mines, to be answered with any degree of assuredness. There are those, of course, who believe that prisons ought not to be in the business of rehabilitation, that time endured behind bars is righteously intended to punish, to inflict emotional and physical pain upon those who have caused distress in the lives of others. An eye for an eye. Justice in the most biblical sense of the term.

One might reasonably counter that a criminal justice system erected on a foundation of misery and degradation is doomed not only to failure, but virtually guaranteed to aggravate an already grim situation. There is no shortage of sociologists and reformists eager to share the view, typically bolstered by statistics related to violent crime and recidivism, that American jails and prisons excel at one thing and one thing only: honing the aberrant tendencies and survival instincts of criminals, the majority of whom are warehoused for a period of time and then spit back, devoid of any useful skill, with anger freshly stoked, into a society that perceives them as beneath contempt.

No great leap is required to view Tyson through this prism, to regard him as a casualty, first, of the child welfare system and personal and familial circumstances beyond his control. It's a bit of a cliché to suggest that Tyson is a product of the streets and a broken home, of reform schools and juvenile detention centers and prisons. But there is at least a kernel of truth in the cliché.

Observed Tom Patti, Tyson's closest confidant: "I think Mike's challenges are to try to undo damages and try to forge forward. How can you be a good father when you don't know what a father is, when you come from such a fantastically challenged childhood?"

An equally sympathetic, though ostensibly objective, portrait was etched by Tom Junod, who wrote of the tormented champion in *Esquire:* "There are no baby pictures of Mike Tyson. Nobody cared enough either to keep them or to take them in the first place, and so there are no pictures of Mike Tyson smiling without teeth, or sleeping in a crib, or being held aloft in the arms of his father against some white stain of sunlight; no pictures of Mike Tyson's first step, or his first day at school; no way of knowing whether Mike Tyson was a cute infant, a cute toddler, or even a cute little boy. He is around twelve years old by the time of his first extant photograph, and because no pictures of him exist before that one, it's almost as though he didn't, either, until the first click of the shutter nudged him into being, and he was born, on film, fully formed, already finished: already stocky, already strong, already brave, already scared, already heartbroken, already truant, already violent, already in trouble, and already captured, thirty-eight times between the ages of ten and thirteen, and delivered into the hands of the law."

Fair and accurate enough, but it's also true, as Lennox Lewis pointed out, that Tyson is not alone in having been born into unfortunate circumstances, and that indeed over the years he has received innumerable opportunities to escape, or at least transcend, his past, and, by his own admission, flushed most of them away. Precisely what role the Indiana Youth Center played in the evolution—or devolution—of Tyson is open to speculation. Veritable forests were felled during this period so that authors and journalists could chronicle their jailhouse discussions with Tyson or merely speculate from afar on reports of his voracious literary and philosophical appetites. The incarcerated fighter was prone to introspection, it was said, and he filled his time not by watching television, but rather by devouring books. He claimed to have been influenced by the works of a disparate group that included Voltaire, Machiavelli, W. E. B. DuBois, Francis Bacon, and Gertrude Stein, just to name a few. There were rumors that he had found tranquillity and solace in religion and that he was seriously considering a formal conversion to Islam. Maybe, it was suggested, the fighter was no longer a fighter; maybe he had become a man of peace. Prison, perhaps, had done the unthinkable: sucked the anger and bitterness out of Tyson, and left in its place a shell open to the prospect of a different, more spiritual existence.

Then again, given the fact that his postprison years would be checkered by behavior at least as bizarre and disturbing as the years prior to his sentencing, one might be tempted to look back on this rather naïvely optimistic assessment with skepticism.

This much can be said with a degree of certainty: While Tyson was away, professional boxing, the heavyweight division in particular, began a long and precipitous slide toward the margins of mainstream sports. Granted, there would be hiccups along the way, pay-per-view bouts that made mountains of money, temporary infatuation with a particular champion (such as the genial giant Foreman), but the overarching theme was one of a sport in decline. And that decline continues to this day. With its principal attraction out of the picture, boxing soon returned to the fractured and quizzical position it had held prior to Tyson's arrival: too many divisions, too many "governing" bodies, too many champions (especially too many champions of little regard), and not nearly enough charisma or drama. For better or worse, Tyson had been a unifying force in professional boxing, not simply because he held championship belts from multiple organizations, but also because virtually anyone who had even the slightest interest in the sport followed his every move. He was *newsworthy*.

"Away from the ring, Tyson was bigger than life," said the *Daily News's* Vic Ziegel. "He was, in a way, exactly what we want our heavyweight champions to be. We don't want them to be gentlemen. We really don't."

The dominoes of the heavyweight division began tumbling the night Tyson was knocked out in Tokyo and gained momentum primarily through two events: Holyfield's obliteration of Douglas and Tyson's reluctant sabbatical. By the end of 1990, two upstart organizations had been formed: the Intercontinental Boxing Council (IBC) and the International Boxing Organization (IBO); in early 1992, a third governing body, the World Boxing Organization (WBO), which had been formed in 1989, gained a measure of respectability, if not interest, by stripping its champion, Ray Mercer, of the heavyweight title for refusing to face George Foreman or Michael Moorer, its top contenders.

Confusing? It only gets worse.

On November 13, 1992, Riddick Bowe earned a twelve-round decision over Holyfield to become the champion of the IBF, WBA, and WBC, still considered at the time to be the three most legitimate (albeit not free of scandal or corruption) organizations in professional boxing. One month later, in a snit attributable to the organization's insistence that he defend his title against top-ranked contender Lennox Lewis, Bowe tossed his WBC championship belt unceremoniously into a trash can. To the surprise of absolutely no one, the WBC responded by stripping Bowe of his title and promoting Lewis to the rank of "champion."

The next year would see the ascendance of heavyweights such as Tommy Morrison, Michael Bentt, Poncho Carter, Lionel Butler, and

Mike Weaver, fighters of modest repute, each of whom nonetheless held at least one of the lesser titles in that period. Holyfield continued to be the division's top draw, thanks to his reclaiming the WBA and IBF titles with a decision over Bowe in November 1993, although just five months later he would surrender both belts to Moorer, who survived a knockdown to post a majority decision. Similarly, on September 24, 1994, the heavyweight division's other rising star, Lewis, demonstrated his glaring fallibility with a stunning second-round knockout at the hands of former Buster Douglas victim Oliver McCall. Six weeks later, Foreman, at the almost incomprehensibly advanced age of forty-five, knocked out Moorer to claim the WBA and IBF titles, only to be stripped by the WBA in March for refusing to defend his championship against the organization's top-ranked contender.

And so it went. By the time Tyson emerged from prison in the spring of 1995, professional boxing had reverted to its previous position as a sporting sideshow, garnering attention only from the curious and the hard-core. Indeed, the most talented and interesting practitioners of the sport—Julio Cesar Chavez, Pernell Whitaker, James Toney, and Roy Jones, as well as the emergent Golden Boy, Oscar De La Hoya—now worked in the lighter divisions, which, as anyone who follows boxing knows, is a recipe for obscurity.

"Bottom line—as the heavyweight division goes, so goes boxing," said one of the sport's foremost chroniclers, Bert Sugar, in 1995. "This goes back to John L. Sullivan. And it has something to do with being American. Americans are always obsessed with big things—cars, houses, breasts, fighters. We could have ten Roy Joneses or ten Pernell Whitakers, we'd still be waiting for the heavyweight division to come back."

Not yet thirty years of age (a milestone he would reach in the summer of 1996), Tyson was still sufficiently young and healthy—and, remarkably enough, considering the multiple millions he had earned in the ring, sufficiently short on cash—to be regarded as the most suitable vehicle for boxing's resurgence. Whether he was inclined to assume that responsibility and the workload it entailed was another matter. A gentler and more refined Mike Tyson, one who had come to terms with his own humanity while serving time in prison, might be a better citizen, father, friend, and husband (he had already found a smart and supportive companion in Monica Turner, a medical school student who would later become his wife); he would not necessarily be a better heavyweight boxer. More likely, any predilection for amicability would prove a hindrance in Tyson's cultural and athletic rebirth, impeding the fighter's natural and irrefutably useful (albeit sometimes troubling) inclination toward violent antisocial behavior.

By the end of the year, however, concerns over Tyson's commercial viability and commitment to fighting had largely been erased. His comeback began in Las Vegas, on August 19, 1995, with a knockout of Peter McNeeley just eighty-nine seconds into the fight. Slow and hittable, McNeeley was a predictably overmatched opponent, and his hasty departure shed hardly any light on the issue of whether Tyson had regained the speed and skill that once made him the game's most fearsome champion; rather, this fight, and a subsequent third-round knockout of Buster Mathis Jr., on December 16, reaffirmed the drawing power of Tyson. Even at something less than his best, against marginal opponents, he was boxing's biggest star, and clearly capable not only of recapturing the titles he had lost to Douglas, but of reassembling the splintered heavyweight division.

A multifight deal with Showtime helped alleviate some of Tyson's financial concerns (although not for long, since the fighter, as would later be revealed, was spending heroically throughout this period), and by the fall of 1996 he had recaptured two of the division's prominent titles, stopping Frank Bruno (for the second time) on a third-round technical knockout in March to secure the WBC belt, and then acquiring the WBA championship in September with a first-round TKO of Bruce Seldon. That victory came with a price, since it represented a direct refusal on the part the champion to defend his WBC title against Lennox Lewis, the top-ranked contender. Predictably, the WBC immediately announced that it would no longer recognize Tyson as its champion.

Not that it mattered. Tyson had fought four times in thirteen months, and in that span he had demonstrated an ability to galvanize the sport in ways it hadn't known since . . . well, since before Tyson went off to jail. From a strictly economic standpoint, neither did it matter that on November 9, 1996, Tyson, an 8-to-1 favorite, was stopped in the eleventh round by Holyfield, a tough and indefatigable thirty-four-year-old fighter, once retired, whose best days supposedly were behind him. In fact, that fight, a startling upset over a champion who evinced considerable heart (as he had against Douglas, Tyson fought gamely, if not brilliantly, and absorbed a terrific beating), left the distinct impression that a sequel was warranted.

Tyson-Holyfield II, on June 28, 1997, was the most successful pay-per-view event boxing had known, generating a record 1.8 million purchases (surpassing the previous record of 1.6 million for the first Holyfield-Tyson fight). At a rate of $49.95 per customer, the fight generated approximately $90 million in pay-per-view revenue. From the opening bell, however, it was apparent that the rematch would not meet the standards established by the combatants' first encounter, if only because the challenger was markedly less enthusiastic than he'd been seven and a half months earlier. With a sellout crowd of 16,331 at the MGM Grand Arena in Las Vegas divided in its loyalties—chanting the names of Holyfield and Tyson in roughly equal measure—the two fighters pawed and wrestled uneventfully through much of the first two rounds. First blood was drawn by Holyfield, who opened a gash above Tyson's right eye when the fighters cracked skulls while groping in close quarters in the second round. Tyson, uncharacteristically, it seemed, complained vigorously to referee Mills Lane that he had been the victim of a head butt.

And then the weirdness escalated. Tyson emerged from his corner at the beginning the third round without his mouthpiece, an omission dutifully pointed out by Holyfield and corrected by Lane (Tyson was sent back to his corner and instructed to insert his mouthpiece), and one that would later take on enormous significance, signaling, as it did, not just a lapse of memory on the part of the challenger, but perhaps bad intent as well. In the final minute of the third round, with the two fighters again locked in an embrace, Tyson spit out his mouthpiece, nuzzled against the side of Holyfield's head, and then took the champion's right ear into his mouth. At first it was hard to tell what had happened. Holyfield turned and danced away from the assault with almost comical exasperation, wiping at his ear with a glove and wailing in pain. Tyson spat a bloody hunk of flesh onto the canvas, then attacked Holyfield from behind as Lane tried to make some sense of things. The referee eventually deducted two points from Tyson and compelled the men to resume fighting.

They did, too, but not for long. Soon there was another clinch, and again Tyson bared his teeth, this time chomping down on Holyfield's left ear. Having seen enough, Lane stepped in and put an end to the ugliness, disqualifying Tyson and awarding the victory to Holyfield.

"One bite, maybe, is bad enough," Lane said afterward without a trace of irony. "But two bites is the end of the search."

Tyson would later try to rationalize this madness by claiming that he was merely defending himself against Holyfield's equally (and prior) brutish behavior; when that explanation proved implausible, the fighter turned contrite. That approach, too, was ineffective. Eleven days after the bout, in a move at once unprecedented and un-avoidable (given the public outcry over Tyson's actions), the Nevada State Athletic Commission unanimously voted to revoke the former champion's boxing license. Tyson was also fined $3 million.

None of this came as a shock to Tyson; indeed, it may have been precisely the outcome he sought, a respite from the spotlight, and from a sport that no longer held his interest.

"Nobody knows better how Mike has deteriorated as a fighter than Mike," said Jim Lampley. "Few people know boxing better than Mike. Mike knows better than anybody what he sacrifices when he goes to the strip club instead of the gym. Nobody was more aware of how fraudulent the Mike Tyson image became in the late 1990s than Mike. And that's why he was doing so many things to try to get out of the sport. When he bit Evander's ear, he was trying to get banned. He wanted out."

If that was so, then his wish had been granted . . . if only tem-porarily.

If you talk to certain people in Columbus they'll tell you I'm depressed. They'll say I've put on weight because I'm down over all that happened, that I'm hiding from the world here. But it isn't true. I'm happy.

—James Douglas, Spring 1993

The morning-after press conference is a staple of professional boxing, an opportunity for one man to graciously and gratefully bask in the glory of victory and the other to humbly accept defeat. It's an intensely personal thing, fighting, and it isn't at all unusual for the two combatants to come away from the experience with a deep and unspoken bond. Mutual respect, typically, is the order of the day.

On the morning of October 26, 1990, Evander Holyfield dutifully held up his end of the bargain, quietly and thoughtfully answering all questions, even going so far as to praise the man he had pummeled into apparent submission just a few hours earlier.

"Buster did something everyone thought could not be done," Holyfield said. "He beat Mike Tyson. He's in the books of history now as a heavyweight champion of the world."

Whether Douglas was similarly respectful of Holyfield and his place in the boxing pantheon was anyone's guess, for the deposed champion was nowhere to be found. Left to deflect the slings and arrows of a cynical press corps inclined to report the obvious—that

Douglas had neither prepared properly for his first title defense, nor reached deep into his heart to produce an effort seemingly worthy of a $24 million payday—were the fighter's supporting crew. They chose their words carefully, preferring to defend (albeit with something less than wholehearted vigor) rather than excoriate their fighter.

"Sometimes you have nights when it's just not your night," said J. D. McCauley.

Added John Johnson: "I believe James Douglas, in great shape, could beat anybody."

The real nastiness was left to others, and it came in torrents over the coming days and weeks, a veritable flood of criticism and hostility directed at the former champion. With remarkable swiftness, the folk hero who had captured the heart of the sporting world by pulling off the upset of the century had fallen from grace. Overnight, it seemed, Buster Douglas had become *Blubber* Douglas, the butt of jokes on late-night talk shows, the same shows that had lauded him after the Tyson fight.

Far worse than the satirical jabs or the hatchet jobs by acerbic columnists was the clearheaded analysis offered by people who actually understood and cared about the fight game, and who were understandably offended by what they had witnessed in the ring. When the esteemed trainer Eddie Futch, a seventy-nine-year-old veteran of the sport who rarely indulged in mudslinging of any sort, had this to say of your performance—"I thought Buster Douglas was disgraceful tonight"—it carried more than a little weight. "He allowed himself to get into such poor condition, he had nothing," added Futch. "His judgment of distance, his timing—he had no snap." And then there was the bigger issue, the one everyone wanted to tap dance around because it cut to the core of what it means to be a fighter. There was no disputing the obvious, that Douglas had failed to train properly and entered the ring in woeful physical condition. But what about the fight's ignoble ending, and Douglas's apparent lack of resolve? Could he have risen?

"The things he did—rubbing his face and looking at his gloves to see if there was blood—I'm sure he was perfectly aware of what was going on," said Futch. "In my opinion he could have got up in time. But he chose not to do so, so maybe he had his own reasons."

Whatever those reasons might have been, they were insufficient to placate Mirage owner Steve Wynn, whose $24-million investment in Douglas now seemed embarrassingly ill-advised, particularly for a man with a well-deserved reputation as one of the shrewdest businessmen in the history of Las Vegas. Forget about the fact that the fight was a virtual sellout and generated more than $10 million in live gate revenue; forget that pay-per-view orders would gross another $35 million; forget about the increase in "drop" (money wagered at the gambling tables) that a casino enjoys when it hosts a championship fight. To Wynn, this was about principle and reputation. In declining to take himself or his opponent seriously, and by not making every effort to beat the count of ten, Douglas had not only failed to live up to his end of the bargain, he had compromised the integrity of those who had invested in him and promoted the fight. All of these things were implied by Wynn the day after Holyfield's victory in a statement released by the promoter's publicist: "We compliment Evander Holyfield for coming into the ring well-prepared . . . however, our attitude is that fight purses should be more along the lines of winner-take-all so that the only incentive is for victory."

This was a sentiment echoed often in the aftermath of the Douglas-Holyfield fight; it was even shared by McCauley, who years later clung to the belief that Douglas (like most fighters) needed motivation beyond simple honor.

"I felt terrible about the way things went, and I felt terrible about the way the fight ended up," McCauley said. "I know we could have won. I know we could have beat that man. I can't get anyone to see it that way, but I'm telling you: Buster could have beat Holyfield. But what happens is, the most horrible thing in boxing— and in sports, period—is you get these guaranteed contracts. It's like you're guaranteed twenty-four million dollars, win or lose. The champ gets twenty-four million, the opponent gets eight. Now, wait a minute. Make it winner gets twenty-four, loser gets eight, Holyfield gets his ass beat! Think about what I just said. It makes a lot more sense."

Considerable time would pass before Douglas weighed in on this or any other matter related to the sport of boxing. To the casual observer, it seemed, he fell to the canvas against Holyfield and slid sideways toward the edge of the earth, eventually plummeting headlong into oblivion. In reality, Buster merely stepped away from the spotlight and from boxing and went on with his life, although it would be simplistic (and inaccurate) to suggest, as some did, that he laughed all the way to bank.

After the Holyfield fight Douglas felt no great inclination to return to Columbus, where he'd likely be showered with pity (which was worse than scorn), so he headed west instead, spending a week hanging out in Los Angeles with his buddies. The partying grew old, however, and soon Douglas returned to Columbus, although not before parting with a bit of his newly acquired wealth. The first major purchase, picked up at Beverly Hills dealership, was a Porsche 930S Turbo convertible, a laughably small (although undeniably muscular) vehicle for such a big man, with a price tag of $125,000, an auto that fairly shouted, "Success!"

Next came a parcel of land in a blighted section of Columbus, which Douglas hoped to transform into a thriving example of new urbanism, complete with a youth center. And yet, at the same time that he funneled resources into the revitalization of his hometown, Douglas felt the undeniable urge to flee. He liked the warmth and sun of Las Vegas but considered it an unappealing place to raise children, so, in 1992, he and Bertha went on a fact-finding mission in Florida. They came away with a new home: a 6,400-square-foot mansion on Marco Island, a onetime sleepy fishing village that had blossomed into a thriving resort town. As is true with much of coastal Florida, an inland waterway snakes through Marco Island, so it isn't unusual for homeowners to have a pair of cars in the driveway and a boat docked canal-side out back. Buster's was a beauty: spanned forty-plus feet from bow to stern, slept six comfortably, trimmed in teakwood. It set the champ back about 150 grand. On the hull there was a painting of a seashell and a gleaming white pearl, along with the name of the vessel: *Lula Pearl.*

"James loved his mother dearly," said Bertha Douglas. "You

know, he always wanted to buy a home for her and give her every-thing she wanted, all that material stuff that you give, just because you can and you love your mother. He never got an opportunity to do that, to live the dream the way he wanted to live it."

If this was a version of that dream, intended to honor his mother, it wasn't nearly as fulfilling as it might have appeared on the surface. In May 1993 *Sports Illustrated* published a lengthy profile of the onetime champion. Written by John Ed Bradley, the story depicted Douglas as an ostensibly jolly man of leisure whose days were filled with trips to the video store and fishing excursions with his friends. And eating. Lots of eating. More disturbing than the piece itself, with its unmis-takable undercurrent of emptiness and regret, were the accompany-ing photos, including one of Douglas peering longingly through the window of a local deli during off hours ("Even the delicatessen on Marco Island, one of Buster's favorite places to pig out, has to close sometime," read the caption), and another of a magnificently corpu-lent Douglas, dreadlocked and wearing shades, sitting astride a Harley-Davidson motorcycle (license plate: "Boss Hog"), grinning like the Joker, Batman's nemesis, a character described in the story as being a favorite of Douglas's. The title of the article: "Get a Load of Me!"

The author made numerous references to Douglas's girth, though his estimate (320 pounds) appeared distressingly low, and a reader couldn't help but come away from the story feeling that this was a man in crisis. Douglas was offended and angered by the *SI* piece: "That was a horrible story, man. That guy set me up . . . writing all that shit about me, like I was doing so bad . . ."

He paused, shrugged, smiled. "Okay, maybe I was pretty fucked up."

Never let it be said that Buster Douglas lacks introspection. It was one of the characteristics that made him, simultaneously, such a lik-able fellow and reluctant fighter. One senses upon meeting Douglas that it also contributes to his being a thoughtful and involved father, as well as a man who generally, and genuinely, wants to do right. And it almost certainly contributed to the crushing sense of disappoint-ment and shame that enveloped Douglas in the wake of the Holyfield fight. He ate too much, drank too much. (On February 14, 1992, while driving with friends near Columbus, Douglas was pulled over by police, who clocked him at eighty miles per hour, and was subsequently charged with driving while intoxicated. A jury trial that summer resulted in an acquittal.)

"James was depressed," observed Bertha Douglas. "He was in a downward spiral. He needed to hit rock bottom, I guess. Like when you're on drugs or whatever, doing things that are not good for you, and nobody can help you. You have to go there yourself."

It's a strong word, depression, and one that gets thrown around a bit too casually. But Douglas does not deny that it was applicable to his situation.

"That was all depression, everything from 1990 on," he said. "I moved down to Florida to be in my own little world, my own little space. Leave me be. I didn't care about anything. It was like, I'm going to go ahead and get big and ride my hog. That's what it was. That was living. That was me being Boss Hog! But I was miserable. I missed my mom. I was depressed. I wasn't good. Only good thing is that I was down there doing it, instead of up [in Columbus] doing it. Because if I'd been up here doing it I don't think I would have made it. I would have hurt somebody or somebody would have hurt me. I wasn't in the right frame of mind. I was bad, man. Bad."

He wasn't alone. John Johnson, too, uses the word "depressed" to describe his state of mind in the months and even years following the Douglas-Tyson fight. McCauley prefers "sad." Both men remained in Columbus after the Holyfield debacle, although neither saw much of Buster Douglas. Circumstances and familial responsibility occasionally brought McCauley and Douglas together, uncomfortably and briefly, but Johnson was exiled on a more permanent and immediate basis. Contractually bound to Douglas, he was, at least as far as Douglas was concerned, a manager in name only, since Buster had no intention of returning to the ring (periodic claims to the contrary notwithstanding). In the summer of 1995, more than five years after the Tyson fight, and very nearly that long since the two men had spoken, Johnson settled a long-standing legal dispute with Douglas. Johnson had claimed in a 1993 lawsuit that he was owed a portion of $250,000 in "training expenses" received by Douglas from the Mirage while preparing for the Holyfield fight. According to the lawsuit, a check for that amount had been assigned to both Johnson and Douglas but had been improperly cashed by the brokerage firm Merrill Lynch and deposited into Douglas's account. Johnson had sued Merrill Lynch (but not Douglas) for $250,000 in actual damages and another $750,000 in punitive damages. The brokerage firm, in turn, filed suit against Douglas, arguing that the fighter was responsible for any damages incurred by Johnson. In any event, the case was settled on the eve of trial, with Johnson receiving $147,500. This was in addition to the $4.3 million managerial share he had earned for the Holyfield fight.

Many of those who held professional relationships with Douglas in 1990 enjoyed a financial windfall; few, if any, emerged from the experience with anything resembling happiness. John Russell, the trainer who had grown so fond of Douglas, and who was chiefly responsible for the fighter's preparation for both Tyson and Holyfield, withdrew from everyone and everything.

"I'd basically had enough of boxing," Russell said. "I saw the other side of it. There had been so much confusion in our camp on that second fight that I basically burned myself out on it."

So Russell moved back to Akron, tried to pass the time by playing a lot of golf, found himself drinking heavily and taking out his anger and frustration on his longtime girlfriend. ("I put her through hell.") Eventually he left Akron and moved to a little town called Chagrin Falls, Ohio, where people were less likely to stop him on the street and ask what had happened that night in Las Vegas against Holyfield, where they weren't so quick to request an update on the condition of Buster Douglas, with whom the trainer no longer communicated on a regular basis. Eventually, Russell stopped drinking and starting working out. He lost weight. In solitude, interestingly enough, his spirits improved. But still he was left with a nagging sense of remorse.

"I wasn't happy, mainly because I knew Buster was a better fighter than that," Russell said. "To be on such a high, such a peak, beating Tyson, and then to go out like that—not putting forth the effort against Holyfield. And then everybody went from saying, "Buster's a hero," to "Oh, fuck.""

"*Oh, fuck.*" Meaning, perhaps, "*He stole the money*"?

"Yeah," Russell said. "And I kept hearing that shit, which is why I went into seclusion: I didn't want to hear it anymore."

Understandable, because the trainer was implicated as well. Guilt by association. Russell felt compassion for Douglas, but he was angry, too. Angry with the fighter for letting him down; angry with himself for not figuring out a way to get past all the bullshit and motivate his fighter; angry with Johnson and McCauley . . . Nallie and Rogers . . . Don King. Everyone who had interfered with the important stuff: the training and preparation. Russell had been a worker all his life, a hard-core trainer who labored in the shadows, shunned the spotlight, and liked to keep things simple. He was content that way. Suddenly he had the heavyweight champion of the world, and he was miserable. How did that happen?

The search for an answer took Russell eventually to Marco Island, Florida, and a resuscitation of his friendship and working partnership with Douglas. But it was a circuitous route. In the late winter of 1993 Russell had been approached about the possibility of working the corner for a young boxer managed by Douglas. Open to the idea of returning to the sport and eager to help his friend, Russell flew to Atlantic City on March 25, arriving just in time for the pre-fight weigh-in. As Russell entered the ballroom, he spotted Bill Douglas, looking as lean and hard as he'd ever been. Next to Dynamite was a mountain of a man with short, sweaty dreadlocks, fairly bursting out of his clothes. Russell blinked, uncertain at first whether his eyes were deceiving him. Then the big man smiled and Russell knew: *James.*

"If he hadn't been sitting beside his dad, I wouldn't have known who he was," Russell recalled. "True story. I would not have recognized him. That's how big he was. And then—I'll never forget this— the matchmaker comes up to me and says, 'John, I don't want to introduce Buster because he looks so bad.' That tells you where we were at."

The passing of time had done nothing to diminish the trainer's affection for the fighter, and when the two men met each other, they embraced warmly and fell into an easy conversation. Physical changes notwithstanding, it was almost as if time had stopped in 1990 and they'd never parted ways. The following night Russell worked the corner for Douglas's fighter, and then he left town; the two men agreed to stay in touch. Two months later Russell picked up a copy of *Sports Illustrated,* and there was Buster in all his grinning glory, his body spilling down the sides of an overmatched Harley. Russell's breath caught as he read the story.

"I don't think he was on a suicide mission or anything," Russell said. "I just think he didn't care. He had lost his will."

Russell phoned Douglas and the two chatted amiably. They began communicating more frequently. Russell had been spending some time in Naples, Florida, so he figured he might as well reach out to Douglas in a more personal fashion. Eventually they made arrangements to meet at Douglas's home on Marco Island. Douglas promised to take Russell out on the *Lula Pearl.* They'd fish for marlin, talk about old times, just kick back and hang out.

"It was like we never left," Russell said. "Our friendship was still there. But he looked awful. I'll never forget the first time I went down there and saw him, and it was like, *Wow, what happened?*"

The two were out on the boat that first day, basking in the warmth of the Florida sun, when Russell was moved to action by something he witnessed. He'd been on deck, fishing, and had gone inside to check on Douglas. Russell found his friend sitting on the cabin floor, tossing back doughnuts by the fistful and washing them down with a six-pack of beer. Russell turned on his heels and, without saying a word, left the cabin. He stood on the deck, alone, and started to cry.

"It broke my heart," Russell said. "All I could think was, *Jesus, how could this guy do this to himself?*"

The trainer gathered his composure. He took a deep breath and went back below deck.

"Look, man," he said to Douglas. "We need to talk. You need to get yourself together or you're going to die. Please, talk to me."

Douglas dismissed Russell's concern with a wave of a hand. "Come on, have a beer."

Life wasn't so bad, Douglas insisted. Sure, he was a little overweight, but so what? It wasn't like he was training to fight or anything.

That part of his life was dead. Ancient history. The new James Douglas was a man of leisure. He had a loving wife, three healthy children, and a pile of money in the bank. He owed nothing to anyone.

"I didn't give a shit. I wasn't ashamed. I guess it was just something I had to go through to get where I am today," Douglas recalled. "I had to walk that journey—alone. Nobody could say anything to me, because the people I really listened to were gone. My mom—she would have been like, What the hell is this? She would have told me I was in denial."

By the summer of 1994 Douglas's health had deteriorated to such an extent that he often lacked the energy to leave his house. He suffered from a variety of maladies, ranging from chronic sinusitis to blurred vision. In early July, after his family had returned to Ohio for the summer, he came down with what at first seemed to be a nasty case of the flu. Antibiotics did nothing to alleviate the symptoms. Buster slept for hours on end, rising only to use the bathroom or ask his wife for a glass of water. Bertha thought it was odd that her husband couldn't seem to slake his thirst. Then again, nothing seemed right to her. There was the odor that wafted from Buster's body, a fruity fragrance she'd first noticed back in Florida. And the foot fungus that seemed impervious to all manner of treatment. Doctors, according to Bertha, told her that James was suffering from a bacterial infection. Give the antibiotics a few days, they suggested. He'll be fine.

More time passed. On July 4, with her husband lying in bed, babbling incoherently, Bertha made a decision.

"James, we have to take you to the hospital," she said. "Either you get up and I take you right now, or I call the paramedics."

Douglas dragged himself out of bed and downstairs to the living room, where he promptly fell asleep on the couch.

"Come on, baby, we're not there yet," Bertha implored.

She roused him after a time, and together they made their way to the car, all the while James mumbling and wheezing. She raced through Licking County with no regard to speed limits or radar guns. By the time they arrived at Columbus's Grant Medical Center, James had lost consciousness. In the Emergency Room doctors discovered the source of Douglas's distress: a critically elevated blood-sugar count.

A normal range for blood sugar is between 80 and 120; Douglas's blood-sugar count at the time he was admitted to the hospital was 850. By the time Bertha received this news, her husband had lapsed into a diabetic coma and been whisked away to the Intensive Care Unit.

The next day, with tubes pumping fluid and medication into his 400-pound body, and a catheter draining waste from his bladder, Douglas began to wake from his slumber. Delirious, but clearly unhappy with his surroundings, Buster tugged at the tubes and tried to sit up in bed. Bertha wasn't surprised—he was a fighter, after all— and while she viewed his irritability as a good sign, she knew measures had to be taken to ensure her husband's safety, so she consented to have him restrained. Soon Douglas was strapped down. Didn't matter. Buster "ripped the cords apart," Bertha recalled. "Tore them like they were paper."

Standing at the edge of the bed with Bertha was Bill Douglas. Dynamite watched James struggling against his illness, literally and figuratively, and felt a strange mixture of concern and pride.

"Kiss me!" he shouted. "Come on, son, kiss me again!"

So they strapped him down once more, this time even tighter. Buster eventually grew weary of the struggle and relented. He spent the better part of a week in the hospital, sleeping and recuperating. Word of Douglas's condition seeped out slowly, at first, until reports of his hospitalization appeared in the media. When John Russell heard the news, he immediately drove from Akron to Columbus, only to be told upon arrival that his name had not been placed on a list of approved visitors. John Johnson said he was also rebuffed.

"Larry Nallie was in charge," Johnson said. "And I was told, 'You are not fucking welcome here.'"

Doctors diagnosed Douglas's condition as diabetic ketoacidosis, an early form of diabetes. To avoid serious, life-threatening consequences in the future, Douglas would have to make dramatic changes in his lifestyle. He would have to change his diet and embrace a regimen of daily exercise. He would have to lose weight. He would have to learn how to inject himself with insulin. Buster heard the words and took them in. The admonishment didn't frighten him as much as it irritated him.

"They almost killed me," Douglas said, without explaining who "they" might be. "I'm going to let them kill me? Uh-uh. I decided to turn my life around . . . get back in the game."

Later that summer, after he'd regained some of his strength, Douglas picked up the phone and called John Russell.

"I have to take some of this weight off," he said to the trainer. "Can you come down? I'll get up on my feet and we can get back together."

When he got off the phone with Douglas, Russell called his mother to let her know that he'd be leaving town for a while. The next morning he rose early, packed his car, and drove to Columbus.

12

I remember reading with some melancholy that Douglas had blown up, was a has-been, resting on his laurels, a shadow of the man I saw in the ring . . . When did he die?

—James Sterngold

They began slowly, warily, their first steps nearly as tentative as a toddler's. The trainer and the fighter walked quietly in the early morning hours, when the park belonged to a cadre of anonymous joggers and cyclists and in-line skaters. Few people recognized the fighter; fewer still took the time to ask how he was doing. That suited James Douglas just fine. Not long ago there had been reports in the media about a possible rematch between Douglas and Mike Tyson. The timing of the news was odd, to say the least, considering that less than one month earlier Douglas had been hospitalized in a diabetic coma and Tyson remained incarcerated in an Indiana prison. If ever a boxing match seemed unlikely, this was it. Then again, maybe that was precisely the point.

"Where are you going to find a better story line than that one?" asked Mike Marley, a former newspaperman who had become a publicist for Don King Productions, in a fit of inspired rhetoric. "One guy is railroaded into prison, the other guy becomes a happy fat man with a terrible illness. I don't think you can find a better soap opera than that."

Quibbles aside—one might have disputed the claim that Tyson was "railroaded," and while Douglas was undeniably "fat," he certainly wasn't "happy"—Marley had a point. Tyson-Douglas II had all the makings of an epic boxing match; at the very least, it had the potential to be the richest event in the history of the sport. So, decorum be damned. Boxing has never been overly concerned with restraint or modesty; why waste time fretting over the fact that neither man had been near a gym in nearly three years? (In Douglas's case, more like four years.) Crank up the hype!

Somewhere in the back of his mind Douglas indulged in a bit of fantasy. He envisioned a series of fights against opponents of escalating abilities, culminating with a rematch against Tyson . . . maybe even a redemptive showdown with Holyfield. For the most part, though, he kept these thoughts to himself, for they seemed so distant, so unattainable, that it was silly to give them voice. It was enough of a challenge now to go for a leisurely stroll, to put one heavy foot in front of the other.

"At the time, I know James was thinking, 'Well maybe I can fight again.' But there was no concern on my part about trying to train him to fight," John Russell recalled. "I just wanted to help him stay alive. The goal was just to get some weight off him, because I knew he was going to die if he didn't lose weight. So I took him to the park that first morning, and I said, 'We're going to walk a little bit, then we'll run some.' That was the plan: walk, run, walk, run. Well, when we started out, James was so bad and so overweight that there was no running, none at all. I thought he was such a good athlete that he could handle it, but he couldn't."

There is a perverse game enjoyed by those with a particularly skewed sense of humor. It's called "Dead or Alive," and the ground rules are morbidly simple: A celebrity (more typically, a celebrity whose fame has dissolved into a blur) is named, and the players must respond with one of two words: dead or alive. It sounds easier than it is, for there exists a vast and heavily populated realm of actors, musicians, athletes, politicians—some lifelong B-listers, others A-listers who fell from grace—who for one reason or another have faded from the public consciousness. They are linked by their passage into anonymity or outright obscurity, and, often, by hazy reports of failing health. So it was that Buster Douglas seemed to disappear in 1990, resurfacing only briefly and sadly a few years later. Most people, if they think about Douglas at all, presume his boxing career ended with the loss to Holyfield; they wonder, not unreasonably, given his sorry physical condition, if his life ended shortly thereafter.

It did not. There was a second career, or at least a second phase, and this, as much as anything, saved his life. Walking evolved into jogging; jogging became running. The weight came off in heaps. As Douglas's health improved he became less reluctant to share his aspirations, and though Russell remained skeptical, he saw no harm in supporting his friend's desire to get back in the gym. They worked out at the Fitness Trend, the same Columbus Gym where Douglas had trained prior to the Tyson fight, only now they trained during off hours, early in the morning or late at night, when the gym was essentially empty. Sometimes Bill Douglas would join them. Buster felt comfortable in this setting, working the heavy bag, speed bag, skipping rope. Time went by and eventually they began talking about stepping into the ring against a live opponent. Nothing too serious, just a few rounds of sparring, a chance to see if there was anything left in the tank.

"I'll never forget it," said Russell. "I couldn't even get James's cup on him. It wouldn't fit. He was so fat I could hardly get his head-gear on. He was still big as hell, probably three hundred pounds, but he sparred. We let him go a couple rounds, and I saw that he still had his hand skills. I couldn't believe it. *Jesus, this guy can still fight.*"

On February 20, 1995, Douglas went public with plans to resurrect his boxing career. Though he wouldn't say exactly how much he weighed at the time, Douglas told reporters that he had crossed (in a good way) the three-hundred-pound threshold. He was training every day; having weaned himself from daily insulin injections, he now controlled his diabetes through diet and exercise. Doubters naturally wondered why Douglas would entertain the possibility of a comeback. It was widely known that he did not need the money. He had invested wisely; by the admittedly loose standards of heavyweight champions, he had been virtually parsimonious. Yes, there was the home on Marco Island and the Porsche convertible, but compared to the mansions, cars, jewelry, and exotic animals Tyson would famously accumulate, these seemed modest accoutrements. Equally well known was Douglas's distaste for the sport that had made him wealthy. He had a wife and three children now. He had business interests. His health was on the mend. Why risk all of that?

"I was at the top of the boxing world, fulfilling a dream, with all these plans of how I wanted to do things and how I wanted it to end," Douglas explained. "And then it didn't end that way."

Every comeback needs a hook, and Douglas seized on the obvious: a return engagement with Tyson. This was problematic, given Tyson's address at the time, but since the former champ was scheduled to be released from prison in a few months, there was no harm in chatting up a possible rematch, say, one year down the road. In the meantime, if all went according to plan, Douglas would remain in the gym, cutting weight and sharpening his skills.

As it happened, nearly a year and a half would pass before Douglas returned to the ring, and neither the opponent nor the circumstances would resemble anything close to championship caliber, but that was almost beside the point. It was the journey that mattered, and this one would take some time and effort.

When Russell began working with Hector Camacho, another former champion whose best days were behind him, the training schedule took him to Orlando, Florida. Russell did not want to abandon Douglas, for their arrangement was rooted in friendship more than business, but this was his life and his work. Russell invited Douglas to join him in Orlando, figuring one of two things would happen: He'd either decline the invitation and put aside the dream of fighting, or he'd accept and benefit from a change in locale and proximity to a fighter who was apparently serious about getting back in the fight game. Camacho was a flamboyant lightweight who, although only thirty-three years of age, was well past his prime. But he could still sell a few tickets, and there was sufficient money attached to his name to establish a solid and professional training camp. Whether Douglas was serious enough about his own venture to accept the offer was debatable.

"I thought he would say, 'No way,'" Russell remembered. "But he didn't even hesitate. He was ready."

Nor did Douglas balk in the spring of 1996, when Russell suggested they move there training camp to the mountains of North Carolina. They went there together, Camacho and Douglas (along with Russell, Bill Douglas, and a small group of supporting staff), renting three houses at a mountainside ski resort not far from Asheville. Douglas, smart and deadpan, got a kick out of the chatty and hyperactive Camacho. Training runs at nearly five thousand feet seared his lungs and left him doubled over, gasping for breath, but they served a purpose. Within six weeks Douglas had achieved a level of fitness he hadn't known since 1990. It was time, Douglas decided, to test himself in a real fight.

His "debut," appropriately enough, came on the undercard of a fight between Camacho and Roberto Duran (combined ages: seventy-nine), against a Chicago club fighter named Tony LaRosa. If this seemed on the surface to be a precipitous fall for a heavyweight champion—from $24 million headliner to $100,000 opening act—well, Douglas didn't really care. He had to start somewhere, so why not here, against an eminently beatable opponent? LaRosa had spent most of his professional career as a cruiserweight and light heavyweight, and not a particularly distinguished one at that. Against Douglas he would be fighting as a heavyweight for only the second time in his career; however, neither inexperience nor physical stature (he stood only five foot nine) guaranteed that LaRosa would be an easy conquest. Six years is an eternity in the life of a professional athlete, and in Douglas's case the natural withering effects of time had been compounded by serious health issues. Regardless of the quality of the opponent, the boxing ring was a dangerous place for Douglas, a fact largely ignored by the fighter himself, but not by those closest to him.

"I was happy he was healthy and in shape," said Bertha Douglas. "But I was nervous, because I knew for certain that James was not the same person that he had been before. The fact that he was older didn't really bother me. I was just really concerned about the diabetes. Physically, I knew he had changed, and James knew it, too. But he had always been smart when it came to his boxing career. He didn't fight a hundred and fifty times. He only had forty or fifty fights."

It's fair to say that Douglas had always been at the upper end of the boxing curve in terms of general cognitive ability and, especially, thoughtful introspection. He was, in other words, a smart guy with a good heart, qualities that had not been diminished through repeated battering in the ring. On some level it was pure folly for him to risk so much at this point in his life. The slurred speech, reduced coordination, tremors, and confusion symptomatic of pugilistic dementia—a disorder that has ravaged countless boxers who stayed too long in the game (Floyd Patterson, Joe Louis, and the Quarry Brothers, Mike and Jerry, among them)—were altogether absent in Douglas. He was the antithesis of the punch-drunk boxer. A reporter once said to Douglas, after a particularly insightful observation, "You don't act like most fighters. You have a very sensitive view of your life."

To which Douglas replied, "Could be my problem, huh?"

That depends on the circumstances. Certainly, in the boxing ring instinct is more valuable than sensitivity. It helps not to think too much.

Douglas need not have revisited any of this, but something told him there was work still to be done. He'd shed nearly 150 pounds since being hospitalized, and now, for reasons even he could not quite articulate—pride, and curiosity, perhaps—the ring pulled him back. But sitting in his dressing room on the night of June 22, 1996, as Russell wrapped his hands, Douglas felt a surge of anxiety. He wondered whether he'd made a colossal mistake. As he walked to the ring with his father and trainer and heard the buzz of the crowd, saw the glimmer of lights, the nervousness became nearly overwhelming.

"What an experience that was," Russell recalled. "It was sort of like we never left, but also like we were just starting out. Like it was all brand-new. We were out there in the tunnel, waiting to go, and there were a lot of people. It was close to a sellout. Donald Trump was there, Shaquille O'Neal. It seemed like everybody still loved Buster. But as we were coming out of the tunnel, I turned around and said something to James, and when I looked up at him, I could see it in his eyes, like, 'What have I gotten myself into?'"

Only two words, however, passed through Douglas's lips: "Oh, shit."

Russell tried to calm the fighter. "No, man, you're all right. We're going to take care of business."

Douglas shook his head, smiled warily. *Whew. Now I remember.*

Russell again offered reassurance.

"You're in great shape, James. It's okay." The trainer looked out at the arena. "This is beautiful."

Bill Douglas, too, tried to calm his son, promising him that everything would be fine. And indeed it was, although the fight was not without its difficult moments. Despite giving up more than seven inches to his opponent, LaRosa was fearlessly (and perhaps foolishly) aggressive.

"You all right?" Russell asked Douglas after the first round. "Everything good?"

Douglas nodded. "One thing's for sure: I know I'm in a fight."

Although his determination and energy got Douglas's attention ("He hit me pretty good, that little fucker"), LaRosa was simply too small and inexperienced (and not sufficiently skilled) to compete against Douglas. At 244 pounds, Buster was actually two pounds lighter than he'd been for the Holyfield fight, and although it took some time to shake off the ring rust, he displayed enough of his old prowess—the sharp jab and elegant footwork—to make the fight seem like a legitimate attempt at a comeback and not merely a geriatric sideshow.

Douglas's best moments came in the third round, when a series of combinations compelled LaRosa to drop to one knee. The respite ultimately proved insufficient. With a gash across the bridge of his nose and the rest of his face a mass of cuts and welts, LaRosa was examined between the third and fourth rounds. On the advice of two ringside physicians, referee Wayne Hedgepath stopped the fight and declared Douglas the winner by technical knockout.

Appearances to the contrary notwithstanding, LaRosa insisted afterward that Douglas's punches lacked effectiveness: "He didn't hurt me. He didn't hit me hard at all." Then the club fighter excused himself. "I have to get going. My nose is all busted up."

Douglas was more gracious, offering praise for LaRosa's pluck and punching power. As testament to those characteristics, Douglas held an ice pack against his eye. Standing next to him, patting his son proudly on the back, was Bill Douglas.

"Back in 1981 I told people I had a champ," the father said. "And everybody laughed at me. Now I've heard the laughter again. Look out."

In another corner of the dressing room sat John Russell, who hung his head and wept at the enormity of his friend's accomplishment.

"The guy almost died," Russell would later explain. "I know what he went through, mentally and physically, after the Tyson fight. Especially mentally. What that kid went through . . ." Russell's voice trailed off. "There's no comparison between how proud I was the first time and the second time. Not that I wasn't proud of him when he beat Tyson, but there's just no comparison between that and how proud I was when he got his life back. I mean, this guy should be dead."

Nearly seven months passed before Douglas fought again, and though he was significantly heavier (261 pounds) and less impressive than he had been against LaRosa, the result—a ten-round decision over Rocky Pepeli—was enough to sustain interest in his comeback. To ensure a higher level of fitness, and to fuel the publicity machine, Douglas then embarked on a more rigorous campaign, fighting four times in the next six months. It was the type of hectic schedule more commonly embraced by younger, less established fighters, but it seemed to work for Douglas, who with the backing of promoter Bob Arum and Top Rank took to barnstorming with surprising ease. Not one of the victories was achieved at the expense of a highly ranked opponent. Indeed, history will not look back with anything other than a quizzical glance at the likes of Louis "the Facelifter" Monaco (an uninspiring 6-6-2 when he met Douglas in May of 1997) or 272-pound Brian Scott (a sixth-round knockout victim in March). They served a purpose, though, permitting Douglas to hone the skills that had once made him the heavyweight champion and to fight the never-ending battle of the bulge. (Admittedly, progress came in fits and starts. Monaco, for example, knocked Douglas cold with a punch after the bell ended the first round of their bout; Douglas was unable to continue, and was therefore awarded the victory by disqualification.) By the time Douglas fought Quinn Navarre on July 13, in Biloxi, Mississippi, he had slimmed down to 235 pounds, just three and a half pounds more than he weighed for the Tyson fight.

A rematch with Tyson had become Douglas's grail, primarily because Tyson, since emerging from prison, had once again come to define, if not dominate, the heavyweight division. But there were obstacles to a rematch, most of which pertained to the twin issues of money and ranking. Buster's second choice was Holyfield, but since Holyfield and Tyson were busy tangling with each other (they fought in November 1996 and June 1997), Douglas had no choice but to look for other opponents. There was talk of a fight with Roy Jones Jr. and with Lennox Lewis. Either of those opponents would have lent an air of credibility to Douglas's comeback; both deals, however, fell apart at the negotiating table. Time passed, which wasn't a good thing for Douglas, who, after all, wasn't getting any younger. Months went by without a fight. Douglas, who had been training in Akron, went home to Columbus. He visited the gym with less regularity. Predictably, he ballooned.

On June 25, 1998, at Foxwoods Resort and Casino, Douglas met 234½-pound Lou Savarese for the vacant International Boxing Association heavyweight title. Douglas weighed in at 242 pounds, a deceptive figure considering that he'd been far bigger just a few weeks prior to the fight. He'd lost a lot of weight in a short time, and the struggle had left him weakened and sick (he suffered from a sinus infection prior to the fight). Russell thought about postponing the bout, but figured even in his compromised condition Douglas could handle Savarese. He was wrong.

"I probably shouldn't have let him fight," Russell said. "But I thought Savarese wasn't much and wouldn't be a problem. But the guy was ready. He got himself in tremendous shape, and the result speaks for itself."

Although his overall record was impressive, the twenty-eight-year-old Savarese had defeated few opponents of any merit, and in fact had lost two of his three previous fights. Against Douglas he seemed to have been reborn. He presented a stark contrast to his opponent; his skin stretched taut across a muscular frame. With a flap of flesh hanging like an apron across his midsection (the result of having cut weight so quickly), and the hollow-eyed countenance of a man who hasn't slept well, Douglas looked to be in trouble before he even entered the ring. Indeed, shortly after the opening bell, Douglas walked into a right hand that buckled his knees and sent him to the canvas.

This time, at least, no one could accuse him of quitting. If he was plodding and ineffective, every inch the fighter on the precipice of middle age, Douglas nevertheless demonstrated uncommon heart, particularly for one whose heart had so often been questioned. He rose at the count of four and tried to gather himself, holding his opponent at bay with a few lazy jabs. Savarese, who had studied Douglas in great depth and knew his weaknesses, circled patiently, waiting for another opening. It came soon enough, and Savarese seized the opportunity, driving Douglas into the canvas a second time with a solid right to the side of the head. Douglas struggled to his feet again, only to be smothered instantly by his stronger, younger opponent. Savarese unleashed a torrent of blows to Douglas's face and head, until the former champion, with his hands dangling helplessly, plunged facefirst to the ring floor.

Ordinarily this might have signaled an automatic end to the proceedings, three knockdowns in one round typically resulting in an immediate stoppage by the referee. The three-knockdown rule, however, had been waived for the evening (it is inapplicable in IBA title fights), meaning Douglas had the option, if not the requirement, to come back for more. As Savarese leaped into the air in premature celebration, Douglas somehow emerged from the fog once again. He staggered to his feet as referee Steve Smoger steered Savarese to a neutral corner. A bit befuddled but prepared to finish the job, Savarese did as he was instructed, only to witness Douglas wobble and fall once more, without another punch being thrown. By this time Smoger had seen enough and stopped the fight. Officially, the carnage ended at 2:34 of the first round.

Just like that, the comeback of Buster Douglas came to a stop.

"Buster gained the weight and I got it off him, but we did it too quick," Russell said. "I'll take the blame for that."

Douglas was quick to wrest that responsibility from the trainer, saying, simply, and with only a hint of regret, "I fucked it up."

There would be two more fights, and though each ended with Douglas winning on a first-round knockout, neither bout did much to advance the argument that there was still something left in the tank. This had less to do with Douglas's expanding girth (he weighed 253½ pounds for the first fight and 258 for the second) than it did with the declining quality of his opponents, and the increasingly remote outposts where he fought. Warren Williams was a pedestrian 12-8-1 on the December night he lost to Douglas in Boise, Idaho. And then there was the spectacularly ineffective, yet admirably irrepressible Andre Crowder, who had won only eight of sixty-one fights prior to meeting Douglas on February 19, 1999, in Burlington, Iowa. Douglas swiftly and predictably dispatched Crowder. The fight was stopped at 1:11 of the first round, raising Douglas's record to 38–6–1.

And that is where it would remain. Over the next several months Douglas slipped quietly away from the sport of boxing. Out of necessity and preference, more time was devoted to his personal life. Douglas had lost a second brother to a violent death in December 1998. According to police reports, Robert Douglas, thirty-five, was fatally shot after becoming involved in an altercation with two men in the parking lot of a Columbus Laundromat.

"The streets are mean," Douglas said in the fall of 2005, while standing on those very streets. "But there ain't nothing but cowards out there, anyway. Everybody's got a gun. There aren't any real men out there. That's what I found out. It doesn't matter how big you are, or how strong you are. It just doesn't matter."

Even as Douglas drifted from boxing there was talk of a rematch with Tyson; again, this was complicated both by Tyson's lack of availability (he was incarcerated a second time in the spring of 1999) and a significant disagreement between the Tyson and Douglas camps regarding an equitable division of the purse. According to John Russell, who by this time was handling negotiations for Douglas (the fighter's contract with Johnson had expired), Tyson's promoter, Dan Goossen, initially offered Douglas only $750,000. Tyson, meanwhile, would receive approximately $10 million.

Russell found the terms unacceptable.

"If they weren't going to make it very attractive for James, I wasn't interested in doing it," said Russell. "I told them, 'Look, Tyson goes to bed every night, and wakes up every morning, knowing that Buster kicked the shit out of him. If I remember right—and I think I do—in 1990, I'm almost sure that was Tyson on his knees in front of me, trying to find his mouthpiece. I don't think that was Buster. And now you want to give Tyson $10 million, and give us $750,000? Go fuck yourself!'"

Douglas had plenty to keep him busy: three sons; business interests; a sprawling, hundred-acre homestead known as Quick Jab
Ranch, located in rural Licking County, not far from Columbus; and,
most pressing of all, a father in failing health. Bill Douglas had been
diagnosed with colon cancer in early 1999 (though he had been ill
for much longer), and James soon became his constant companion and
caretaker. Father and son had grown closer during Buster's comeback,
and whatever tension might have remained, by all accounts it melted
away in the last months of Bill's life.

"Once James's father got back in the corner with him, their relationship was really nice," said Bertha Douglas. "They had a great last
few years together."

Bruce Trampler was involved in the promotion of the Douglas-
Savarese fight. That was the last time he saw Bill Douglas.

"He had kind of an ashen, gray pallor," Trampler recalled. "I
knew he was sick, but I didn't know the degree of it. Even though
James got whacked out that night, you could tell Bill was a proud
papa. And that was his boy. I was glad to see they had some kind of
closure at the end."

In some odd way, though, it was reassuring to know that not even
cancer could take the sting out of the old man. He remained hard to
the core, true to his nature, until the very end. Not everyone finds religion in their waning days; not everyone is overcome with sweetness
or melancholia. Dynamite, on his deathbed, suffered fools with no
more patience than he had when he was younger. Russell likes to tell
the story of a man who visited Bill near the end, when he'd shrunk
to less than a hundred pounds and required hospice care to get
through the day. The visitor was not a close friend of Bill's; the two
hadn't even spoken in some time. Why, Bill wondered, was the guy
coming around now, when he felt like shit?

"Get that guy out of here," Bill grumbled. "Asshole . . ."

Friends were a different story. Russell last saw Bill Douglas in the
final week of his life. He'd heard that Dynamite was gravely ill and
wanted to say goodbye, but before leaving Akron he called James, just
to make sure a visit would be appropriate . . . or even welcome. Sure,
James told the trainer. He'd like that. So Russell drove to Columbus
and spent the day with Buster and Bill. Russell was so shaken by

Bill's frail appearance that he nearly fainted when he first walked into the house. But he quickly found that whatever else the disease might have taken, it hadn't robbed Dynamite of his spirit.

"He was amazing," Russell recalled. "Five days before he died he was telling Buster to go out and play the numbers for him. It was unbelievable. You never would have known he was sick. I mean, he looked awful, but he wasn't going to say he was in pain or feel sorry for himself. He'd just say, 'I'm fine.' I was amazed."

Knowing this was probably the last time he'd ever see Bill, Russell wasn't quite sure how to excuse himself at the end of the day. He waited until they were alone, just the two of them, Russell standing in the middle of the room, Dynamite resting on the sofa. There was an awkward silence as Russell fumbled for the right words.

"I'll see you later, Billy," he finally said, knowing it wasn't true.

Bill held up a bony hand. "No, wait."

Russell walked to the couch, took Bill's hand in his.

"You get that Tyson fight for Buster again, okay?" Bill said.

Russell laughed.

"I mean it. And don't let them bullshit you either, John."

"Okay, Bill."

Dynamite pulled him closer, until their faces were an inch apart. He squeezed Russell's hand and whispered, just in case anyone might be within earshot.

"Thanks for taking care of my son."

Five days later, on October 7, 1999, Bill Douglas passed away at his home. He had been so weak the previous night that he'd been unable to walk from the living room to his bed, so James had tried to pick him up and carry him. Bill had responded by smacking his son's hand away. "I'm all right," he said. "I got it."

"That was Billy," Russell said. "The guy lived by the sword and shield. He was a gladiator."

By the time Bill died, James Douglas was thirty-nine years old and many months removed from serious training. There would be no more fighting in his future, although periodically he'd talk about making a comeback, getting another shot at Tyson or Holyfield. Those closest to him would usually just nod in agreement and wait for the urge to pass. If he persisted, they would try to talk some sense into him. Maybe he listened. Maybe he didn't. It was hard to tell sometimes with Buster. But this much is certain: He never took another punch.

"I said, 'James, if you're coming back, you're coming back without me,'" Russell said. "The fact is, I love the guy, I'd do anything for him, but I knew it was over. And I don't think he would have come back without me. They could have said, at that time, 'We'll give you ten million to fight Tyson,' and I would have said no. I wasn't going to let him end up like some of those guys. You know, the guys who are walking on their heels."

I'm going to go down as probably one of the most outstanding fighters—not just heavyweights, but one of the most outstanding fighters—since the beginning of this sport.

—Mike Tyson

I'm working on a book right now called Boxing's Greatest Fighters, *and [Tyson] is in it. I have him at number one hundred. And I had to shoehorn him in.*

—Bert Sugar

Athletes in general, and boxers in particular, are notorious for outstaying their welcome, plying their trade even when common sense dictates that it is time to move on. And so, as often as not, we are left with juxtaposed images of the fighter as champion and chump; a pure and exuberant youth one moment, an aging mercenary the next. The drop is rarely that sudden or precipitous, of course. Careers play out in undulating fashion, rising and falling over time, until the curve finally begins to flatten and never rises again.

Any attempt to evaluate or analyze the career of Mike Tyson is muddied by the static of his personal life—a hundred different episodes that, superficially at least, had nothing to do with boxing, except to the extent that they subverted his ability to perform in the ring. Not that the responsibility for this rests anywhere but with Tyson himself, a fact he readily acknowledges. While he believes that history will regard him as one of boxing's most accomplished practitioners, Tyson also realizes that he is destined to be viewed as something of a poster child for opportunity squandered. If that seems contradictory, well, it really isn't. This is a man who earned approximately $400 million during his career, yet somehow wound up filing for bankruptcy; a fighter who, for a time, was brilliant in the ring, winning his first thirty-seven bouts in a span of less than four and a half years, before compiling a pedestrian record of 13–6 (with two no contests) over the next sixteen years.

"Mike had as good a run as any heavyweight ever had, including Rocky Marciano," argued Kevin Rooney. "Some people try to say—and they have a little bit of a point—'Oh, the fighters of the eighties weren't as good as the fighters in the fifties.' Well, maybe, maybe not. But whoever you put in front of Mike, he knocked them out. My goal was for Mike to be 100–0. I wanted him to break Marciano's record, and that was definitely within his reach."

Tyson knows boxing as well as well as any athlete has ever known his sport; he knows what he might have accomplished and the standard against which he will be measured: not merely the accomplishments of fighters such as Marciano and Ali, but of Tyson himself. It is almost as if he had two careers: pre-Douglas and post-Douglas (one might argue that an equally significant line of demarcation would be "pre–Don King" and "post–Don King," or "pre-Catskill" and "post-Catskill"), and the second career fell woefully short of delivering on the promise of the first.

"I fucked my whole career over," Tyson said during in an interview in January 2006. In his voice was more than a hint of resignation. Not regret, really, but something more like cold acceptance. "But you know," he continued, "I've come to grips with that. I've come to grips with who I am and what I had happen to me and what I brought on to myself. And I'm content with myself."

It's an interesting adjective, "content," and one that should not be considered interchangeable with "happy." Whether either word applies to Tyson is debatable. Tom Patti knows the fighter as well as anyone, and even he considers Tyson at times to be complex to the point of impenetrability.

"Listen, do you have complete, utter happiness in your life?" Patti said. "To be more philosophical about it, to me, happiness is a fleeting moment of enjoyment. And after that you've got life struggles, issues, your own salvation . . . Mike has definitely grown in so many capacities as a human being, but he definitely remains challenged to find his peace and his happiness."

Tyson himself put it more succinctly: "My life is pretty fucked up." This was said with a hearty laugh, as if Tyson wanted the listener to understand that no one gets the joke more than Tyson himself. And, indeed, it's difficult to look at his life and career and not see it as some sort of darkly comic epic. A tragedy with a laugh track, if there is such a thing. But there is legitimate pain, too, even if Tyson himself is reluctant to acknowledge it or embrace it or share it with anyone else.

"Mike remembers being a hero, and he remembers being loved, and he has none of that right now," said Steve Lott. "That bothers him every time he goes to sleep at night. He remembers going to sleep in 1985, '86, '87, and he was sleeping like a baby. Now, in his mind, just the thought of having to exist every day is painful. He hides it very well. One thing Cus taught him was, 'Don't let your opponent know what you're thinking.' His opponent now is the public. They can't see what he's thinking. But any human being examining the situation, putting themselves in his position for a moment, just for a moment . . . you've gotta have tremendous pain. Knowing you were loved and adored, and now being hated and despised and laughed at. *Laughed at!* The brunt of every joke in the world!"

Lott then launched into a diatribe about common sense and reputation and the importance of surrounding oneself with the right people. In his eyes, as in the eyes of so many left in Tyson's wake, the collapse of Mike Tyson is due largely to the fighter's neediness, his tendency to be easily manipulated by those who may not have his best interests at heart. As an example, Lott pointed to the infamous tattoo that appeared on Tyson's face in 2003, on the eve of a fight with Clifford Etienne, a stark and swirling bit of artwork around his left eye and cheekbone that, for no particular reason, suggested a link to the *moko* (full-face tattoos) traditionally worn by warriors in the Maori culture.

"It doesn't signify basically anything," Tyson told ESPN's Jeremy Schapp. "It's a New Zealand tattoo. I just feel like I wanted to tattoo my face. I didn't like the way it looked. I wanted to change it."

New Zealanders, the Maori in particular, were not flattered by this endorsement. Others were simply confounded.

"The thinking process around Mike . . . ," Lott said, his voice trailing off in disbelief. "The tattoo on his face? What brilliant thought process went into that? *Hey, Mike, you'd be cool with that tattoo on your face!* Here's the opposite side of the coin: In '86, Mike was going to do an interview with one of the morning [network television] shows. He gets up early, wears a sweater and a big chain. A gold chain. I called him over before he went on, and I said, 'Give me the chain.' Mike said, 'Fine.' Afterward he says, 'Why'd you take the chain?' I said, 'When people watch the interview, I want them to see you and the sweater, not the chain. I want them to get a picture of what you are like. The chain gives them a different image. You understand?' He thanked me. See, Mike used to demand that I make him look good."

The contradiction in Lott's observation is that it simultaneously endorses and criticizes Tyson's neediness; it insinuates that the fighter is incapable of making decisions for himself or accepting responsibility for his actions, and therefore success or failure is determined almost exclusively by the quality of the people he employs and befriends. While it may indeed be true that Tyson received better guidance and advice from the original Team Tyson than he did from any of his subsequent entourages, it is also true that, for better or worse, he *chose* to make changes in his life.

Granted, many of those choices have cost Tyson dearly, a fact he recognizes and acknowledges, albeit only in his more reflective moments. One of those occurred on June 8, 2002, in Memphis, Tennessee, the night Tyson was knocked out in the eighth round of a heavyweight championship fight against Lennox Lewis.

Their meeting, much anticipated and heavily funded, had been years in development, owing largely to the personal, legal, and financial difficulties faced by Tyson. Indeed, the period between June 28, 1997 (when Tyson was disqualified against Evander Holyfield), and the Lewis fight, nearly five years later, was among the most tumultuous of Tyson's career, chockablock with images and incidents of a profoundly unsettling nature, a half decade of spectacularly manic behavior, punctuated by childish tantrums, profanity-laced outbursts, misogynistic posturing, assaults, lawsuits . . . and the occasional foray into the ring. It was during this time that Tyson's public persona sank to depths previously unfathomed.

Even when incarcerated, Tyson had remained, in some corners anyway, a character capable of engendering some sympathy. This, after all, was a man who courted his second wife, Monica Turner, while serving time in prison on a rape conviction.

With each successive public meltdown, however, disdain for Tyson mounted and indulgence withered, a process facilitated in part by the obvious erosion of the fighter's skills. The natural inclination to forgive or indulge Tyson's "eccentricities" diminished more or less in direct proportion to his stature as a boxer. Between June 28, 1997, and October 23, 1999, Tyson fought just once, and yet his name continued to appear in the headlines of newspapers around the world with alarming regularity, above stories chronicling misadventures of one sort or another. Herewith, culled from an Associated Press timeline, a sampling of news items from that period in Tyson's life:

October 29, 1997—Tyson breaks a rib and punctures a lung when he loses control of his motorcycle on a Connecticut highway.

March 5, 1998—Tyson files a $100 million lawsuit in U.S. District Court in New York against promoter Don King.

March 9, 1998—Tyson sues former managers Rory Holloway and John Horne, claiming they betrayed him by facilitating a deal that made King the former champ's exclusive promoter.

March 9, 1998—Sherry Cole and Chevelle Butts file a $22 million lawsuit against Tyson, claiming he verbally and physically abused them at a Washington, D.C., restaurant after his sexual advances were rebuffed.

July 16, 1998—The 2nd U.S. Circuit Court of Appeals reinstates a $4.4 million award that a jury decided Tyson owes former trainer Kevin Rooney.

July 29, 1998—Appearing before the New Jersey Athletic Control Board in an attempt to regain his boxing license. Tyson chokes back tears as he apologizes for biting Evander Holyfield. At the conclusion of his appearance, however, Tyson loses his temper and begins cursing in front of regulators after being continually questioned about the Holyfield incident.

August 31, 1998—Tyson's bodyguards prevent him from attacking another motorist following a minor auto accident in Gaithersburg, Maryland.

September 2, 1998—Richard Hardick files an assault charge against Tyson, claiming he was kicked in the groin by the fighter after Hardick's car struck a Mercedes driven by Tyson's wife, Monica, on August 31.

September 3, 1998—Abmielec Saucedo files a complaint against Tyson, claiming Tyson struck him as Saucedo conversed with another driver following the accident of August 31.

October 13, 1998—A psychiatric report on Tyson is released. The report states that Tyson is depressed and lacks self-esteem but he is mentally fit to return to the sport of boxing. Doctors and psychiatrists who evaluated the fighter over a period of five days conclude that Tyson is unlikely to "snap" again, as he did when he bit Holyfield.

October 19, 1998—The Nevada Athletic Commission votes 4–1 to restore Tyson's boxing license.

December 1, 1998—Tyson pleads no contest to misdemeanor assault charges stemming from the August 31 auto accident in Maryland.

January 16, 1999—Fighting for the first time in nineteen months, Tyson posts a fifth-round knockout of Francois Botha. It is only Tyson's seventh fight in eight years, and the rust is apparent: at the end of four rounds, Tyson trailed on the cards of all three judges.

February 5, 1999—Tyson is sentenced to two concurrent two-year sentences on the assault charges of the previous summer. A judge suspends all but one year of jail time. Tyson is also fined $5,000 and sentenced to two years' probation following his release.

March 5, 1999—Tyson is ordered to serve an extra sixty days in a Montgomery County, Maryland, jail for violating terms of his probation following a 1992 rape conviction.

May 24, 1999—Tyson is released from jail after serving three and a half months for assault.

Five months after his release from jail, Tyson returned to the ring against unheralded Orlin Norris at the MGM Grand in Las Vegas. The fight lasted three minutes and ended in controversy, with Tyson flooring Norris after the bell signaling the end of the first round. Norris injured his knee in the fall and was unable to continue, resulting in the fight being declared no contest. A second-round knockout of Julius Francis followed in January of 2000, and five months later, on June 24, in Glasgow, Scotland, in a performance at once infuriating and mesmerizing, Tyson knocked out Lou Savarese in the first round. This was Tyson at his most perplexing, raining furious and crippling blows on Savarese, only to ruin (or accentuate, depending on your point of view) the evening by failing to heed the directive of referee John Coyle, who, having seen enough, stepped in between the two fighters thirty-eight seconds into the fight and shouted, "Stop boxing!"

Savarese, knocked silly with the very first punch thrown by Tyson, was more than willing to oblige; Tyson was not. Riled apparently to the point of sensory deprivation, Tyson ignored both the words and the presence of the referee, and continued to flail at Savarese. One of the punches, a sweeping left hook, tagged Coyle, sending the referee to the canvas. Coyle quickly scrambled to his feet, and this time Tyson got the message. The fight was over. He was fortunate to avoid disqualification, but the rage that had fueled his performance continued unabated in the moments afterward, when Tyson was interviewed on camera by Showtime's Jim Gray, and asked about a potential date with Lewis:

"Lennox Lewis, I'm coming for you!" Tyson proclaimed. "I'm the best ever. I'm the most brutal and vicious and most ruthless champion there's ever been. There's no one who can stop me. Lennox is a conqueror? No, I'm Alexander! He's no Alexander! I'm the best ever. There's never been anybody as ruthless. I'm Sonny Liston, I'm Jack Dempsey. There's no one like me . . . There's no one that can match me! My style is impetuous, my defense is impregnable, and I'm just ferocious! I want your heart, I want to eat his children. Praise be to Allah!"

Afterward, Tyson's camp dismissed the outburst as the residual effect of a fight that failed to demand enough of the former champion; in short, the argument went, there were copious amounts of anger and adrenaline left in the tank. It wasn't an implausible excuse, really: Boxers, who face critical damage, are required to work themselves into a lather before entering the ring. It's a survival mechanism, and one that isn't easily shut down on a moment's notice. Tyson's behavior, however, was particularly disconcerting, not merely because it was so overtly grotesque, but because of the fighter's history. Watching Tyson sauntering about the ring, clubbing the referee, and threatening to eat the offspring of another fighter (who, by the way, did not have any children), one couldn't help but wonder, *He might just do it.*

Certainly his comments and general lack of decorum were viewed with great displeasure in the United Kingdom, where Tyson was once held in the highest regard.

"Boxing is a sport; [Tyson] is a devil," offered Barry McGuigan, the former Irish champion who served as a television analyst for the fight. "To push a referee out of the way to get past him and inflict further pain on an already defeated opponent is disgraceful."

In apparent agreement with that sentiment was the British Boxing Board of Conduct, which in August fined Tyson $187,500 for misconduct. Two months later, on October 23, 2000, Tyson administered a savage beating to Andrew Golota, who quit after two rounds and was subsequently pelted with garbage as he left the arena in Auburn Hills, Michigan. The fight, hardly memorable in the first place, was declared no contest (and thus virtually wiped from the record books) in January, when it was revealed that traces of marijuana had turned up in Tyson's system following a routine postfight drug test. Tyson had refused to submit to a prefight urinalysis, an act that resulted in his being fined $5,000 and suspended for ninety days by the Michigan Board in Control of Athletics.

Over the course of the next year Tyson engaged in fights with Brian Nielsen, who was stopped after six rounds in Copenhagen, on October 13, 2001; Monica Turner (the mother of two of Tyson's children), who sued for divorce on January 18, 2002, citing, among other factors, Tyson's adulterous behavior; and Lennox Lewis, who was doubtless surprised to feel Tyson's teeth sinking into his leg during a ridiculous melee at a press conference to promote an April showdown between the two fighters.

The event, staged January 22, 2002, at the Hudson Theater in New York, began innocently enough, with a video package featuring highlights from the careers of both fighters. Tyson, the challenger, was then introduced. Dressed casually in black, he sauntered onto the stage and stood motionless, arms at his side. Lewis, wearing a suit, was introduced next, but before the champion could get comfortable, Tyson threw his leather cap to the floor and charged across the stage, a move that precipitated one of the more bizarre events in boxing history—which is saying quite a lot. One of Lewis's bodyguards stepped in front of Tyson and absorbed a left hook; Lewis countered with an overhand right to the challenger, and then all hell really broke loose, with some two dozen members of both entourages forming a massive scrum on the stage.

Several minutes passed before order was restored. Lewis appeared relatively unscathed, although he would later claim to have been bitten by Tyson. WBC president Jose Sulaiman fared worse; he was knocked unconscious after hitting his head on a table during the brawl and was later treated at a hospital for a concussion. Tyson, meanwhile, looked like a man in his element, emerging with a trickle of blood along his forehead and a welt on his temple, battle scars that only seemed to energize the fighter. When a member of the audience had the temerity (and perhaps the bad sense) to suggest, rather loudly, that Tyson belonged in a straitjacket rather than a boxing ring, Tyson, standing at the edge of the stage, cupping his genitals with one hand and gesticulating wildly with the other, erupted with one of the more memorable tirades of his career:

"Fuck you, you ho! Come and say it to my face. I'll fuck you in the ass in front of everybody. You bitch . . . Come on, you bitch, you scared coward. You're not man enough to fuck with me. You can't last two minutes in my world, bitch! Look, you're scared now, you ho, scared like a little white pussy . . . scared of the real man. I'll fuck you till you love me—faggot!"

Tyson later attempted to explain his actions as being the result of miscommunication between representatives of the two fighters. His intention was merely to hype the fight with a bit of theatrical posturing.

"My motivation for approaching Lennox was to stage a face-off, which I was told both camps had agreed to," Tyson said. "It was Lennox's bodyguard who panicked and shoved me. Lennox then threw a right. I was here to promote the fight, not be intimidated. I will never be intimidated by anyone, and Lennox will pay in April."

Whether Tyson was misled, as he suggested, or just plain loony (the natural conclusion reached by many in the wake of the incident) was open to debate. Another theory, one that would gain support as he became increasingly self-destructive—both in and out of the ring—was that Tyson had simply lost the will to fight and was looking for an exit strategy.

"If it was planned, then everybody would have known," Steve Lott said of the brawl. "Does that make sense? If you're the manager of Mike Tyson, and someone says, 'We're going to have a mock melee, and Mike is going to come running over and throw punches,' you're going to say, 'Oh, fine, that should be fun! They'll both have absolute control.' No way."

Tyson's penance following the outburst included another hearing before the Nevada State Athletic Commission. On January 30, 2002, in an appearance at once poignant and painful, Tyson, accompanied by his attorney, Bob Faiss, and his advisor, veteran boxing manager and promoter Shelly Finkel, offered contrition in support of his application for a boxing license and vowed to behave better in the future: "You will never see that happening again. I give you my word. I'm not Mother Teresa, but I'm not Charles Manson either." Revealed during the proceedings was Tyson's ongoing struggle to quell his demons through therapy and medication. Since 1998, the fighter had regularly been prescribed antidepressants, most commonly Zoloft, although he often was weaned in the weeks prior to a fight in order to mitigate the drugs' calming effects (which might be useful in daily life, but an impediment in the boxing ring).

Some of this was old news. Tyson had first publicly acknowledged use of antidepressants in 2000, although his explanation hardly proved endearing ("I'm on the Zoloft to keep from killing y'all," he told reporters prior to the Golota fight), and by the end of the three-hour hearing it was clear that the commission, while not unsympathetic, suffered from Tyson fatigue. The five-member board ultimately rejected Tyson's application by a vote of 4–1.

It is, sadly, a measure of the apparent madness of Mike Tyson that a prefight press conference looms larger in the collective consciousness than the fight itself, despite the fact that the fight was not without historical, athletic, and commercial significance (with 1.8 million "buys" it remains the second most popular pay-per-view fight in history, trailing only Tyson-Holyfield II; in terms of total revenue, it is ranked first).

The unlikely venue for Tyson-Lewis was an arena known as the Pyramid in Memphis, representatives of which had landed the fight in a bidding war after Tyson was denied a license in Nevada. Lewis, by this time, was the dominant fighter in the heavyweight division, and he provided boxing fans with a seemingly ideal foil to Tyson. Where Tyson was often crude and obnoxious, Lewis was well-spoken (with a British accent, no less!) and genteel. Born in London, Lewis had moved to Toronto when he was twelve and had gone on to win a gold medal while representing Canada at the 1988 Olympics. In reality, Tyson and Lewis had more in common than appearances might have suggested. Each had used boxing to rise above impoverished surroundings; they had even trained together briefly and sparred as teens. By this point, however, their careers had diverged rather dramatically.

Big (six foot five, 249¼ pounds) and mobile, with a punishing jab—and a huge reach advantage with which to employ that weapon—Lewis was precisely the type of fighter known to give Tyson problems. Even at his peak, Tyson could be flustered and frustrated by a taller opponent, especially one with skill and speed and strength. Lewis, the reigning IBF and WBC champion, possessed all of those characteristics, while Tyson was left with only a smattering of the traits that had once made him unbeatable.

And yet, he fought bravely against Lewis, absorbing a terrific beating for nearly eight rounds. By the time Tyson was counted out by referee Eddie Cotton at 2:25 of the eighth he was bleeding from cuts over both eyes and from his nose. Afterward, in a moment of poignancy, Tyson stood in the ring next to Lewis—a man he had bitten and repeatedly insulted, and whose children he had vowed to consume—while the two answered questions. As the champion spoke, Tyson reached over and delicately brushed away a streak of blood that had begun to dry on Lewis's cheek.

"I'm very Freudian about fighters," said Jim Lampley, part of the broadcasting team for the fight. "I think they're easily psychoanalyzed because they wear so much on the surface. To me, when Mike reached across and wiped that blood off Lennox's cheek, he was paying tribute to the fact that Lennox is everything Mike in his heart of hearts might have desired to be. Lennox is the champion. Lennox is someone who has, most critically, a mother who loves him, and who is with him all the time. You have to figure Mike deeply envies that. A mother who bent her life to get in a position to take care of her son. Lennox has the real title. Lennox has basically saved most, if not all, of his money. Lennox is respectful and dignified in a lot of ways. Lennox has all the things that deep in his heart Mike would love to have . . . and won't have. Lennox is a real fighter who went into the gym, day after day, polished his craft, and got better later in his career, because he honored the sport in a way that Mike would have loved to honor the sport. But he was too fragmented a personality to do that. So Mike was saying, *This is what I would love to have been, but couldn't be.*"

Earlier in their respective careers, when Tyson was fighting regularly on HBO and Lampley was broadcasting his fights, the two had forged a professional relationship that went beyond the merely cordial. It would be a significant stretch to suggest they were friends—a journalistic distance was maintained—but one sensed that Tyson, whose relationship with the media was always tempestuous, had some degree of affection for Lampley, and the feeling was mutual. But as Tyson gravitated away from HBO (and generally fought less), they had rarely spoken. Lampley on several occasions had used his syndicated radio program as a forum for airing criticism of Tyson. In essence, Lampley had implied (and, in some cases, stated outright) that Tyson's career had become a joke, and that Tyson was a fraud, a fighter who had lost the stomach for fighting.

Now, as Lampley walked to Tyson's dressing room for an interview arranged by HBO (which had formed a temporary and unlikely alliance with Showtime in the promotion of the event), he wondered whether Tyson might greet him with animus. Lampley passed through a phalanx of thick-chested men in black suits and bowler hats ("a pretty intimidating scene"), and finally came upon Tyson, who was seated in a chair at the center of the room, holding a small child on his lap.

"He looked up at me and said, 'I know all the shit you've been saying about me on the radio all these years,'" Lampley recalled. "I said, 'Okay, yeah.' And the next thing he said was, 'I've missed you.'

"Now, I know that wasn't personally about me," Lampley continued. "That was about a long time ago . . . What he was saying was, I left the scene in which I had been nurtured and brought to public eminence, and I know I lost something when I left all that behind. At least that was my interpretation. He wasn't saying, I miss you, Jim. He was saying, I miss HBO, I miss the aura I enjoyed when I was at HBO, I miss the trappings that all that implied. I miss being the Mike Tyson who was Mike Tyson before all that other stuff began. Obviously, at that point, he's suing Don King for $100 million, and he knows what's happened to his career, and he can see more clearly the way the business has used him. Then we sat down and had a very cordial interview. He was happy that night, and my judgment was that he was happy because he was pretty sure that . . . it was over. He was done and wouldn't have to go through that charade again. But he underestimated, of course, the degree to which he was imprisoned by financial forces and the agendas of the people around him. He had to keep going."

Tyson earned approximately $20 million for the Lewis bout. Two years later, in June 2004, a settlement was reached in the fighter's dispute with Don King. Terms of the agreement called for King to pay Tyson $14 million. Remarkably, neither of those windfalls did much to alleviate Tyson's financial concerns. The previous summer Tyson had filed for bankruptcy protection, a highly public disclosure that was shocking only if one was unfamiliar with Tyson's prodigious appetite for spending. Court documents filed in support of Tyson's lawsuit against King recounted not only the promoter's allegedly slippery accounting (King, according to Tyson's attorneys, somehow earned more from Tyson's work than did the fighter himself during their partnership), but also served as a handbook for anyone trying to spend more than $100 million in a span of roughly three years. Among the more interesting items in Tyson's ledger were: $4.47 million on automobiles and $411,777 for the care and feeding of "pigeons and cats" (the latter classification including a pair of white Bengal tigers), a figure representing more than twice the amount listed under the heading of "child support."

In an effort to satisfy his creditors (including his second ex-wife, who received $10 million in a divorce settlement; and the IRS, which claimed Tyson owed more than $13 million), Tyson sold off the cars and the mansions and went back to work, although he possessed neither the skill nor the inclination to do the job well. From 2001 through 2005, he fought five times, once per year, an unenthusiastic annual pilgrimage to the ring that invariably failed to fulfill the promise of the publicity that preceded it (the lone exception being the Lewis fight in 2002). A first-round knockout of Etienne proved less revealing than the next bout, in July 2004, when Tyson was knocked out by 9-to-1 underdog Danny Williams of Great Britain. Tyson's camp tried to minimize the impact of that defeat, attributing it largely to a knee injury that limited Tyson's mobility. But it was clear that other factors were involved, namely, a cynical approach to the sport that precluded any purity of purpose, something a thirty-eight-year-old boxer desperately needs.

There would be one more fight, on June 11, 2005, at the MCI Center in Washington, D.C. The opponent was Kevin McBride, a six foot six, 271-pound Irishman whose nickname, "the Clones Colossus," was markedly more impressive than his résumé. Heavy-footed and lantern-jawed, McBride was the type of opponent a younger Tyson might have dispatched in a matter of seconds. But that fighter was long gone, replaced by a wheezing, slugging, tattooed target, a man who fought only because there was nothing else for him to do.

Nevertheless, more than fifteen thousand people showed up at the MCI Center that night, presumably hoping to see one man beat another into submission. And, indeed, if that is what they sought, then their money was well spent. To hype the event, Tyson had tried to muster a little of the old bile in the days prior (of his opponent he had said, "I'll gut him like a fish"), but the threats and taunts that had made Tyson the object of scorn and fascination seemed empty; one sensed in the fighter's demeanor an understanding that he was merely playing a role, and that it had long ago gotten stale.

Regardless, Tyson was no match for McBride. Although in the first few rounds he demonstrated a renewed devotion to movement and hand speed, Tyson eventually grew frustrated with McBride's refusal to yield. The bigger man withstood the early pressure and then began leaning on Tyson and landing punches with relative ease. By the fifth round Tyson had resorted to the sort of dirty tactics that by now had become a hallmark of his career: hitting his opponent below the belt and attempting to drive the thumb of his glove into McBride's eye. In the sixth round Tyson crumbled, both physically and emotionally. He twisted McBride's arm early in the round (an act that recalled one of Tyson's earlier fights, when he rather obviously tried to break the arm of Francois Botha). Then he invoked images of the Holyfield fight by attempting, unsuccessfully, to bite McBride. Next came a head butt . . . and another, the second opening a cut above McBride's left eye. McBride, sensing Tyson's desperation, seemed unfazed by any of this. Referee Joe Cortez deducted two points from Tyson, but chose not to disqualify the fighter. Disinclined to engage, and left with no other viable exit, Tyson simply quit.

Twice, actually.

The first attempt came after a McBride uppercut drove him into the ropes. The two fighters then clinched, and when McBride pressed his weight against Tyson's back, Tyson slid to the canvas. As the fighter sat, motionless, his opponent began to move away. Cortez, surprised by what he was witnessing, stepped in and informed Tyson that he had not been knocked down, and urged him to resume fighting. Tyson rejected the offer, choosing instead to remain seated. Before Tyson could be counted out or disqualified (for inactivity), the round came to an end. When the bell sounded, Tyson pulled himself up and walked slowly to his corner, where he was met by trainer Jeff Fenech. Having seen enough, Fenech, the chief second in the ring, surrendered on behalf of his fighter.

If the sight of the once invincible Tyson, bewildered and broken, sitting impassively on the canvas, refusing to fight, was not sufficient evidence that his career was over, then surely his postfight comments left no doubt.

"I do not have the guts to be in this sport anymore, and I don't want to disrespect the sport that I love by continuing to fight like this," Tyson told Showtime's Jim Gray before leaving the ring. "My heart is not into this anymore. I'm sorry for the fans. I wish I could have done better. I want to move on with my life."

And that was merely the beginning. In the postfight press conference, a remarkable and revealing dialogue with the media that stretched out for more than an hour, Tyson meandered through his life and his psyche.

"Smart too late and old too soon," he said at one point. "This is just my ending."

And it was the end, Tyson assured the audience. If nothing else, this evening had presented irrefutable evidence that the Mike Tyson who once ruled the ring was long gone. And he wasn't coming back.

"My career's over . . . It's been over since 1990," said Tyson, obviously alluding to his encounter with James Douglas. "I'm not interested in fighting no more. I can't beat Father Time. I don't have the desire to do this stuff anymore. I don't want to take anything away from Kevin. He fought a great fight. But we all know his résumé. If I can't beat him, I can't beat Junior Jones."

No disrespect to Jones (a former champion who usually fought at 130 pounds), either, but the point was valid. Somehow Tyson had become merely an opponent, an old man fighting on the fumes of fading glory. At this point he wanted neither sympathy nor adulation; he wanted only for others to respect his decision. When Rock Newman, the promoter of the event, publicly lauded Tyson at the press conference, and encouraged others in the audience to do the same, a standing ovation predictably ensued. Almost, anyway. No sooner had the applause begun than Tyson waved a disapproving hand.

"No, no, no, no . . . Sit down. Sit down, please," he shouted. "People have given me enough applause in my life. When I hear bullshit, I've got to call it. I'm as hard and as cold as they get."

In support of this self-assessment, Tyson added, "I'm not used to sensitivity anymore. When I see people cry when I lose . . . Save your tears. I don't know how to handle people crying any more. I lost my sensitivity like that. Please, you embarrass me when you cry because I don't know what to do when you cry. I don't know what to say . . .

"I'm just Mike," Tyson continued. "I'm a peasant. I'm here to entertain the people. I'm no elite person. At one stage in my life, I had my little jewelry and all my little girlfriends and my big cars and things. At one point, I thought life was about acquiring things. But as I get older . . . life is totally about losing everything. As life goes on, we lose more than we acquire."

A year after the loss to McBride, Tyson had surprised even his most ardent critics by failing to break his retirement vow. But there were bills to be paid and a celebrity status that could not be denied, a combination that resulted in Tyson appearing in the news on at least a semiregular basis. There were reports that he would embark on a career as a star of adult films (denied); or that he would seek fulfillment through missionary work in Rwanda or Bosnia (acknowledged, but, as yet, not attempted). He lived in a modest ranch house in Phoenix but seemed to spend much of his time globetrotting. He talked of establishing a foundation and raising money for a children's hospital.

During an interview in January 2006. Tyson said he didn't miss boxing in the least, didn't even really follow the sport anymore. This hardly made him unique. Professional boxing, by this time, had been pushed to the fringe of the sporting world, its relevance increasingly indistinguishable from that of niche sports like ultimate fighting and even pseudo sports like professional wrestling. Which is not to suggest that boxing lacked talent, intrigue, or marketable personalities, characteristics on display in abundance whenever the likes of Floyd Mayweather, Jermain Taylor, or Oscar De La Hoya stepped into a ring. And yet, if a barometer of success is the extent to which a sport captivates a large and diverse audience, crossing ethnic and socioeconomic boundaries, then it's fair to say that their accomplishments failed to lift boxing out of its doldrums.

The lighter weight classes, as usual, were dominated by Hispanic and Latino fighters, and indeed boxing maintained a devoted following in those communities. The marquee division, however, suffered from a distinct lack of charisma as a progression of immense, leaden heavyweights lumbered out of eastern Europe. The Klitschko brothers (Vitali and Wladimir), Nikolay Valuev (at seven foot three, 330 pounds, the biggest champion in history), Sergei Liakhovich, Oleg Maskaev—all were solid fighters who became champions of one or more of boxing's myriad organizational bodies, and all had the misfortune not only to speak English as a second language, but also to be almost dogged in their pursuit of blandness.

And so, despite their achievements they sank into anonymity, their careers followed by a dwindling audience of boxing fans who, by this time, had few outlets for their passion. Along with the occasional pay-per-view event, they settled mostly for the agate section of the newspaper and late-night bouts on basic cable, and vented their frustration through Internet chatter. Whether anyone was listening, however, seemed questionable.

"Boxing is almost exclusively a Latin sport now," said *Sports Illustrated*'s Richard Hoffer. "That's how it's promoted and marketed, and promoters make no bones about it. It will only be mainstream again to the extent that Latins become mainstream in [American] culture. It's sort of happening now, of course. [Los Angeles] is more Latin than not. Still, [boxing] will not ever again be the national sport it once was."

HBO analyst Larry Merchant, a member of the World Boxing Hall of Fame who has reported lovingly and often eloquently on the sport for more than three decades, took a somewhat less pessimistic view, supporting the notion that the popularity of boxing, more than most sports, has been cyclical in nature, with peaks coinciding with the emergence of a particularly engaging personality, such as Ali or Tyson. But he acknowledged that the current climate is less conducive to the nurturing of such a fighter; moreover, the appearance of one great fighter would not necessarily signal the rebirth of boxing.

"I think it's a sport that's been declining as a mainstream sport for a long time," Merchant said. "It's no longer a part of the social fabric of the country. Once upon a time you didn't have every kid graduating high school, much less college, and boxing was one of the ways out. You could go to Rochester, Minnesota, and find a fight club. There were gyms in every town, and in most cities it was a place where kids went to test their manhood or to get away from influences; it was something in the dreams of youngsters, the dream to be a champion. And I think that's gone, except in some pockets of the Hispanic world.

"So I'm not in denial about the decline of boxing as a mainstream sport, which was once up there with horse racing and baseball. They were the only three [sports] that mattered for a long time. Now, when people say, 'Where are all the heavyweights?' I say, 'There are hundreds of them out there . . . and they're all playing linebacker.' "

It was an indication of boxing's ill health that Tyson continued to serve as the game's most compelling and newsworthy practitioner, even when he wasn't practicing. In the fall of 2006 plans were announced for a worldwide tour in which Tyson would stage a series of exhibition matches. There would be no winners or losers, nothing at stake other than attempting to put on a reasonably entertaining show, nothing promised other than an opportunity to see the former champion "in action," and perhaps even shake his hand and get an autograph. Participants could choose to wear headgear. A portion of the proceeds (tickets for early events, which also included legitimate boxing cards, ranged from $25 to $250; pay-per-view access was available for $29.95) from the tour would be donated to charity; presumably, a percentage would be applied to the task of helping Tyson climb out of debt. "Opponents" would cover a broad spectrum—from Tyson's former sparring partners to boxers and boxing fans from the entertainment industry (Welsh pop star Tom Jones, at sixty-six years of age still apparently in fighting trim, was among the first to claim interest in queuing up for a shot at Iron Mike; whether he was serious or not seemed almost beside the point). Tyson even suggested, with tongue planted loosely in cheek, that he would be willing to fight against a woman.

The news of Tyson's descent into a lower circle of entertainment hell provoked only a modest amount of self-righteous indignation or moralizing, in part, perhaps, because he handled the matter with an unusual degree of poise. He poked fun at himself and the very nature of an exhibition tour, and cheerfully pronounced that the former Mike Tyson—the ear-biting, crotch-grabbing, baby-eating, arm-breaking, invective-spewing menace of the 1990s—was as good as dead.

"It's all fun. I'm not Mike Tyson," he said. "I'm not twenty years old. I'm not going to smash anybody. I'm not going to talk about smashing anybody's brains. You're not going to see that guy no more."

Historian that he is, Tyson surely took comfort in knowing that while his tour might have appeared pitiable or even seamy to the uninitiated, it hardly represented a reinvention of the wheel; indeed, Tyson was merely traveling a path well worn by the likes of Jack Johnson, Joe Louis, Max Baer, and even Jack Dempsey, whose exhibition matches outnumbered his appearances in championship bouts.

Conventional wisdom was that Mike Tyson would be dead by the age of forty, a victim of his own self-destructive tendencies. But here he was, precisely that age, trying, at least halfheartedly, to figure out a way to live the next forty years with some degree of dignity and peace and productivity. To that end, paradoxically, he attempted to shed the grotesque baggage that came with being Mike Tyson while simultaneously trading on the Tyson brand. A certain degree of dexterity and self-deprecation was required, and Tyson, on the surface at least, seemed up to the task.

Still, one couldn't help but wonder what might have been, and what Cus D'Amato might have thought about the degeneration of his prodigy. Aside from Tom Patti, Tyson said he remains close to no one from the Catskill days (nor, for that matter, the Don King days); he returns home once a year or so to visit the grave sites of D'Amato and Camille Ewald (who died in 2001, at the age of ninety-six).

"I go up there when I'm depressed," said Tyson. "When I go through my . . . I don't know . . . judging my whole perspective on my decision making, I guess. I go up there and I talk to those guys. I'm a New Yorker, I'm a city boy, but I'm a Catskill New Yorker, too. I'm a small-town, northern New York guy. That's what I became, really. That's what I am."

The conversation travels in one direction, of course, but Tyson has an idea what D'Amato would say if he could talk to him now.

"Cus had his ego, too, you know?" Tyson said. "He was my trainer. He would probably say, 'You're a great fighter, but if you had listened to me you would have been the greatest fighter God ever created.' But then again, he would be really disappointed in me because I don't spend enough time with my children, and that would really . . . that would have devastated him more than anything—all my losses, me going to prison . . . not spending enough time with my children, that would have affected him a great deal. I'm not a good father, I don't believe."

It isn't surprising that this disturbs Tyson, who grew up without a father and now has six children of his own. When it was suggested to him that there was time to rectify this situation, and countless others—that in actuality he might have many years left on the planet—Tyson chuckled.

"I don't think so, sir. I'm not feeling too good these days."

There was a pause. Then, more soberly, quietly, Tyson added, "I don't know where to start sometimes."

EPILOGUE

November 29, 2005

It's difficult to imagine James Douglas passing unnoticed almost anywhere, but his arrival at a cozy little neighborhood coffee shop in suburban Bexley, on the outskirts of Columbus, Ohio, causes hardly a stir. Neatly but casually dressed in jeans, sport shirt, and wool overcoat, he walks slowly and with surprising lightness for such a big man (precisely how big, Douglas won't say—he doesn't own a scale—but somewhere in the vicinity of 300 pounds does not appear to be an impolite guess, although at six foot four, with the wide shoulders and thick neck of an NFL lineman, he carries it reasonably well); and there is a softness reflected in his face—a complete lack of scars, physical or otherwise—that one might find incongruous in a former heavyweight champion.

Douglas is something of a regular here, stopping by on occasion to break up days that are filled mostly with the duties of fatherhood and the leisure of semiretirement. A good deal of time, he says with a tone of satisfaction, is devoted to shepherding two of his sons to school and to various athletic endeavors. Twelve-year-old Cardae, also known as B.J., is the youngest; Artie is fifteen. (Lamar, who stood in the ring with his father in Tokyo on the night Douglas beat Tyson, is a grown man now, twenty-seven years old.) Thus far, they've shown little interest in boxing, which is fine with James. He knows how that works, how hard it is to follow in your father's footsteps. Football, though, is a different story.

"They play all the time," Douglas says, smiling. "I'm all over the place for games and practices."

Douglas notes with obvious parental pride that Artie already weighs more than 180 pounds, a figure achieved in part through serious weight training and off-season conditioning, fundamental aspects of twenty-first-century high school sports that barely existed when James was growing up, and which, frankly, he would have been disinclined to embrace, anyway. It's too early to tell whether either of the boys might have a future beyond high school ball, but they will have a future, their father says; they will have options.

"Whatever they decide to do, they have to have a college education first," Douglas says. "That's my wife's only requirement. And I do know they can go to school. Their grades are great." He hesitates, smiles. "Way, way better than mine."

As he talks, Douglas withdraws a slip of wrinkled paper from the breast pocket of his coat. Indecipherable script covers both sides of the page. It is, he explains, a Christmas list. Douglas plans to get an early jump on shopping for the kids.

"Video games, mostly," he says. "Lots of them. They have the little ones now that you can carry around in your pocket. Amazing."

I tell him that I have a daughter in high school and that she never expressed much interest in video games. Douglas nods.

"Yeah, it's a man thing, for sure."

When I tell him that I also have a son, age six, Douglas laughs.

"Oh, you're done, man. You . . . are . . . done."

A few minutes later, just as Douglas settles into a comfortable rhythm of storytelling, the shop's espresso maker erupts, spewing a whistling geyser of steam into the air. Judging by the frantic reaction of the barista, this is not an ordinary occurrence. As the machine roars, a cloud rises to the ceiling.

"Must be a new guy," Douglas shouts over the noise. "Think we should be scared?"

Despite his imposing physical presence, Douglas is genial to the point of being disarming. Close acquaintances and family members say he's always been this way, friendly to a fault. Certainly there is nothing in his demeanor that suggests the hardness required of a boxer, let alone a boxer capable of pulling off the upset of the century. In the right moment, though, under the right circumstances, a man is capable of almost anything, as Douglas demonstrated so vividly in Tokyo. It was a long time ago, that fight, although Douglas says there are moments when it seems like just yesterday. Hardly a day goes by, he notes, that someone doesn't ask him about Mike Tyson and February 11, 1990. This is fine with Douglas, who appears neither perturbed nor overly impressed by the fact that his life will forever be defined by and measured against that single event.

"I understand it. Everybody knows where they were that night," he says. "And I opened the door for all those other guys to make a hell of a lot of money. Holyfield, Bowe . . . Had I not done what I did in Tokyo that night, those dudes wouldn't have made all that money, because I don't think they would have beaten Tyson if I hadn't beaten him first."

Holyfield.

That's a different story. Douglas has rarely (and never fully) addressed the issue of whether or not he quit against Holyfield, in part because it is a question too painful and accusatory for most people to ask (Douglas's likability only heightens the awkward nature of the discussion), but also because the evidence seems to speak for itself. More than fifteen years later, it is a topic that continues to cause him discomfort. He is, after all, a fighter.

"About Holyfield. Did you really get knocked out?"

There is no response. Douglas fidgets a bit, gazes out the window.

"Or did you just say, 'Enough'?"

He sips from a bottle of water, considers the question for several seconds. He looks around the coffee shop. It almost seems as though he wonders whether anyone is listening. Quietly, almost in a whisper, without making eye contact, he says, "I was exhausted, man. Exhausted . . . just exhausted."

There is a brief silence. Douglas shrugs and smiles. "Holyfield is a good man. I just wish I had gotten a chance to show him my best, too. He did it right, though. He was a good champion."

A few minutes later, in a tone betraying both pride and resignation, Douglas will add, "I had my moment. It was a beautiful thing; now I've moved on to bigger and better things."

Generally speaking, his pursuits are quiet and dignified. Indeed, given his physical stature and the size of his achievement (singular though it might have been), Douglas has over the years proved unusually adept at avoiding the spotlight and all manner of publicity—good, bad, or indifferent. Six months after this meeting he would face a misdemeanor charge of complicity stemming from an odd and embarrassing incident in which his brother, William "Billy" Douglas, falsely identified himself as James Douglas in an attempt to obtain a motorcycle permit. (On September 26, 2006, James Douglas pleaded guilty; he later paid $406 in fines and court costs.) But that incident is noteworthy not merely for its staggering imprudence (Douglas was accused of lending his driver's license and Social Security number to his brother, which says something about the fighter's indifference toward celebrity, particularly his own), but for the anomalous nature of the transgression, the sole entry in the Buster Douglas canon that makes him a potential candidate for *The Surreal Life*.

Douglas has not crossed paths with Tyson since February 1990, specifically, not since the day the two met at a New York television studio to tape interviews for HBO's rebroadcast of their fight. When asked if he's surprised by the way their respective lives have unfolded—that Tyson squandered hundreds of millions of dollars and is now reduced to fighting exhibition matches to pay off his debts, while Douglas, who earned a fraction of that amount, is financially secure—Douglas shakes his head.

"It's just unfortunate that he never had control of his life. He was always controlled by others. I feel bad for him sometimes, but I think he'll be all right. It seems like a lot of people still like him . . . or care about him."

Except to the extent that he will always be regarded as a fighter, boxing plays only a peripheral role in Douglas's life. He is neither a manager nor a trainer and only occasionally attends amateur or professional boxing matches. His younger brother is a fighter, and Douglas offers guidance and advice when it's sought. Billy Douglas sometimes trains at the same Columbus gym where John Johnson works, so Buster and his former manager have had a chance to patch things up over the years. Johnson refers to Douglas as a "friend." Douglas says that the two men are "cordial," but adds, wryly, "We don't hang out."

James sees a bit more of his uncle and former trainer, J. D. McCauley. The two are related, after all, and periodically a family function brings them together. McCauley continues to train fighters for Johnson, so there are times, albeit infrequent, when the three of them are all together in the gym. But that is merely coincidence. Like Tyson, Douglas has shed most of the professional (and many of the personal) relationships from that period of his life. A notable exception is John Russell, the Akron trainer who now refers to Douglas as one of his dearest friends.

"We're real close," says Douglas. "John and I talk almost . . . shit . . . pretty much every day. I do events with him, and when he trains other fighters, sometimes I'll go to camp and help out."

The two are close enough that Russell has long owned a set of keys to Douglas's Marco Island retreat. It was during a visit to Florida, in March 2003, that Russell (who had all but retired from boxing) was involved in a horrific automobile accident. He was less than a half mile from home when he lost control of his Mecedes E-320. Russell remembers almost nothing about the accident, although he later learned that the car was traveling at roughly seventy miles per hour when it rammed a mailbox and rolled over six times before coming to a stop and bursting into flames. Russell was not wearing a seat belt at the time, and that bit of carelessness, ironically, may have saved his life, since he was thrown from the vehicle. Russell was airlifted to a hospital in Fort Meyers, where he spent the next eleven days, the first five on life support. To assist in his recovery, Russell eventually returned to Akron and began working out in a gym. That led to a renewed interest in training, a pursuit he maintains with great vigor to this day.

"It got me moving and feeling good again," Russell says. "Thank God for boxing."

Much of Douglas's passion is reserved not for boxing, but for business. His dream involves the development of a 3.8-acre parcel of land on the East Side of Columbus, just a few blocks from the Black-burn Recreation Center, where Bill Douglas used to work and where Buster learned to box. The property was once home to Pontifical College Josephinum, a Roman Catholic seminary that relocated to Worthington in the 1930s, eventually making way for a roller-skating rink. As a youngster Douglas liked to hang out at the rink, and his mother, who worked as a cook nearby, often stopped by to pick him up on her way home.

"I spent a lot of time on the East Side when I was a kid," Douglas says, somewhat whimsically.

A combination of restlessness, nostalgia, and entrepreneurial ambition prompted Douglas to purchase the site for $200,000 in 1992, with dreams of resurrecting the rink as part of a neighborhood revitalization project. Reality quickly intervened, however, as the project became bogged down in environmental concerns, political posturing, and financial pressures. Abandoned gas stations had left behind underground tanks that threatened to poison groundwater; old buildings requiring renovation or demolition were choked with asbestos and lead paint.

"And I got stuck with the cleanup," notes Douglas.

The initial out-of-pocket cost for meeting Environmental Protection Agency standards, Douglas says, was more than $200,000; over the years he's pumped more money into the project, and still it hasn't taken flight. But Douglas is nothing if not an optimist. He has a new partner in the project, and his vision, supported by the Main Street Business Association, has expanded considerably. It now reads like something out of a guide for urban renewal: three- and four-story buildings vibrant with mixed usage—retail shops on the first floor, condominiums or apartments above; modern town houses; elegant brownstones; a thriving commercial and residential district.

"Want to see it?" he asks. "Come on. I'll show you."

Covering roughly a square city block on the southeast corner of East Main and South Eighteenth streets, hard by Interstate 70, Buster's dream for now isn't much more than a vast vacant lot, although he observes with some satisfaction that this represents a substantial improvement from the 1980s, when the area was rife with "poverty, prostitutes, and pimps." There are designs on paper somewhere, but

Buster has already committed them to memory. He stands on a street corner, pointing to various empty spaces, explaining how and when they will be occupied.

"It's going to turn the whole community around," Douglas says, his coat billowing in the afternoon chill of a blustery Midwestern day.

For now, the only activity on the site is a tractor trailer pulling off Main Street and into a cleared lot. The driver cuts the engine and sits. It would appear he's simply killing time before getting back on the highway.

"Not supposed to park there," mutters Douglas, shaking his head. He is the guardian now, walking slowly, purposefully across his land. As Douglas approaches the truck, the driver rolls down his window.

"Hey, man," Douglas tells him, "you gotta move."

The driver does not question Douglas's authority, but merely starts the engine and suggests, before pulling away, that if parking is not permitted, then someone ought to put up a sign indicating as much. Douglas nods.

Moments later, snow begins to fall as a pair of Columbus police cruisers (there is a substation nearby) emblazoned with the acronym SWAT pulls into the lot. Douglas waves politely. The officers respond in kind.

It's a rough neighborhood, Douglas explains once more, but it used to be a lot worse. He looks around, smiles. "They're just keeping an eye on things for me."

ACKNOWLEDGMENTS

By November 2005 I was more than six months into the research and writing of this book and still had not spoken directly with either of the principal figures, Mike Tyson and James Douglas. Given Tyson's enigmatic nature and general dissatisfaction with the media in all forms, this wasn't a complete shock. Tyson by this time had announced his retirement from boxing and embarked on a global walkabout that seemed to regularly place him, Zelig-like, in the oddest of circumstances: jet-skiing in the Mediterranean, touring war-torn Chechnya. He had become a citizen of the world, rootless and wandering, supporting himself and whacking away at a mountain of debt through the only means possible: by exploiting what remained of his own celebrity.

I had attempted to contact Tyson through numerous channels, formal and informal, and had repeatedly run into dead ends. Again, this was not a surprise. There was no reason for Tyson to cooperate with this project, which, after all, served no purpose to him, financial or otherwise. In retrospect, the loss to James Douglas on February 11, 1990, can be seen as a watershed event in the life of Mike Tyson, the first step in a long, steady decline. One could understand why Tyson might not be eager to revisit that night or to discuss the long-term effect it had on his life and career. Indeed, when Home Box Office produced a half-hour retrospective on the Tyson-Douglas fight (which served as a terrific source of information while I was in the early stages of this project) in 2003, Tyson's involvement was noticeably lacking; his only contribution was a brief, twelve-year-old sound bite praising Douglas. Having long been fascinated by the Tyson-Douglas fight and the fallout it produced—the ways in which it affected the two participants and the sport itself—I was committed to writing this book. I knew, of course, that it would be a better book if I could secure the interest and involvement of the two fighters themselves, but I was prepared to move forward regardless.

As it happened, neither Tyson nor Douglas was initially eager to cooperate. Douglas, I had heard, was considering a book of his own, and was understandably wary of the possibility that indulging a related project by another writer might not be in his best interests. After several months, however, I was able to speak with Douglas directly, thanks in no small part to the intervention of John Russell, Douglas's close friend and former trainer. I had already interviewed Russell for many hours as part of my research, and we had developed a comfortable rapport. I believe he respected my commitment to producing a narrative that would be fair and uncompromising. Douglas ultimately agreed, and within a few days of our first telephone conversation, I was in Columbus, Ohio, meeting with him in person. Douglas's willingness to share many of the details of his personal and professional life, including some that were extraordinarily painful and intimate, was crucial to making this book.

Predictably, tracking down Tyson proved a bit more difficult. On more than one occasion it was suggested to me that I "try to catch him at an airport somewhere." This seemed impractical, if not downright quixotic. A breakthrough came in late 2005 when I spoke with Tom Patti, one of Tyson's oldest friends and a sometime advisor. I had heard that Patti was still close to Tyson, that their friendship had somehow survived the tests of time and turmoil. I had left messages for Patti at his place of business in California, and one day he called back and we chatted amiably for a while. I told him I was working on a book about the Tyson-Douglas fight and that I was wondering if he had any suggestions for contacting Tyson about the possibility of an interview. Patti said he might be able to arrange something, but that Mike typically received no less than $100,000 for participation in any project.

My counteroffer was zero. It wasn't merely that a hundred grand sounded a bit steep, I explained to Patti; any exchange of currency would make Tyson a partner in the project and so compromise the book's integrity. I told him that I planned to write the book with or without Tyson's participation, but that I thought it would be a better and more fully realized story if he were to offer some observations about the importance of the fight and its effect on his life. My hope was that this might appeal to Tyson's fondness for boxing history.

"I'll take it to him," Patti promised.

Frankly, I did not expect much to come of that conversation, so I was surprised to receive another call from Patti a week later. Tyson had agreed to be interviewed for the book, Patti reported, but there would be strict parameters. First of all, we would have to speak by phone; Tyson would not agree to a face-to-face interview. Second, the topic of conversation would be limited to the Tyson-Douglas fight.

"Fine," I said. "When can we talk?"

Patti laughed. "You never know with Mike. Just be ready."

Two weeks passed. One morning my cell phone rang. Tom Patti was on the other end. He and Tyson were in a car together and Mike was ready to talk.

"Let's go, Mr. Joe!" Tyson yelped. "Busy day, today. Busy day."

We chatted briefly and superficially about matters unrelated to boxing. Tyson wanted to know where I was calling from, and when I told him Saratoga Springs, New York, he launched into an enthusiastic monologue about the city's colorful, mobbed-up past, casually and expertly dropping the names of Arnold Rothstein and Diamond Jim Brady and even lesser-known figures such as casino magnate Richard Canfield. Tyson used to spend a fair amount of time carousing in

Saratoga when he was younger and still living in upstate New York, and he wanted to know what had become of a particular haunt, one that had a reputation for robust late-night activity that sometimes spilled into the street.

"Gone," I told him. "They turned it into a coffee bar for a while. Now it's kind of a Yuppie tavern."

Tyson groaned. "Oh, man."

We talked for a while about the Douglas fight, the preparation for the fight, and the aftermath of the fight. When the conversation strayed occasionally from the established boundaries, Tyson would sometimes go along for the ride; usually, though, he would quickly change the topic.

"You keep asking me questions, next thing you know it's gonna be my story," he joked. "It'll be like, 'Hey, man, fucked that up! Met this girl, she dumped me . . .' Then the pity party starts all over again."

When the interview ended, following another attempt to push the envelope, it did so without warning. Tyson veered from a cogent observation to a friendly farewell.

"Don't want to go there, brother," he said. "Give my best to Buster and his kids, okay? God bless."

And that was that.

In the end it wasn't quite what I had hoped for, but more than I expected. Tyson believes now that his career essentially came to an end on February 11, 1990, in Tokyo, and I respect him for taking part in a book that illustrates precisely how important and catastrophic a day that was for him. And I appreciate Tom Patti's efforts in facilitating an interview that helped form the backbone of this story.

As with any work of narrative nonfiction (particularly one that deals with recent history), this book could not have been written without the efforts of numerous contributors. I would like to gratefully acknowledge the following people, each of whom generously agreed to be interviewed for this project: Paul Antonelli, Matt Baranski, Paul Bauman, Jay Bright, Bertha Douglas, James Douglas, Ross Greenburg,

Richard Hoffer, John Johnson, Jim Lampley, Steve Lott, Blanca Eugenia Meyran, Octavio Meyran, J. D. McCauley, Larry Merchant, Tom Patti, Kevin Rooney, John Russell, Gary Smith, James Smith, Aaron Snowell, James Sterngold, Bert Sugar, Bruce Trampler, Mike Tyson, Vic Ziegel.

I also received assistance and suggestions from numerous people within the journalism, broadcasting, and public relations communities, and while their contributions may not be immediately evident to the reader, I am indebted nonetheless. So thanks to Marty Appel, Wayne Coffey, Brian Doogan, Mike Lewis, Joe Maxse, Leigh Montville, Tom Reed, and Jon Saraceno. Thanks, especially, to Ray Stallone at Home Box Office for helping to set up interviews and providing videotapes of fights and documentaries, as well as important statistical information.

Every author of narrative nonfiction relies, to an extent, on the accumulated contributions of writers who have already walked a similar path. While the bulk of this book is the result of firsthand research, reporting, and interviews, as well as endless hours of video review, I would be remiss if I did not credit the many fine authors and journalists whose work helped me to fashion a blueprint for this project. They are duly noted in the source notes and bibliography that follow this text.

Thanks to everyone at St. Martin's Press, most notably my editor, Marc Resnick, who fought for this project from the very beginning, and who has supported it vigorously every step of the way.

As always, thanks to my agent, Frank Weimann, and everyone at the Literary Group, along with Neil Reshen and Dawn Reshen at Benay Enterprises.

Writing is a lonely and sometimes maddening exercise; it helps to have someone with whom you can share the myriad frustrations and small triumphs, someone who understands precisely what you are experiencing. My brother, Tim Layden, is not only my best friend, but a fine writer and tireless reporter. He also shares my fascination with boxing and has a wealth of information on the subject of Mike Tyson. Tim patiently listened to my stories over the last two years and helped me separate the important from the trivial, the interesting from the mundane. Thanks also to Bob Whitaker, friend, author, entrepreneur, fellow skeptic, and newspaper alumnus, who knows all too well what a long journey this has been.

Finally, and most important, I would like to thank the home team—Sue, Emily, and Max—for their unwavering love and support.

SOURCE NOTES

Prologue

1 So exhausted: Details of Douglas's illness and hospitalization based on author interviews with James Douglas and Bertha Douglas.

2 Meanwhile, two hundred miles down the road: Much has been written about Tyson's time in prison; the information here owes a particular debt to Pete Hamill, "The Education of Mike Tyson," *Esquire,* March, 1994.

Chapter 1

5 For him the love affair: Much of the biographical information about George Chuvalo is attributed to Stephen Brunt, *Facing Ali: 15 Fighters, 15 Stories* (Guilford, Conn.: Lyons Press, 2002), 47–51.

7 "He was very friendly and accommodating": Bruce Trampler interview.

8 "wore his emotions": James Douglas interview.

9 "At a time when the middleweight division": "Douglas Was a Feared Middleweight," J. Russell Peltz, ESPN.com, October 13, 2005.

10 "Peltz responded . . . with a list of ten names": Bruce Trampler interview.

11 "did what he wanted to do": James Douglas interview.

13 The fight itself: Account of the Soto-Douglas fight attributed to Deane McGowan, "Soto Bows to Fill-in; Bobick Wins," *New York Times,* February 7, 1976; and Wallace Matthews, "A Journeyman's Journey," *Newsday,* February 18, 1990.

13 "Bill was the kind of guy": Bruce Trampler interview.

14 And then Bill and Lula Pearl: Gary Smith, "The Fight of His Life," *Sports Illustrated,* October 22, 1990.

14 "My mom was the mediator": James Douglas interview.

16 "What's wrong with you?": Ibid.

16 A few years later: Smith, "The Fight of His Life."

17 "I was going to be a basketball player": James Douglas interview.

18 "Jesus!" he'd rail at Lula Pearl: Ibid.

Chapter 2

19 June 27, 1988: The account of the fight presented in this chapter is taken from my own reporting in combination with other sources. The anecdote about Butch Lewis and his opposition to Tyson's gloves owes a particular debt to Pat Putnam, "I'm Gonna Hurt This Guy," *Sports Illustrated,* July 4, 1988; as well as Jose Torres, *Fire and Fear: The Inside Story of Mike Tyson* (New York: Warner Books, 1989), 198–200; and Peter Heller, *Bad Intentions: The Mike Tyson Story* (New York: Da Capo Press, 1995), 1–5.

19 Over the years these transgressions: Gavin Evans, "Backpages: Tools of the Trade . . . Boxing Gloves," *Guardian,* January 15, 1999; James P. Dawson, "Miller Reinstated by Boxing Board," *New York Times,* November 11, 1925; "Miller Yarns Hit at Jack Delaney," *Hartford Courant,* November 5, 1925.

20 In fact, just two years earlier: "Boxer and manager sentenced to prison for glove tampering," Associated Press, October 28, 1986.

20 "Pulling his usual bullshit": Kevin Rooney interview.

20 "Get rid of that": Putnam, "I'm Gonna Hurt This Guy."

21 "You know, I'm gonna hurt this guy": Ibid.

24 "There were all kinds": Bert Sugar interview.

25 Holmes defended the WBC title: Biographical material on Larry Holmes and Michael Spinks, along with Holmes's quotes, relies heavily on Gavin Evans, *Kings of the Ring: The History of Heavyweight Boxing* (London: Weidenfeld & Nicolson, 2005); and Stephen Brunt, *Facing Ali: 15 Fighters, 15 Stories.*

26 "I can say to the judges": "Holmes Again Raps Officials After Decision," Associated Press, April 20, 1986.

27 "Yeah, Mike was thirteen": Matt Baranski interview.

28 "It's funny": Ibid.

28 "Mike, I think": Tom Patti interview.

29 "Mike lived in my apartment": Steve Lott interview.

30 "My opponent was game": Tom Callahan, "Boxing's Allure," *Time,* June 27, 1988.

32 "I knew he had potential": Kevin Rooney interview.

32 Rooney had witnessed: Details of the altercation between Tyson and Atlas taken from Teddy Atlas, *Atlas: From the Streets to the Ring* (New York: Ecco, 2006), 100–105.

32 "Let's say it was true": Steve Lott interview.

33 "Cus D'Amato": Bert Sugar interview.

36 On that date: Callahan, "Boxing's Allure," *Time,* June 27, 1988.

38 "I was with Gil Clancy": Matt Baranski interview.

38 "When I worked with Mike": Ibid.

38 "Fear is like fire": Torres, *Fire and Fear,* 50.

39 "Most fighters": Kevin Rooney interview.

40 "In my opinion": Ibid.

Chapter 3

42 "The first major blowup": Wallace Matthews, "A Journeyman's Journey," *Newsday,* February 18, 1990.

43 "I don't think any significant punches hit him": Ibid.

43 "Artie was tough": James Douglas interview.

44 "Number one": John Russell interview.

44 "I grew up with boxing": John Johnson interview.

44 Another love was football: Tim May, "Manager Sure of Standing," *Columbus Dispatch,* January 21, 1990.

45 "It was the best thing": John Johnson interview.

45 The connection to Hayes: Richard Hoffer, "Hey, Champ!" *Sports Illustrated,* February 26, 1990.

45 "The last job, I left": Ibid.

46 When they gathered: Michael Madden, "After Upset, Douglas a Bust," *Boston Globe,* August 18, 1995.

47 "I didn't trust white people very much": Elmer Smith, "Father Carves Path for Son's Shot at Title," *Philadelphia Daily News,* May 29, 1987.

47 "Bill and I were real close": J. D. McCauley interview.

47 "We were friends way back when": John Johnson interview.

48 "When we first got together": James Douglas interview.

48 "James, at heart": John Johnson interview.

49 Douglas accepted the offer: David Iamele, "Buster Douglas Looks Back at the Night He Rocked the Boxing World," *Utica Observer-Dispatch,* May 1, 2004.

50 "My dad was bickering": James Douglas interview.

5I "Nothing too serious": J. D. McCauley interview.

5I There was another time: Gary Smith, "The Fight of His Life," *Sports Illustrated,* October 22, 1990.

52 "Going into that [training] camp": James Douglas interview.

52 A week before the fight: Smith, "The Fight of His Life."

53 "J.D. and I sat in the audience": John Johnson interview.

53 "He had shown": Bert Sugar interview.

53 "I was just going through the motions": James Douglas interview.

54 "Tony Tucker was a very good fighter": Larry Merchant interview.

55 Not long after that: Story and subsequent quotes gleaned from James Douglas interview.

Chapter 4

57 "It's very simple": Steve Lott interview.

58 Never one to be preoccupied: Phil Berger, *Blood Season: Tyson and the World of Boxing* (New York: William Morrow, 1989), 63.

59 As the late Phil Berger wrote: Ibid, 64–65.

59 "Mike moved into Cus's house": Kevin Rooney interview.

60 To the extent: Background material on Robin Givens from Phil Berger, *Blood Season,* (New York: William Morrow, 1989); and Peter Heller, *Bad Intentions* (New York: Da Capo Press, 1995).

6I A story often has been told: Berger, *Blood Season,* 242.

62 With Jacobs out of the picture: Background material on Ruth Roper attributed to Heller, *Bad Intentions,* and Berger, *Blood Season.*

62   So, too, was Don King: Biographical material on King, including details of his conviction on charges of manslaughter, and subsequent rise to prominence in boxing, from Jack Newfield, *Only in America: The Life and Crimes of Don King* (New York: William Morrow, 1995), 1–21.

64   "Don King is the most": Kevin Rooney interview.

64   Throughout 1988: Gerald Early, "Mike's Brilliant Career," *Transition,* no. 71 (Fall 1996).

66   If this is so . . . they did their jobs well: Rudy Gonzalez, with Martin A. Feigenbaum, *The Inner Ring* (Miami: Oliver Publishing Group, 1995); excerpted in Daniel O'Connor, ed. *Iron Mike: A Mike Tyson Reader* (New York: Thunder's Mouth Press, 2002), 112.

66   A slightly more generous perspective: Donald McRae, *Dark Trade: Lost in Boxing* (New York: Mainstream Publishing, 1996); excerpted in *Iron Mike,* 214–215.

67   "At the time of the Spinks fight": Steve Lott interview.

68   "Robin's lawyers": Ibid.

69   It was on that morning: Story of Tyson's hospital stay taken from Heller, *Bad Intentions,* 297–301.

70   Media outlets predictably had a ball: Mike McAlary, "Tyson Tried to Kill Self," New York *Daily News,* September 7, 1988.

70   "Mike wrecked a lot of cars in his life": Paul Antonelli interview.

71   When the end came: Story of Tyson's *20/20* appearance and subsequent altercation with police at his Bernardsville home, taken from Heller, *Bad Intentions,* 309–317.

72   "Robin and me": Dan Rafael, "Mike Tyson Sounds Off About his Past, Present and Future," ESPN.com, June 11, 2006.

73   As a reminder: Ron Borges, "Cayton Enduring Unkindest Cut of All," *Boston Globe,* July 20, 1989.

73   "I have integrity as a manager": Ibid.

74   "Mike could have been a billionaire": Kevin Rooney interview.

74 "I like to hurt women": Jose Torres, *Fire and Fear* (New York: Warner Books, 1989), 107.

Chapter 5

77 John Russell came straight out: Background material gleaned from a combination of author interviews and Tom Reed, "Roped In Again," *Akron Beacon Journal,* July 14, 2002.

79 "Billy was forty or forty-one years old": John Russell interview.

79 In later years: Ibid.

79 "I wasn't friends with James at the time": Ibid.

80 As if that weren't enough pressure: Steve Wulf, "Adversity's Adversary," *Sports Illustrated,* February 19, 1990.

80 The almost inexplicable calm: Gary Smith, "The Fight of His Life," *Sports Illustrated,* October 22, 1990.

81 In the middle of August: Joe Maxse, "Columbus Boxer Is Tyson's Next Opponent," *Cleveland Plain Dealer,* August 15, 1989.

82 "It ain't about if [Tyson] knocks a guy out": Richard Hoffer, "KO'd," *Sports Illustrated,* February 19, 1990.

82 Sometimes James eased the pain: Douglas C. Lyons, "New Champ Samples the Sweet Life," *Ebony,* June 1990.

82 "That was a tough time": James Douglas interview.

83 "I thought he was just a patron": Bertha Douglas interview.

83 "A lot of strangers came into our lives": Ibid.

84 Regardless, with Ruddock out of the way: "Tyson Bout in February," *New York Times,* November 16, 1989.

84 "John [Johnson] wasn't very happy": James Douglas interview.

85 "Actually, some fighters don't bother": Richard Hoffer interview.

85 "I honestly resent": John Johnson interview.

86 "I went back to James": Ibid

86 "They called me to come in": John Russell interview.

86 "It was just there": Ibid.

87 When informed of Johnson's claim: Ibid.

87 "We brought [John Russell] in as a cut man": James Douglas interview.

87 "John [Russell] was there": Ibid.

88 "If you're standing on the railroad tracks": John Russell interview.

89 "James, this guy is about five foot ten": Ibid.

89 The great majority of Douglas's workouts: Ibid.

90 Las Vegas oddsmakers: Kevin Iole, "Upset of the Century," Las Vegas Review-Journal, February 13, 2000

90 "Everybody quotes the forty-two-to-one odds": Bert Sugar interview.

90 "I never had any doubt": James Douglas interview.

90 "Tyson has to be planted": Ibid.

91 This was the fight Dynamite never got: Ibid.

92 "I don't give a shit": Ibid.

92 "Most of the guys who fought Tyson": John Russell interview.

92 At a New Year's Eve party: James Douglas interview.

93 A few days later: Story and quotes, Ibid.

94 "See, I think she just needed to see it herself": Ibid.

94 Three days later: Gary Smith, "The Fight of His Life," Sports Illustrated, October 22, 1990.

95 "Yeah, I had an out": James Douglas interview.

Chapter 6

97 As darkness lifted: Joe Maxse, "Douglas Tokyo-Bound to Fight Tyson," *Cleveland Plain Dealer,* January 27, 1990.

98 "The mayor was supposed to be there": John Russell interview.

98 "There was very little indication": Ross Greenburg interview.

100 "Mike basically had to be dragged onto the plane": Jay Bright interview.

100 But given Tyson's indelicate history: Neil Allen, "The Real Iron Mike," *Boxing Monthly,* February 2 000.

100 "I didn't see anything": Paul Antonelli interview.

100 The most glaring indication: Wallace Matthews, "Knockdown a Hyper Event," *Newsday,* January 25, 1990.

101 "Greg was ready for Mike": Aaron Snowell interview.

102 "So it was kind of like fireworks going off": Ibid.

103 Cayton, ever the shrewd observer: Dave Anderson, "Is Tyson Sabotaging Himself?" *New York Times,* February 6, 1990.

103 "The first press conference was funny": James Douglas interview.

104 "Neil called me out of the blue": James Sterngold interview.

105 "It was one of the most thrilling": Ibid.

105 In reality, Western heavyweights: Bernard Fernandez, "Japanese Have a Yen for Tyson," Philadelphia Daily News, February 8, 1990.

106 "He was on a couch": James Sterngold interview.

106 A highly publicized meeting: Fernandez, "Japanese Have a Yen."

106 A visit to the Ueno Park zoo: Tim May, "Tyson's Brash Style Rubs Douglas Wrong Way," *Columbus Dispatch,* February 9, 1990.

106 "That was kind of interesting": Vic Ziegel interview.

107 King rather obviously: Jack Newfield, *Only in America* (New York: William Morrow, 1995), 282.

107 "I just kept thinking": James Douglas interview.

108 "My whole thing was": John Russell interview.

108 "Pritchard rocked him with a left hook": Ibid.

108 Later, in the dressing room: Ibid.

109 "You looked like you were on roller skates": Ibid.

109 Back in Ohio: Tim May, "Douglas Arrives for Bout on the Run," *Columbus Dispatch,* January 28, 1990.

109 "You know, one day I'm going to come out here": J. D. McCauley interview.

110 "Just like in that movie": Ibid.

110 "What makes a great fighter": Aaron Snowell interview.

110 That rarely happened: Ibid.

111 "Look, I thought he was going to quit": Mike Tyson interview.

111 "Snowell had known Douglas for some time": Aaron Snowell interview.

112 "I started putting pressure on him": Ibid.

112 "We talked a lot": Ibid.

112 The selection of Snowell and Bright: Larry Merchant interview.

114 As Snowell remembers it: Aaron Snowell interview.

114 "As a trainer": Ibid.

114 Unlike Tyson: Donald McRae, "Me and Mike Tyson," *Guardian,* January 22, 2000.

115 "I think that Cus's ideology and style": Jay Bright interview.

115 "Jay Bright": Matt Baranski interview.

115 "When you hear things like that": Jay Bright interview.

116 "I have total respect for Buster Douglas": Ibid.

116 "Tyson was really [messing] with Douglas's head": James Sterngold interview.

117 Tyson himself would acknowledge: Duncan Campbell, "Painful Hearing as Commission Shows No Mercy," *The Irish Times,* January 31, 2002.

117 As for psychiatric counseling: Allen, "The Real Iron Mike."

117 "Part of my task": Ibid.

118 The day before the fight: Ross Greenburg interview.

119 "About thirty seconds in, I start to realize": Ibid.

119 "Douglas had a lot of conviction": Ibid.

120 "The way he acts": Tim May, "Douglas Winning Bout with Flu," *Columbus Dispatch,* February 10, 1990.

120 Johnson's theory: Ibid.

120 Jose Sulaiman, chairman of the World Boxing Council: Ibid.

120 "He said, 'Oh, my God' ": John Russell interview.

121 "It may have just been a wisecrack": Larry Merchant interview.

121 On the eve of the fight: Allen, "The Real Iron Mike."

122 "I sat down and threw a towel over his head": John Russell interview.

122 "Let your hands go": James Douglas interview.

Chapter 7

123 "The whole camp was with me": James Douglas interview.

123 At approximately 11:15 local time: Story and quotes, Ross Greenburg interview.

126 "Usually on the day of a fight": John Russell interview.

127 "As I sat him down": Ibid.

127 "Usually I would have sent someone else": Ibid.

128 "So I said, 'You've gotta take [the gloves] off' ": Ibid.

128 "By that time": Ibid.

128 "Can I tell you something?": Mike Tyson interview.

129 "Like, 'I don't really want to be here'": Aaron Snowell interview.

129 "You're ready, James": J. D. McCauley interview.

129 Russell, meanwhile, continued to emphasize strategy: John Russell interview.

130 There is an oft-repeated story: HBO broadcast of Tyson-Douglas fight.

130 His entrance was accompanied by gloomy proclamations: Ibid.

130 "It was supposed to be just a walk": James Douglas interview.

131 "Mike has termed this phase of the fight": HBO broadcast of Tyson-Douglas fight, February 10, 1990.

131 "I don't get into the staring stuff": James Douglas interview.

132 "Two minutes into the fight": Jim Lampley interview.

133 "Use the jab, baby": HBO broadcast of Tyson-Douglas fight.

133 "A lot of what I told Mike": Aaron Snowell interview.

135 "Tyson fought the way James made him fight": John Russell interview.

136 "I think we were going to run something either way": Richard Hoffer interview.

136 "It became something of a joke among the writers": Ibid.

137 "Cus's style is a very precise style": Jay Bright interview.

137 "As soon as Mike walked into the ring": Kevin Rooney interview.

140 "The corner was woeful": Jim Lampley interview.

141 "Unbelievable. They didn't even have the right equipment": Matt Baranski interview.

141 "The cut man is responsible": Aaron Snowell interview.

142 "No," Snowell said with a laugh: Ibid.

142   "Hey, it wasn't their fault": Mike Tyson interview.

142   The quiet of the crowd: HBO broadcast of Tyson-Douglas fight.

142   "During the first round": Ross Greenburg interview.

143   "An incredible thing happened": Jim Lampley interview.

143   "There was a focus by the broadcasters": Ross Greenburg interview.

144   "You're getting your ass kicked, Mike": HBO broadcast of Tyson-Douglas fight.

144   "It wasn't the most ethical thing": John Russell interview.

144   "We're in the eighth round, folks": HBO broadcast of Tyson-Douglas fight.

144   "You got him, Buster": Ibid.

144   "Can you imagine": Ibid.

144   "It's not over yet": Ibid.

144   "It boggles the mind": Ibid.

145   "That was the only time": James Douglas interview.

145   "When I saw that": John Russell interview.

145   "Frankly," said *The New York Times*'s James Sterngold: James Sterngold interview.

146   "It was a good shot": James Douglas interview.

146   "The referee is counting": Steve Lott interview.

146   "God damn it, James!" John Russell interview.

147   "Mike showed a lot of heart": James Douglas interview.

147   "I didn't fight well, but I took my beating pretty good": Mike Tyson interview.

148   "When James hit him with that uppercut": John Russell interview.

148   "Finishing was always a struggle for me": James Douglas interview.

288 / SOURCE NOTES

149   "That was poetry": James Sterngold interview.

149   "When Mike went down": John Russell interview.

150   "I'll never forget hitting the canvas": Mike Tyson interview.

150   "It was shocking": Paul Antonelli interview.

150   At ringside: HBO broadcast of Tyson-Douglas fight.

150   In the midst of the postfight chaos: story and quotes, Aaron Snowell interview.

Chapter 8

153   "Don King puts up a good image": Octavio Meyran interview.

153   Into the celebration: HBO broadcast of Tyson-Douglas fight, February 10, 1990.

155   This was back in January 1973: Phil Berger, "King an Artful Dodger Who Lands on His Feet," *New York Times,* February 18, 1990.

156   "I was waiting for him": John Russell interview.

156   "My first thought was": Ibid.

157   "Two knockouts took place": Richard Hoffer, "KO'd," *Sports Illustrated,* February 19, 1990.

157   Eyewitnesses to the fight: Berger, "King an Artful Dodger."

158   There would be a press conference: Hoffer, "KO'd."

159   Here, for example, is an excerpt: Rules governing IBF championship fights, ibf-usba-boxing.com.

159   The World Boxing Association's rules offer even greater detail: Rules governing WBA championship fights, wbaonline.com.

161   "I was coherent": James Douglas interview.

161   "I can handle losing": James Sterngold, "No Heart? Douglas Disproved Doubters," *New York Times,* February 12, 1990.

161   "It was a long count": Mike Tyson interview.

162 As Meyran himself put it: Octavio Meyran interview.

163 That appears to have been the case: Ibid.

164 "The letter of the rule": HBO rebroadcast of Tyson-Douglas, February 16, 1990.

164 "Both boxers, I made the same count": Octavio Meyran interview.

165 "For me, all the time": Ibid.

165 "In the press conference after the fight": Octavio Meyran correspondence, via e-mail, with author.

166 "Personally, I feel there were two knockouts": Phil Berger, "Boxing Officials Could Overturn Defeat of Tyson," *New York Times,* February 12, 1990.

166 Said WBC ratings chairman Dick Cole: Richard Hoffer, "Hey, Champ!" *Sports Illustrated,* February 26, 1990.

166 "The press jumped on it": John Russell interview.

167 "Sulaiman was essentially a King henchman": Richard Hoffer interview.

167 "It was a career performance": Bert Sugar interview.

168 "Buster Douglas was a guy": Larry Merchant interview.

168 "No one outside of King's sphere of influence": Tom Callahan, "When Buster Beat up Godzilla," *Newsweek,* February 26, 1990.

168 "It has made boxing ludicrous": Royce Feour, "Sanctioning Bodies Practice Unfairness," *Las Vegas Review-Journal,* November 21, 1999.

168 So relentless and one-sided was the beating: Phil Berger, "Tyson Concedes; Wants Rematch," *New York Times,* February 14, 1990.

169 A news conference conducted that afternoon: Ibid.

169 For the embattled referee: Octavio Meyran correspondence, via e-mail, with author.

Chapter 9

173 "We were like a close-knit family": James Douglas interview.

173 On his first morning back in Columbus: William Gildea, "From Humbling Start to Humbling Tyson, He's the Same 'Buster,'" *Washington Post,* February 14, 1990.

174 On February 14: Richard Hoffer, "Hey, Champ!" *Sports Illustrated,* February 26, 1990.

174 The original broadcast: Ratings information provided by HBO.

174 "Every Tyson fight": Ross Greenburg interview.

175 First, however, there was business to conduct: Hoffer, "Hey, Champ!"

175 Whatever goodwill King might have engendered: Ibid.

176 The first three questions were directed at the ex-champ: Ibid.

176 When Johnson got word: Ibid.

177 "We never really got a chance": John Johnson interview.

177 The following morning: Tom Archdeacon, "Out Cold Dad Doesn't Receive an Invitation to Son's Celebration as Douglas, Columbus Party Over Heavyweight Crown," *Dayton Daily News,* February 18, 1990.

177 The world, it seemed to Douglas: Hoffer, "Hey, Champ!"

178 "No one could have expected it": James Douglas interview.

178 In some ways the parade in Columbus: Phil Berger, "On Top and Loving It," *New York Times,* March 4, 1990.

178 Douglas and Johnson first visited Vegas: Hoffer, "Hey, Champ!"

178 In this same time frame: Berger, "On Top."

179 "After the Tyson fight": John Russell interview.

180 "John Russell is a good person": Bertha Douglas interview.

180 James Douglas would later refer to Nallie: James Douglas interview.

180 "James basically said to me": John Johnson interview.

180 "He's my father and I want to protect him": Sam Donnellon, "Bubble Buster: Champion of Busted Dreams," *Philadelphia Daily News,* February 10, 1993.

180 "Tyson opened the door": Bertha Douglas interview.

181 "I was there, but I had no say in anything": John Johnson interview.

181 Bob Arum labeled Johnson: Robert Seltzer, "Maverick Manager Is No Hit Outside the Ring," *Philadelphia Inquirer,* October 21, 1990.

181 "There were times": John Russell interview.

182 "John did what he did": James Douglas interview.

183 Negotiations between King and the Douglas camp: Jack Newfield, *Only in America* (New York: William Morrow, 1995), 298–301.

183 "That wasn't a good time at all": James Douglas interview.

183 "I was constantly flying to New York": Ibid.

183 At the time, the Douglas camp: Tim May, "Douglas Shrugs Off All the Legal Maneuvering," *Columbus Dispatch,* March 6, 1990.

184 A Harvard Law School graduate: Newfield, *Only in America,* 306.

184 "Steve Wynn stabbed me in the back": Ibid, 306–307.

185 "That's how we fight our battles in boxing": Pat Putnam, "Of Wheat, Chaff, and Boxing," *Sports Illustrated,* July 23, 1990.

185 As King has demonstrated: Newfield, *Only in America,* 313.

185 Small wonder that afterward: Phil Berger, "King, Douglas Reach Settlement," *New York Times,* July 18, 1990.

185 In reflecting on the settlement: James Douglas interview.

186 Far from being a bloated cruiserweight: Pat Putnam, "Busted," *Sports Illustrated,* November 5, 1990.

186 The plan was for Holyfield to use fitness as a weapon: Ibid.

186 "I want that left hand of yours": Ibid.

186 Twelve days before the fight: Ibid.

187 "And Part Three?": Ibid.

187 "When I got on the scale": James Douglas interview.

188 "Buster wasn't able to focus": John Russell interview.

188 "Let's cancel the fight": Ibid.

188 "I was very concerned": Ibid.

188 "I wish somebody would have": James Douglas interview.

189 At a press conference in early August: Mike Downey, "Buster Delivers Blow to Image," *Los Angeles Times,* August 8, 1990.

190 "You know, fighters are all crazy": Jim Lampley interview.

190 "It don't make no difference": Phil Berger, "Douglas Weighs In at a Surprising 246," *New York Times,* October 25, 1990.

190 Added J. D. McCauley: Ibid.

191 "He fought at that weight his whole life": J. D. McCauley interview.

191 "We're home free": Berger, "Douglas Weighs In."

191 "I don't know how in the hell": John Russell interview.

191 In the first two rounds: Putnam, "Busted."

192 On several occasions: Ibid.

192 "That's a question only he can answer": John Russell interview.

193 "I don't know if he could have got up": Putnam, "Busted."

193 *I'm so tired*: James Douglas interview.

Chapter 10

195 On March 25: Richard Hoffer, "Up from the Canvas," *Sports Illustrated,* March 27, 1995.

195 Since Tyson lost to Douglas: Kevin Rooney interview.

195 "Nearly every day": Steve Lott interview.

196 Anyway, Don King had made certain: Gary Younge, "Out for the Count," Guardian, August 5, 2003.

197 "For me, each time, it was sad": Steve Lott interview.

197 "Testosterone—that's what it is": Mike Tyson interview.

198 "I feel sympathy": Jim Lampley interview.

199 "Mike has said his heart isn't in it": Jay Bright interview.

200 "Mike is an extremely complex individual": Paul Antonelli interview.

200 "On a human level": Larry Merchant interview.

200 "Well, I think what he did": Ibid.

201 "They met by a fluke of fate": Richard Corliss, "The Bad and the Beautiful," *Time,* February 24, 1992.

202 "The stud defense": Sonja Steptoe, "A Damnable Defense," *Sports Illustrated,* February 24, 1992.

203 In contrast, Washington seemed believable: "Tale of the Tapes," *Sports Illustrated,* April 26, 1993.

203 Jemison was later indicted: Katrice Franklin, "Baptist Leader Blames Jemison for Church's Problems," *The Advocate* (Baton Rouge), January 14, 1995.

203 In the end: William Nack, "A Crushing Verdict," *Sports Illustrated,* February 17, 1992.

203 "Here it is": Ibid.

203 On March 26, 1992: "Mike Tyson Sentenced to Six Years, Appeal Filed Immediately," *Jet,* April 13, 1992.

204 The fighter calmly removed: Ibid.

205 Observed Tom Patti: Tom Patti interview.

205 An equally sympathetic: Tom Junod, "The Father's Kiss," *Esquire,* June 1, 1999.

206 He claimed to have been influenced: "*Ebony* Interview with Mike Tyson," *Ebony*, September 1, 1995.

207 "Away from the ring": Vic Ziegel interview.

208 "Bottom line": Hoffer, "Up from the Canvas."

210 Tyson-Holyfield II: John M. Higgins, "Buy Rates Soar for Bite Bout," *Broadcasting and Cable*, July 7, 1997.

210 And then the weirdness escalated: Richard Hoffer, "Feeding Frenzy," *Sports Illustrated*, July 7, 1997.

211 "One bite, maybe, is bad enough": Ibid.

211 "Nobody knows better": Jim Lampley interview.

Chapter 11

213 "If you talk to certain people": John Ed Bradley, "Get a Load of Me!" *Sports Illustrated*, May 17, 1993.

213 "Buster did something": Tim May, "Which Douglas Was It?" *Columbus Dispatch*, October 27, 1990.

214 "Sometimes you have nights": Ibid.

214 "I believe James Douglas": Ibid.

214 When the esteemed trainer: Pat Putnam, "Busted," *Sports Illustrated*, November 5, 1990.

214 "The things he did": Ibid.

215 All of these things were implied by Wynn: May, "Which Douglas Was It?"

215 "I felt terrible about the way things went": J. D. McCauley interview.

216 After the Holyfield fight: Bradley, "Get a Load of Me."

216 "James loved his mother dearly": Bertha Douglas interview.

217 In May 1993: Ed Bradley, "Get a Load of Me."

217 Douglas was offended and angered: James Douglas interview.

217 On February 14, 1992: Sam Donnellon, "Bubble Buster," *Philadelphia Daily News,* February 10, 1993.

218 "James was depressed": Bertha Douglas interview.

218 "That was all depression": James Douglas interview.

218 He wasn't alone: John Johnson interview.

218 McCauley prefers "sad": J. D. McCauley interview.

218 Johnson had claimed in a 1993 lawsuit: Randall Edwards, "Former Manager Settles Lawsuit Against Douglas, Brokerage Firm," *Columbus Dispatch,* December 12, 1995.

219 "I'd basically had enough of boxing": John Russell interview.

219 "I wasn't happy": Ibid.

220 "If he hadn't been sitting beside his dad": Ibid.

221 "I don't think he was on a suicide mission": Ibid.

221 "It was like we never left": Ibid.

221 "It broke my heart": Ibid.

222 "I didn't give a shit": James Douglas interview.

222 By the summer of 1994: Bertha Douglas and James Douglas interviews.

222 "James, we have to take you to the hospital": Bertha Douglas interview.

223 The next day, with tubes pumping fluid: Ibid.

223 "Kiss me": James Douglas and Bertha Douglas interviews.

223 "Larry Nallie was in charge": John Johnson interview.

223 "They almost killed me": James Douglas interview.

224 "I have to take some of this weight off": John Russell and James Douglas interviews.

224 When he got off the phone: John Russell interview.

Chapter 12

225 "I remember reading with some melancholy": James Sterngold interview.

225 "Where are you going to find a better story line": Greg Simms, "Buster Keeping Busy," *Dayton Daily News*, August 5, 1994.

226 "At the time, I know James was thinking": John Russell interview.

227 "I'll never forget it": Ibid.

228 "I was at the top of the boxing world": Bruce Hooley, "Douglas Comes Out of Retirement, Seeks Fight with Tyson," *Cleveland Plain Dealer*, February 21, 1995.

228 "I thought he would say": John Russell interview.

229 Training runs at nearly five thousand feet: Tim Crothers, "The Battle of the Bulge," *Sports Illustrated*, July 1, 1996.

229 "I was happy he was healthy and in shape": Bertha Douglas interview.

230 "You don't act like most fighters": Tim Crothers, "No Doubt About It," *Sports Illustrated*, December 30, 1996.

230 "What an experience that was": John Russell interview.

230 Only two words: John Russell and James Douglas interviews.

230 Douglas shook his head: Ibid.

231 "You're in great shape, James": John Russell interview.

231 Bill Douglas, too, tried to calm his son: James Douglas interview.

231 "You all right?": John Russell interview.

231 Douglas nodded: Ibid.

231 "He hit me pretty good": James Douglas interview.

231 "He didn't hurt me": Bob Hunter, "Douglas Isn't Pursuing an Impossible Dream," *Columbus Dispatch*, June 24, 1996.

231 "Back in 1981": Crothers, "Battle of the Bulge."

232 "The guy almost died": John Russell interview.

233 "I probably shouldn't have let him fight": Ibid.

233 Although his overall record: Ron Borges, "Savarese Derails Douglas's Bid," *Boston Globe,* June 26, 1998.

234 "Buster gained the weight and I got it off him": John Russell interview.

234 Douglas was quick to wrest that responsibility: James Douglas interview.

235 Douglas had lost a second brother: "Ex-Heavyweight Champ's Brother Shot to Death," Associated Press, December 15, 1998.

235 "The streets are mean": James Douglas interview.

235 "If they weren't going to make it very attractive": John Russell interview.

236 "Once James's father got back in the corner": Bertha Douglas interview.

236 "He had kind of an ashen, gray pallor": Bruce Trampler interview.

236 "Get that guy out of here": John Russell interview.

236 Russell last saw Bill Douglas: Ibid.

237 "He was amazing": Ibid.

237 "I'll see you later, Billy": Ibid.

237 Five days later: Ibid.

238 "I said, 'James, if you're coming back'": Ibid.

Chapter 13

239 "I'm going to go down": Mike Tyson interview.

239 "I'm working on a book right now": Bert Sugar interview.

240 "Mike had as good a run": Kevin Rooney interview.

240 "I fucked my whole career over": Mike Tyson interview.

240 "Listen, do you have complete, utter happiness": Tom Patti interview.

241 Tyson himself put it more succinctly: Mike Tyson interview.

241 "Mike remembers being a hero": Steve Lott interview.

241 As an example: "Maori Anger Over Tyson Tattoo," Associated Press, February 21, 2003.

241 "It doesn't signify": Mike Tyson interview with ESPN, February 20, 2003.

242 "The thinking process around Mike": Steve Lott interview.

243 Herewith, culled from an Associated Press timeline: "Boxer Mike Tyson's Life Chronology," Associated Press, January 30, 2002.

245 This was Tyson at his most perplexing: Bill Pennington, "Another Bizarre Ending Taints a Tyson Fight," *New York Times,* June 26, 2000.

246 "Lennox Lewis, I'm coming for you": Showtime broadcast of Mike Tyson–Lou Savarese fight, June 24, 2000.

246 "Boxing is a sport": Pennington, "Another Bizarre Ending."

247 The event, staged: Dan Rafael, "News Conferences Become Hazardous," *USA Today,* January 23, 2002.

248 Several minutes passed: "Tyson-Lewis News Conference Disrupted by Brawl," Associated Press, January 25, 2002.

248 "Fuck you": Videotape of Tyson-Lewis press conference, youtube.com.

248 "My motivation for approaching Lennox": "Tyson-Lewis News Conference Disrupted by Brawl," Associated Press, January 25, 2002.

248 "If it was planned": Steve Lott interview.

249 Tyson's penance: Duncan Campbell, "Painful Hearing as Commission Shows No Mercy," *Irish Times,* January 31, 2002.

249 "You will never see that happening again": Ibid.

249 "I'm on the Zoloft": Ken Peters, "Tyson Hopes to Be Remembered in Bizarre Way," Associated Press, September 15, 2000.

249 It is, sadly, a measure: Richard Sandomir, "Lewis-Tyson Bout Provides a Knockout Revenue Figure," *New York Times,* Jun 12, 2002.

250 And yet, he fought bravely: "Lewis Topples Tyson," Associated Press, June 9, 2002.

250 "I'm very Freudian about fighters": Jim Lampley interview.

251 "Now, as Lampley walked": Ibid.

251 "He looked up at me": Ibid.

252 Two years later: Dan Rafael, "Tyson, King Settle $100 Million Suit," *USA Today,* June 25, 2004.

252 Court documents filed in support: Richard Hoffer, "All the Rage," *Sports Illustrated,* May 20, 2002.

253 Nevertheless, more than fifteen thousand people: Ron Borges, "Tyson Was Badly Hurt Inside," *Boston Globe,* June 13, 2005.

253 Regardless, Tyson was no match for McBride: Ibid.

254 "I do not have the guts": Showtime broadcast of Tyson-McBride fight, June 11, 2005.

254 "Smart too late and old too soon": Michael Wilbon, "It's a Hard Feeling, Not to Be a Violent Man Anymore," *Washington Post,* June 13, 2005.

255 "My career's over": Ibid.

255 "I'm not interested in fighting no more": Borges, "Tyson Was Badly Hurt Inside."

255 "No, no, no, no": Wilbon, "It's a Hard Feeling."

255 "I'm not used to sensitivity anymore": Chuck Johnson, "Tyson Can't Beat Father Time," *USA Today,* June 12, 2005.

255 "I'm just Mike": Ibid.

256 "During an interview": Mike Tyson interview.

257   "Boxing is almost exclusively a Latin sport now": Richard Hoffer interview.

257   HBO analyst Larry Merchant: Larry Merchant interview.

257   "I think it's a sport that's been declining": Ibid.

258   "It's all fun": "Tyson Returning to Ring," Associated Press, October 17, 2006.

258   Historian that he is: Owen Slot, "Tyson Hits Comeback Trail for Money, Not Love," *Times of London,* October 19, 2006.

259   "I go up there when I'm depressed": Mike Tyson interview.

259   "Cus had his ego, too": Ibid.

259   "I don't think so, sir": Ibid.

Epilogue

All material and quotes are from author interviews with James Douglas; supplemental information from the Columbus Main Street Business Association, except as noted:

264   Generally speaking: "James (Buster) Douglas's Arrest Warrant Cancelled After Paying Fine," Associated Press, November 16, 2006.

265   It was during a visit to Florida: Curt Conrad, "After Accident, Hanshaw's Trainer 'Lucky to Be Alive,'" *Mansfield News Journal,* June 20, 2003.

265   "It got me moving and feeling good again": John Russell interview.

BIBLIOGRAPHY

Allen, Neil. "The Real Iron Mike." *Boxing Monthly,* February 2000.

Anderson, Dave. "Is Tyson Sabotaging Himself?" *The New York Times,* February 6, 1990.

Archdeacon, Tom. "Out Cold Dad Doesn't Receive an Invitation to Son's Celebration as Douglas, Columbus Party Over Heavyweight Crown." *Dayton Daily News,* February 18, 1990.

Associated Press. "Boxer Mike Tyson's Life Chronology." January 30, 2002.

Associated Press. "Boxer and Manager Sentenced to Prison for Glove Tampering." October 28, 1986.

Associated Press. "Ex-Heavyweight Champ's Brother Shot to Death." December 15, 1998.

Associated Press. "Holmes Again Raps Officials After Decision." April 20, 1986.

Associated Press. "James (Buster) Douglas's Arrest Warrant Cancelled After Paying Fine." November 16, 2006.

Associated Press. "Lewis Topples Tyson." June 9, 2002.

Associated Press. "Maori Anger Over Tyson Tattoo." February 21, 2003.

Associated Press. "Tyson Returning to Ring." October 17, 2006.

Associated Press. "Tyson-Lewis News Conference Disrupted by Brawl." January 25, 2002.

Atlas, Teddy. *Atlas: From the Streets to the Ring.* New York: Ecco, 2006.

Berger, Phil. *Blood Season: Tyson and the World of Boxing.* New York: William Morrow, 1989.

Berger, Phil. "Boxing Officials Could Overturn Defeat of Tyson." *The New York Times,* February 12, 1990.

Berger, Phil. "Douglas Weighs In at a Surprising 246." *The New York Times,* October 25, 1990.

Berger, Phil. "King an Artful Dodger Who Lands on His Feet." *The New York Times,* February 18, 1990.

Berger, Phil. "King, Douglas Reach Settlement." *The New York Times,* July 18, 1990.

Berger, Phil. "On Top and Loving It." *The New York Times,* March 4, 1990.

Berger, Phil. "Tyson Concedes: Wants Rematch." *The New York Times,* February 14, 1990.

Borges, Ron. "Cayton Enduring Unkindest Cut of All." *The Boston Globe,* July 20, 1989.

Borges, Ron. "Savarese Derails Douglas's Bid." *The Boston Globe,* June 26, 1998.

Borges, Ron. "Tyson Was Badly Hurt Inside." *The Boston Globe,* June 13, 2000.

Bradley, John Ed. "Get a Load of Me!" *Sports Illustrated,* May 17, 1993.

Brook, Sally. "It's Very Hard Being Second Best as a Woman but as a Geisha That's What it's All About." *The Sun* (London), January 24, 2006.

Brunt, Stephen. *Facing Ali: 15 Fighters, 15 Stories.* Guilford, Conn.: The Lyons Press, 2002.

Callahan, Tom. "Boxing's Allure." *Time,* June 27, 1988.

Callahan, Tom. "When Buster Beat Up Godzilla." *Newsweek,* February 26, 1990.

Campbell, Duncan. "Painful Hearing as Commission Shows No Mercy." *The Irish Times,* January 31, 2002.

Conrad, Curt. "After Accident, Hanshaw's Trainer 'Lucky to Be Alive.' " *Mansfield News Journal,* June 20, 2003.

Corliss, Richard. "The Bad and the Beautiful." *Time,* February 24, 1992.

Crothers, Tim. "No Doubt About It." *Sports Illustrated,* December 30, 1996.

Crothers, Tim. "The Battle of the Bulge." *Sports Illustrated,* July 1, 1996.

Dawson, James P. "Miller Reinstated by Boxing Board." *The New York Times,* November 11, 1925.

Donnellon, Sam. "Bubble Buster: Champion of Busted Dreams." *Philadelphia Daily News,* February 10, 1993.

Doogan, Brian. "Buster Back from the Brink." *The Sunday Times* (London), February 27, 2005.

Downer, Lesley. *Women of the Pleasure Quarters: The Secret History of the Geisha.* New York: Broadway Books, 2002.

Downey, Mike. "Buster Delivers Blow to Image." *Los Angeles Times,* August 8, 1990.

Early, Gerald. "Mike's Brilliant Career." *Transition 71,* Duke University Press, Fall 1996.

"*Ebony* Interview with Mike Tyson." *Ebony,* September 1, 1995.

Edwards, Randall. "Former Manager Settles Lawsuit Against Douglas, Brokerage Firm." *The Columbus Dispatch,* December 12, 1995.

Evans, Gavin. "Backpages: Tools of the Trade . . . Boxing Gloves." *The Guardian,* January 15, 1999.

Evans, Gavin. *Kings of the Ring: The History of Heavyweight Boxing.* London: Weidenfeld & Nicolson, 2005.

Feour, Royce. "Sanctioning Bodies Practice Unfairness." *Las Vegas Review-Journal,* November 21, 1999.

Fernandez, Bernard. "Japanese Have a Yen for Tyson." *Philadelphia Daily News,* February 8, 1990.

Franklin, Katrice. "Baptist Leader Blames Jemison for Church's Problems." *The Advocate* (Baton Rouge), January 14, 1995.

Gildea, William. "From Humbling Start to Humbling Tyson, He's the Same 'Buster.' " *Washington Post,* February 14, 1990.

Gonzalez, Rudy with Martin A. Feigenbaum. *The Inner Ring.* Miami: Oliver Publishing Group, 1995.

Hamill, Pete. "The Education of Mike Tyson." *Esquire,* March, 1994.

Hauser, Thomas. *The View from Ringside: Inside the Tumultuous World of Boxing.* Toronto: SportClassic Books, 2004.

HBO. Broadcast of Tyson-Douglas fight. February 10, 1990.

HBO. Rebroadcast of Tyson-Douglas Fight. February 16, 1990.

HBO Studio Productions. *Legendary Nights: The Tale of Tyson-Douglas.* 2003.

Heinz, W. C. and Nathan Ward, eds. *The Book of Boxing.* New York: Total Sports, 1999.

Heller, Peter. *Bad Intentions: The Mike Tyson Story,* updated edition. New York: Da Capo Press, 2001.

Higgins, John M. "Buy Rates Soar for Bite Bout." *Broadcasting and Cable,* July 7, 1997.

Hoffer, Richard. *A Savage Business: The Comeback and Comedown of Mike Tyson.* New York: Simon & Schuster, 1998.

Hoffer, Richard. "All the Rage." *Sports Illustrated,* May 20, 2002.

Hoffer, Richard. "Feeding Frenzy." *Sports Illustrated,* July 7, 1997.

Hoffer, Richard. "Hey, Champ!" *Sports Illustrated,* February 26, 1990.

Hoffer, Richard. "KO'd." *Sports Illustrated,* February 19, 1990.

Hoffer, Richard. "Up from the Canvas." *Sports Illustrated,* March 27, 1995.

Hooley, Bruce. "Douglas Comes Out of Retirement, Seeks Fight with Tyson." *The Plain Dealer* (Cleveland), February 21, 1995.

Hunter, Bob. "Douglas Isn't Pursuing an Impossible Dream." *The Columbus Dispatch,* June 24, 1996.

Iamele, David. "Buster Douglas Looks Back at the Night He Rocked the Boxing World." *Utica Observer-Disptach,* May 1, 2004.

Iole, Kevin. "Upset of the Century." *Las Vegas Review-Journal,* February 13, 2000.

Johnson, Chuck. "Tyson Can't Beat Father Time." *USA Today,* June 12, 2005.

Junod, Tom. "The Father's Kiss." *Esquire,* June 1, 1999.

Liebling, A. J. *The Sweet Science.* New York: North Point Press, 2004.

Lyons, Douglas C. "New Champ Samples the Sweet Life." *Ebony,* June 1990.

Madden, Michael. "After Upset, Douglas a Bust." *The Boston Globe,* August 18, 1995.

Matthews, Wallace. "A Journeyman's Journey." *Newsday,* February 18, 1990.

Matthews, Wallace. "Knockdown a Hyper Event." *Newsday,* January 25, 1990.

Maxse, Joe. "Columbus Boxer Is Tyson's Next Opponent." *The Plain Dealer* (Cleveland), August 15, 1989.

Maxse, Joe. "Douglas Tokyo-Bound to Fight Tyson." *The Plain Dealer,* (Cleveland), January 27, 1990.

May, Tim. "Douglas Arrives for Bout on the Run." *The Columbus Dispatch,* January 28, 1990.

May, Tim. "Douglas Shrugs Off All the Legal Maneuvering." *The Columbus Dispatch,* March 6, 1990.

May, Tim. "Douglas Winning Bout with Flu." *The Columbus Dispatch,* February 10, 1990.

May, Tim. "Manager Sure of Standing." *The Columbus Dispatch,* January 21, 1990.

May, Tim. "Tyson's Brash Style Rubs Douglas Wrong Way." *The Columbus Dispatch,* February 9, 1990.

May, Tim. "Which Douglas Was It?" *The Columbus Dispatch,* October 27, 1990.

McAlary, Mike. "Tyson Tried to Kill Self." New York *Daily News,* September 7, 1988.

McCallum, John Dennis. *The Encyclopedia of World Boxing Champions Since 1882.* Radnor, Pa.: Chilton Books, 1975.

McGowan, Deane. "Soto Bows to Fill-in; Bobick Wins." *The New York Times,* February 7, 1976.

McIlvanny, Hugh. *The Hardest Game: McIlvanny on Boxing.* New York: McGraw-Hill, 2001.

McRae, Donald. *Dark Trade: Lost in Boxing.* New York: Mainstream Publishing, 1996.

McRae, Donald. "Me and Mike Tyson." *The Guardian,* January 22, 2000.

"Mike Tyson Sentenced to Six Years, Appeal Filed Immediately." *Jet,* April 13, 1992.

"Miller Yarns Hit at Jack Delaney." *Hartford Courant,* November 5, 1925.

Nack, William. "A Crushing Verdict." *Sports Illustrated,* February 17, 1992.

Newfield, Jack. *Only in America: The Life and Crimes of Don King.* New York: William Morrow, 1995.

Oates, Joyce Carol. *On Boxing.* New York: Doubleday, 1987.

O'Connor, Daniel, ed. *Iron Mike: A Mike Tyson Reader.* New York: Thunder's Mouth Press, 2002.

Peltz, Russell, "Douglas Was a Feared Middleweight." ESPN.com, October 13, 2005.

Pennington, Bill. "Another Bizarre Ending Taints a Tyson Fight." *The New York Times,* June 26, 2000.

Peters, Ken. "Tyson Hopes to Be Remembered in Bizarre Way." Associated Press, September 15, 2000.

Putnam, Pat. "Busted." *Sports Illustrated,* November 5, 1990.

Putnam, Pat. "I'm Gonna Hurt This Guy." *Sports Illustrated,* July 4, 1988.

Putnam, Pat. "Of Wheat, Chaff, and Boxing." *Sports Illustrated,* July 23, 1990.

Rafael, Dan. "Mike Tyson Sounds Off About His Past." ESPN.com, June 11, 2006.

Rafael, Dan. "News Conferences Become Hazardous." *USA Today,* January 23, 2002.

Rafael, Dan. "Tyson, King Settle $100 Million Suit." *USA Today,* June 25, 2004.

Reed, Tom. "Roped In Again." *Akron Beacon Journal,* July 14, 2002.

Remnick, David. *King of the World.* New York: Random House, 1998.

Roberts, James B., and Alexander G. Skutt. *The Boxing Register,* 3rd ed. Ithaca, N.Y.: McBooks Press, 2002.

Rotella, Carlo. *Cut Time: An Education at the Fights.* New York: Houghton Mifflin, 2003.

Sandomir, Richard. "Lewis–Tyson Bout Provides a Knockout Revenue Figure." *The New York Times,* June 12, 2002.

Schaap, Jeremy. *Cinderella Man: James Braddock, Max Baer and the Greatest Upset in Boxing History.* New York: Houghton Mifflin, 2005.

Schulman, Arlene. *The Prizefighters.* New York: Lyons & Burford, 1994

Seltzer, Robert. "Maverick Manager Is No Hit Outside the Ring." *The Philadelphia Inquirer,* October 21, 1990.

Showtime. Broadcast of Mike Tyson–Lou Savarese fight. June 24, 2000.

Showtime. Broadcast of Tyson-McBride fight. June 11, 2005.

Simms, Greg. "Buster Keeping busy." *Dayton Daily News,* August 5, 1994.

Slot, Owen. "Tyson Hits Comeback Trail for Money, Not Love." *The Times* (London), October 19, 2006.

Smith, Elmer. "Father Carves Path for Son's Shot at Title." *Philadelphia Daily News,* May 29, 1987.

Smith, Gary. "The Fight of His Life." *Sports Illustrated,* October 22, 1990.

Steptoe, Sonja. "A Damnable Defense." *Sports Illustrated,* February 24, 1992.

Sterngold. James. "No Heart? Douglas Disproved Doubters." *The New York Times,* February 12, 1990.

Sugar, Bert Randolph. *Boxing's Greatest Fighters.* Guilford, Conn.: The Lyons Press, 2006.

"Tale of the Tapes." *Sports Illustrated,* April 26, 1993.

Toole, F. X. *Rope Burns: Stories from the Corner.* New York: Ecco 2001.

Torres, Jose. *Fire and Fear: The Inside Story of Mike Tyson.* New York: Warner Books, 1989.

"Tyson Bout in February. *The New York Times,* November 16, 1989.

Wilbon, Michael. "It's a Hard Feeling, Not to Be a Violent Man Anymore." *The Washington Post,* June 13, 2005.

Wulf, Steve. "Adversity's Adversary." *Sports Illustrated,* February 19, 1990.

Younge, Gary. "Out for the Count." *The Guardian,* August 5, 2003.

Youtube.com. Videotape of Tyson-Lewis press conference. (No longer available on this Web site as of March 23, 2007.)